IMAGES
of America

CLAREMONT

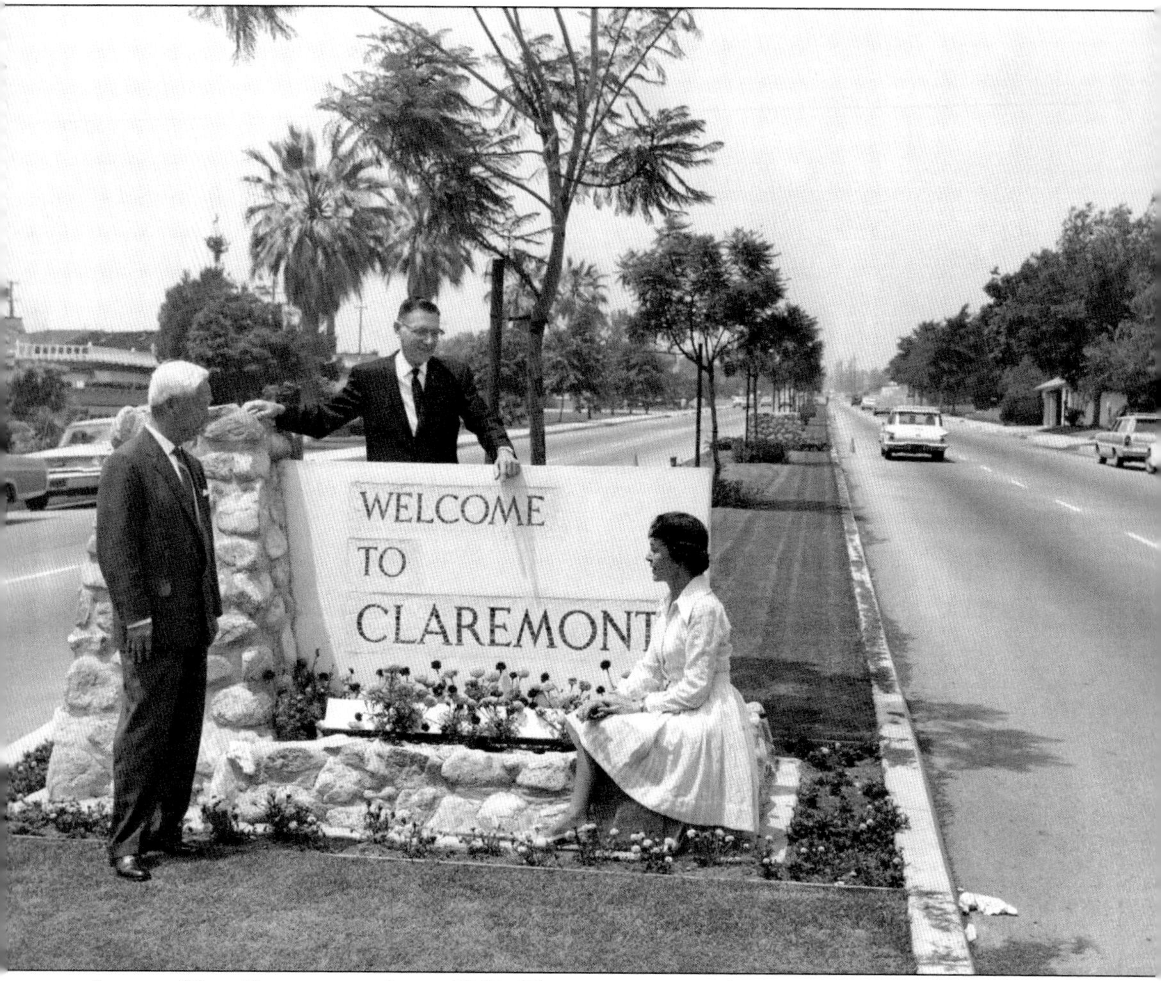

INDIAN HILL BOULEVARD, JUNE 1969. This stone sign welcoming visitors and residents to Claremont stands along one of the most historic streets in the city, near where Native American settlements were once located. In true Claremont fashion, the sign was constructed with money donated from various community organizations. Shown in this photograph are, from left to right, Rotary members J.C. Hsia and Edward J. Dittmer and Mayor Marjorie Spear. (Courtesy of Claremont Heritage.)

ON THE COVER: Claremont's original Gothic-style train depot was built by the Santa Fe Railroad Company in 1887, at the height of the western railroad and land boom. The Santa Fe's Los Angeles–San Bernardino line created many boomtowns along its path, only some of which survived the early years. This depot remained in use until 1928, when it was replaced by the existing Spanish-style depot. (Courtesy of Claremont Heritage.)

IMAGES
of America

CLAREMONT

Eva Landsberg and Sean Stanley,
Claremont Heritage

ARCADIA
PUBLISHING

ISBN 978-1-4671-3191-9

Published by Arcadia Publishing
Charleston, South Carolina

Printed in the United States of America

Library of Congress Control Number: 2013955124

For all general information, please contact Arcadia Publishing:
Telephone 843-853-2070
Fax 843-853-0044
E-mail sales@arcadiapublishing.com
For customer service and orders:
Toll-Free 1-888-313-2665

Visit us on the Internet at www.arcadiapublishing.com

This book is dedicated to the late Judy Wright for her selfless dedication and determination to preserve Claremont's history. Without her, and the support of her family, this book would not have been possible.

Contents

ACKNOWLEDGMENTS

This book is the result of the dedicated work of a number of gifted and conscientious individuals as well as organizations, without whom this publication would not have come to fruition.

I would especially like to thank Claremont Heritage archivist Amy Berssen, who supervised the myriad details involved in the research, writing, and photography permissions that have made Images of America: *Claremont* the comprehensive and accurate publication that it is. Thanks also go to Eva Landsberg and Sean Stanley, the fastidious authors of the book, who spent many hours researching a number of archives to create a well-written and richly illustrated document that is concise and offers a true picture of Claremont's unique and illustrious past. Thanks also to John Neiuber, who offered significant insight in the writing and editing of the manuscript. A special note of gratitude is due to Lisa Crane and the Special Collections Department of the Honnold/Mudd Library of the Claremont Colleges for access to their department and collection.

This book would not exist without the years of dedication and painstaking effort that the late Judy Wright brought to bear compiling and writing the definitive book on Claremont's history, *Claremont: A Pictorial History*, first published in 1980, with a revised and expanded edition printed in 1999. We are exceedingly grateful to the Wright family for the donation of Judy Wright's papers and photography collection to the Claremont Heritage archives.

Ginger Elliott, former executive director of Claremont Heritage, and Mary Ann Barkey, former archivist of Claremont Heritage, deserve recognition for collecting and meticulously cataloging many of the resources used in this book. Unless otherwise noted, photographs used in the book are courtesy of the Claremont Heritage archives. We thank Annie Nguyen for her research contribution to the authors. The support of the Claremont Heritage Board of Directors is recognized for their unanimous approval of this endeavor. Our publisher, Arcadia Publishing, has been enthusiastic about this publication from the beginning, and we are appreciative to them for their guidance and encouragement every step of the way.

—David L. Shearer
Executive Director
Claremont Heritage

INTRODUCTION

"There is an enchanting, yet indescribable something alike in the charming location and in the sublime surroundings that suggests and fills this mind with a peaceful feeling of serene homelike happiness," wrote one *Los Angeles Tribune* reporter in March 1887 about the plot of land destined to become the city of Claremont.

At the time of this pronouncement, Claremont, reportedly named for its clear view of the snowcapped Mount Baldy, looked relatively as it had for the past 1,000 years. Fitted snuggly at the base of the mountain and sustained by San Antonio Creek, its rich land had served as home to Serrano Native Americans, who had been incorporated into the Mission San Gabriel before smallpox outbreaks decimated the population. In 1837, Claremont was legally transferred to become part of the Palomares family's sprawling Rancho San Jose, which it remained until the conclusion of the Mexican-American War. By the 1880s, in the midst of the western railway boom, Claremont had only a few residents, among them hardy pioneer William "Tooch" Martin and a handful of citrus growers.

In their heyday, the railroads had the power to make or break towns, particularly in the West. Thanks to a clever suggestion by early Claremont resident Henry Austin Palmer, the Santa Fe Railroad made the fateful decision to run its Los Angeles–bound line through the north end of the rapidly developing town of Pomona, thus effectively sectioning off the area that was to become Claremont. In January 1887, the railroad subsidiary land company, the Pacific Land Improvement Company, set about "improving" Claremont's land. Rocks and shrubs were cleared, a tiny land office and the grand Hotel Claremont were hastily constructed, and the Santa Fe contributed a clapboard depot. Throughout February and March, promoters advertised "Claremont the Beautiful" through posters and newspaper essays, in preparation for April lot sales and the subsequent arrival of the railroad. Their hard work, it seemed, paid off. By April 15 of that year, Claremont had generated around $80,000 in land sales.

Claremont's success, however, was short-lived. By the spring of 1888, the land boom was essentially over, leaving in its wake a near ghost town. Far from being the bustling, prosperous town promised, post-boom Claremont had only one street and a handful of houses. The imposing hotel stood empty, surrounded by lots sold on paper but never settled. If action was not taken quickly, Claremont was destined to go the way of so many other boomtowns, disintegrating into the dust.

Salvation came in the form of Pomona College, a tiny Congregational school founded in 1887, at the height of the land boom. For years, Congregationalists in the area had been planning for the establishment of a college similar to the ones found in their native New England, and the boom years provided the prime opportunity. The college was intended to be built in the soon-to-be-developed town of Piedmont, which was then considered part of Pomona but is now part of Claremont, and land in that area was quickly snatched up by the dedicated college founders. However, the end of the boom abruptly cut short the cash flow; in September 1888, the cornerstones for the "Central Building" at the Piedmont location were laid with grand fanfare, but they were soon abandoned due to lack of funds.

The Pacific Land Improvement Company seized the opportunity to revive the dying Claremont, capitalizing on the struggling Pomona College. In October, the company offered the empty Hotel

Claremont and the surrounding property to the college; in January of the next year, classes had begun in their new "temporary" location in Claremont. The hotel, which came to be called Claremont Hall and, later, Sumner Hall, comprised nearly the entirety of the college. By 1892, any plans for a move back to Piedmont were abandoned, and Claremont became the permanent home of the contradictorily named Pomona College.

With the growth of Pomona College came renewed life to the decrepit boomtown of Claremont. The spirit of cooperation prevailed amongst the 30-some early residents; there were no city taxes, merely donations, and nearly everyone had some role in the village improvement society. Sagebrush and gravel were quickly replaced with eucalyptus and sidewalk. A volunteer fire department was organized. In 1889, Claremont Grammar School (now Sycamore Elementary School) was established, primarily to teach the children of Pomona College faculty. Claremont was a little slice of New England in the midst of the dry California wilderness; in keeping with their eastern roots, the residents of the unincorporated town used town meetings as their form of self-government.

By 1900, Claremont had a residential population of approximately 250, the majority of whom were connected to either the college or the citrus industry. Pomona College had grown to an enrollment of around 500 students, and the town had developed alongside it. The burgeoning business area, today referred to as the village, soon contained a post office, a bank, and a general store, among other establishments. The town had a Congregational church, in addition to a small Catholic chapel that served the primarily Hispanic citrus workers. The Claremont Inn served as both a hotel and a town hub. There was a high school, a tiny jail, a library, and a local newspaper. In a contentious vote in September 1907, the town was finally incorporated into Los Angeles County, and, by 1910, the population had skyrocketed to 1,114 residents. Its early ghost town days long gone, "Claremont the Beautiful" was beginning to fulfill the promises the optimistic city developers had made decades earlier.

The contributions of the citrus industry to the development of Claremont cannot be overlooked. In 1888, when local rancher Peter Dreher planted Claremont's first citrus trees, the city's survival was uncertain. However, a new boom, the citrus boom, soon replaced the quickly fading land boom. The area's Mediterranean climate proved ideal for the growth of the highly sought-after lemons and oranges, and the convenient proximity to the railroad allowed the citrus industry to become Claremont's largest source of income until almost mid-century.

Just five years after those first trees were planted, Claremont became home to the state's first citrus cooperative, the Claremont Fruit Growers Association, which consisted of the 11 local growers. The tiny town was soon shipping boxes of citrus across the nation, and a box of Claremont oranges even made its way across the Atlantic Ocean to reach England's Queen Victoria in time for her birthday celebration in 1893. The industry came to spawn three separate citrus associations in Claremont alone, and large, cavernous packinghouses soon sprung up alongside the railroad tracks. In 1900, the town was composed primarily of citrus ranches, with their thousands of rows of trees separated into neat tracts of land. The remnants of these can still be found in the numerous orange and lemon trees that dot the backyards of Claremont residents today.

In addition to providing an obvious economic boost to the developing Claremont, the citrus industry also brought a large Hispanic community to the otherwise fairly homogenous town. Citrus pickers were primarily men of Mexican descent, and Mexican American women served as packinghouse workers. Though many were migrant workers, others chose to settle in the Claremont area. By 1920, the city had two main Hispanic districts, the East and West Barrios. Though the Hispanic population was kept generally isolated from town affairs in the early years, their contributions to Claremont were enormous, both economically and culturally.

In April 1917, the United States entered World War I, and Claremont responded accordingly. Pomona College quickly started a Reserve Officers Training Corps (ROTC) program, and barracks to house soldiers were built at Renwick Gymnasium. The influenza outbreak sweeping the world also struck in Claremont, leaving two citizens dead. However, despite these disruptions to the otherwise calm lifestyle of residents, the city continued to develop. The citrus industry grew large enough to encourage the Santa Fe Railroad to build a new, larger Claremont depot in 1927. The all-female Scripps College, with its beautiful campus, designed by Gordon B. Kaufman, held its first classes in 1927. Meanwhile, Pomona College added several new buildings, including the grand Bridges Auditorium in 1931. In 1930, in the midst of the Great Depression, which was devastating to so much of the nation, construction in Claremont totaled over $1 million. "Claremont," wrote the *Claremont Courier* that same year, "has every reason to look forward to continued prosperity and success."

However, Claremont could not avoid the Depression for long. The troubled citrus industry had to receive financial assistance in the form of farm credit loans, Pres. Franklin Roosevelt's Works Progress Administration constructed a new Claremont post office, and the Civilian Conservation Corps provided local men jobs building fire roads in the hillsides. Pomona College saw its enrollment and endowment decline, and the faculty voluntarily accepted a pay cut. However, in comparison to much of the United States, Claremont suffered relatively little during those terrible years, and, by 1937, the citrus industry was once again growing, providing further economic stimulus to the area.

World War II brought about more significant changes to Claremont. The 3,000-plus residents took an active role in the war effort, and Pomona College began an Army Specialized Training Program. The citrus industry, too, was impacted, and German and Japanese prisoners of war, who were kept at the Los Angeles Fairplex, were used as workers on the local citrus farms.

In the postwar decades, the West in particular exploded with growth. In Claremont, three new colleges were added to the consortium: Claremont Men's College (later renamed Claremont McKenna College upon its offering of enrollment to women) in 1947, the science and engineering–focused Harvey Mudd College in 1955, and the originally all-female Pitzer College in 1963. With the addition of these new institutes of higher education, the art scene in Claremont flourished immensely in the mid-1900s. The colleges commissioned famous artists, including José Clemente Orozco and Alfredo Ramos Martinez, to create murals throughout their campuses. Thanks in part to the Servicemen's Readjustment Act, often referred to as the GI Bill, young veterans interested in art poured into colleges nationwide, and the Claremont Colleges—Scripps and Pomona especially—attracted many skilled art instructors.

By the 1940s, Claremont was home to a thriving artist community. Artists flocked to the small town for its temperate climate, inspiring landscape, supportive environment, and the resources provided by the colleges. Among the well-known artists who would come to call the area home were painters Karl Benjamin, Millard Sheets, and Milford Zornes; ceramists Betty Davenport Ford, Harrison McIntosh, and Richard Petterson; furniture maker Sam Maloof; and sculptors John Edward Svenson and Jack Zajac, to name only a few. These artists, many of whom had served in World War II and witnessed the atrocities of war and genocide, turned towards abstract art in particular as a means of expressing themselves and reflecting upon the rapidly changing society.

Meanwhile, the Padua Hills Theatre, situated on a mesa above the town of Claremont, added another aspect of culture to small-town life. The theater and dining room complex was built in 1930 by the influential Garners, Herman and Bess and originally served as the home of the Claremont Community Players, a theatrical group consisting of local residents who for years came together regularly to produce short plays. However, the group struggled to survive during the Great Depression, and it became increasingly difficult to recruit actors and raise funds for performances. Eventually, the Claremont Community Players left the theater and were replaced by the wildly popular Mexican Players, who performed in non-scripted musical plays depicting traditional life in Mexico. These works, which were performed almost entirely in Spanish to audiences that nearly exclusively spoke English, were influential in bridging the gap between white and Mexican communities in the area and promoting cultural understanding.

The artist community and the Padua Hills Theatre were in no way distinct entities. Rather, they were together part of the growing movement that would lead to Claremont being deemed an "Art Mecca" in the 1950s. Many of the local artists set up homes in the Padua Hills area, and the Padua Hills Theatre provided small shops for them to create and display their works. Each summer from 1953 to 1959, the lively Padua Hills Art Fiesta was held. Advertised as "Art in Action," the fiesta brought local artists and craftsmen together with visitors, encouraging interaction between the two groups. The fiestas provided not only the opportunity for the artists to display and sell their work, but also for the local community to gain an increased understanding and appreciation for the art movement. The heyday of the art movement in Claremont may be over, but a strong artist community still thrives in the town and in the greater Pomona Valley.

Today, Claremont's nickname, "the City of Trees and PhDs," is a reflection of both its past and its present. This book traces Claremont's journey from a close-knit, New England–style village to a bustling citrus town to a thriving artist mecca, and those familiar with the town today will recognize the clear impact that each period had on its development. As the town looks forward to future growth, the importance of preserving Claremont's vibrant past must not be forgotten.

One

Sacred Site
Claremont's Early Settlers

For thousands of years, the Los Angeles Basin was home to native tribes who lived in villages throughout the region. Claremont was home to at least one such village, which was located at the base of the sacred Mount Baldy, or Joatnga ("Snowy Mountain"). Appropriately, the village at its base was named Torojoatnga ("The Place Below Snowy Mountain"). In 1771, the Catholic Church established Mission San Gabriel nearby. The mission incorporated most local natives, now called Gabrielinos, who were brought to work as laborers and sheepherders.

The missions were soon dealt a blow, however, when they were secularized in 1834. Two friends, Ygnacio Palomares and Ricardo Vejar, petitioned for and received a large tract of ex-mission land, which they called Rancho San Jose. They used the land to raise sheep, which were tended to by Gabrielinos. Palomares built his original Adobe de Palomares in present-day Ganesha Park, in Pomona, in 1854. Later, he built the one that remains today on Arrow Highway. Meanwhile, Palomares's sister's family, the Alvarados, built their adobe, El Alisal, just outside the rancho boundaries in what is today Claremont's Memorial Park.

In the 1860s, a drought devastated the area, hitting the rancheros hard. Palomares died in 1864, and his wife was forced to sell off parts of the rancho to American settlers. The Alvarados left their home, which lay abandoned for many years. The Gabrielinos continued to live on Indian Hill, the mesa northeast of what are now Indian Hill and Foothill Boulevards, until 1873, when they were struck by a deadly smallpox outbreak.

The 1880s marked the beginning of a new era. With the arrival of the railroads, eastern land buyers now had easy access to the open expanses of California. The Palomares family had already sold their land in 1874, and in December 1882, the Pomona Land and Water Company bought the Alvarados' land in Claremont. Symbolically, the Alvarados' adobe was torn down and replaced with a clapboard house.

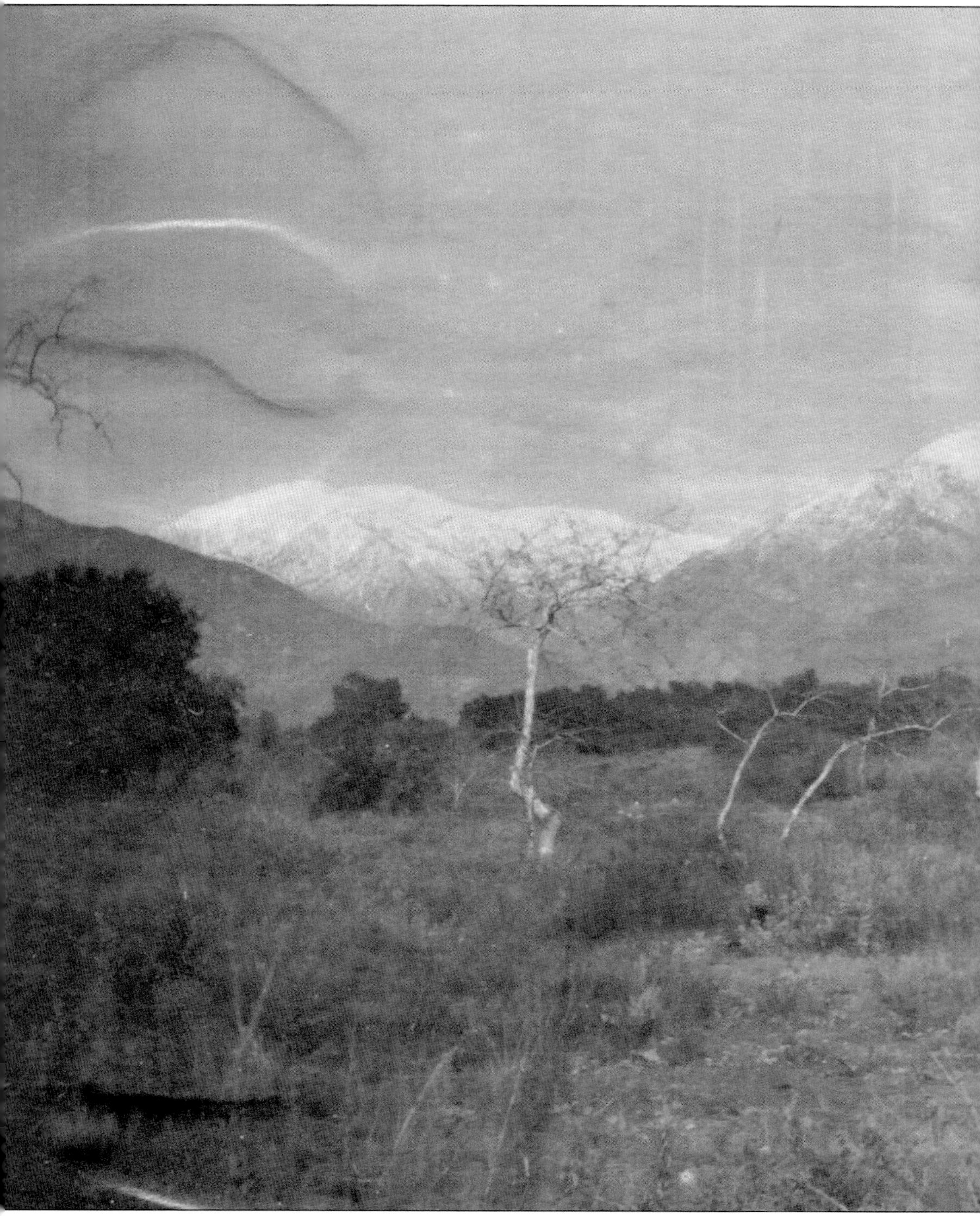

Mount Baldy, c. 1910. Mount San Antonio, commonly referred to as Mount Baldy, is the highest peak in the San Gabriel Mountains, with an elevation of 10,064 feet. Native American encampments are known to have existed in the mountains and foothills surrounding Mount Baldy, with people moving seasonally from the mountain to the valley. The mountain was home

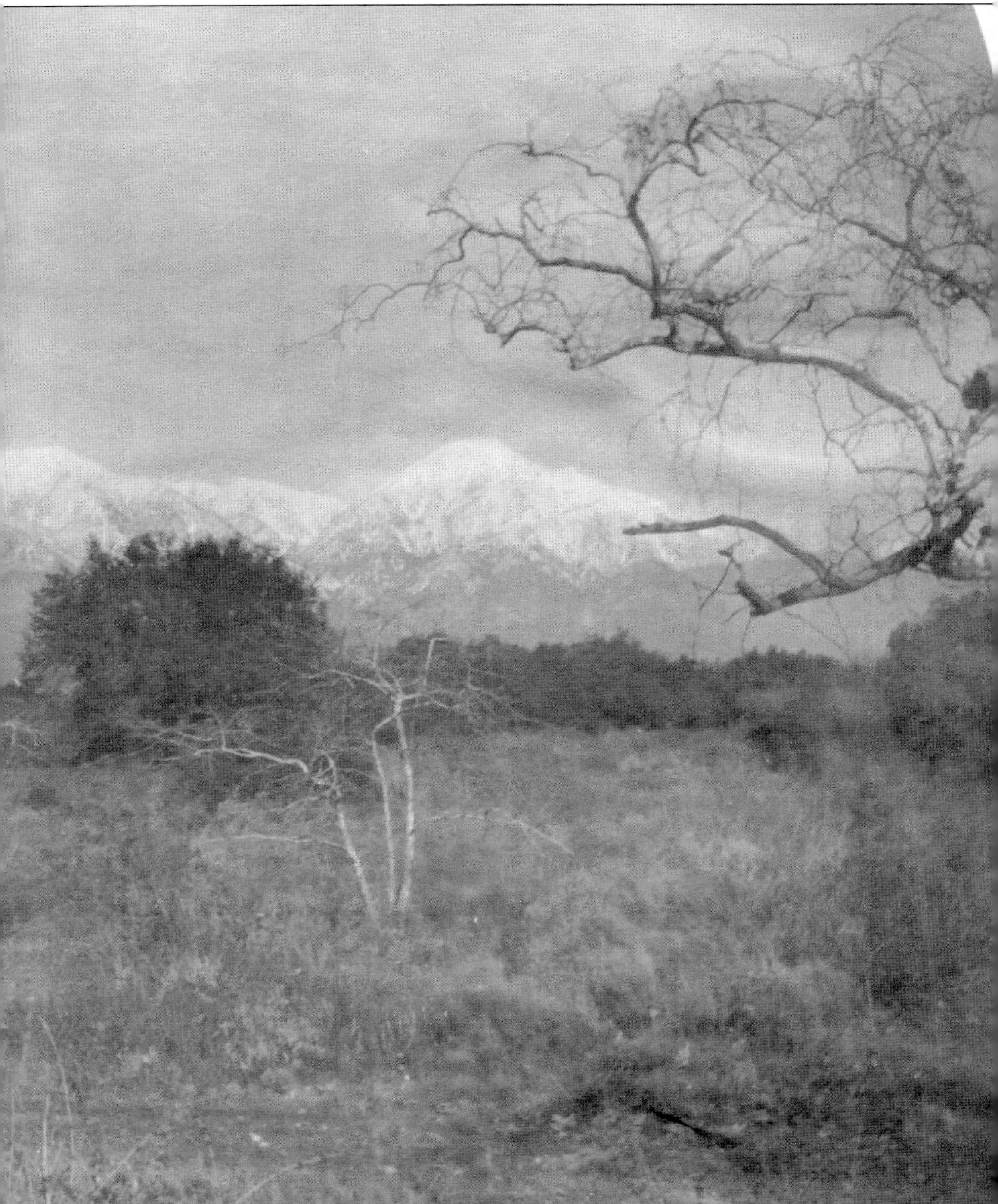

to much plant life and game, and snow runoff made San Antonio Creek an excellent source of fresh water. To many tribes, the mountain, called Joatnga, was sacred. As white settlers came to Claremont, the mountain received the nickname "Old Baldy" due to its bare peak.

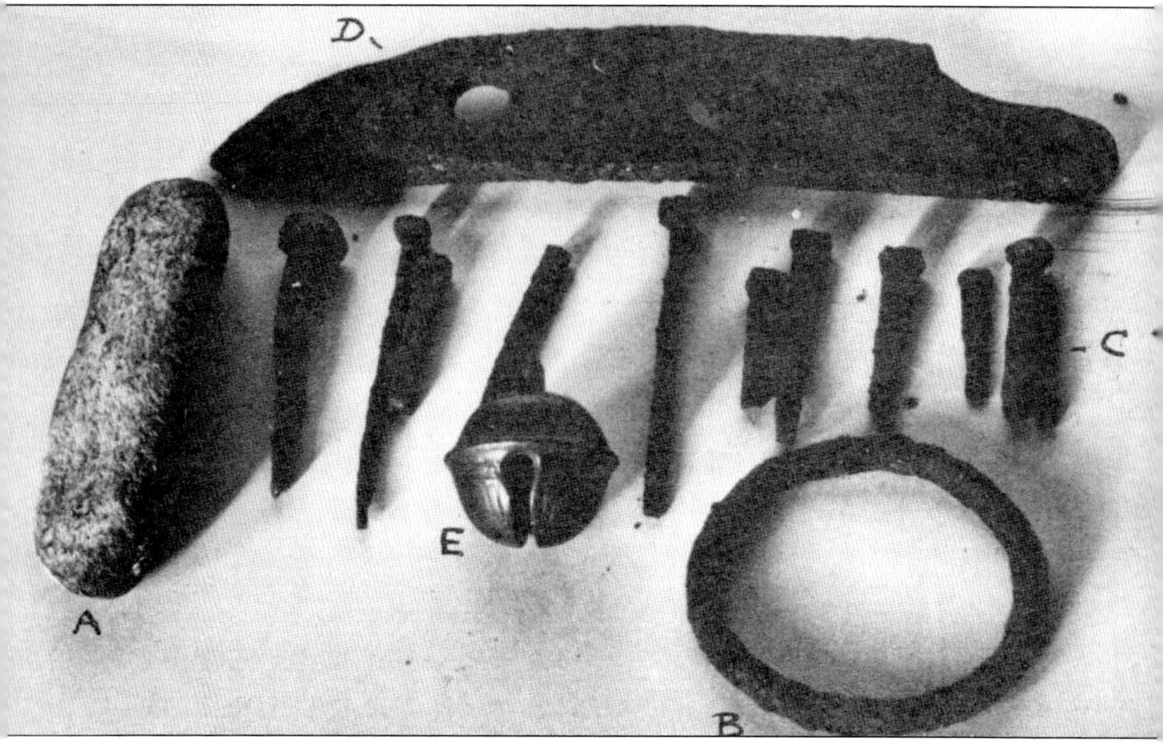

Tongvan Village Artifacts. For centuries, the Pomona Valley was home to several Native American tribes, including the Serrano, Cahuilla, and Tongvan peoples. The Tongvan are believed to have arrived in the area as early as 7000 BC, relying on the abundance of the area's natural resources to survive. Like other tribes in the region, the Tongva utilized freshwater from San Antonio Creek and had tribal encampments scattered along the river throughout the Pomona Valley and into the San Gabriel Mountains. Seen here are artifacts from a Gabrielino encampment on the north side of Indian Hill Boulevard, including an iron ring, nails, and a cast-bronze bell. In 1870, this settlement was home to about 200 Native Americans, who traveled to ranches in Spadra and Puente to work. After a smallpox epidemic hit the community in 1873, their numbers dwindled. By 1883, the settlement was abandoned.

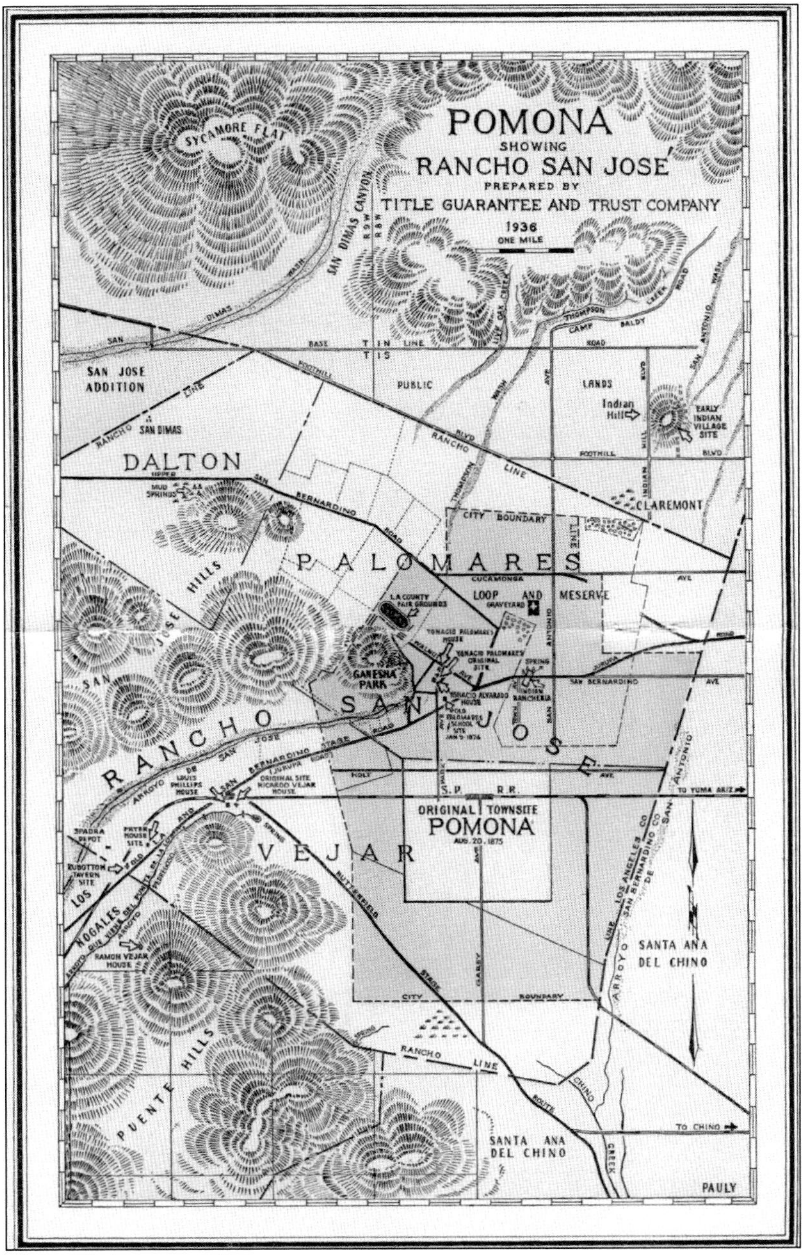

Map of Rancho San Jose. After the Mexican government secularized Mission San Gabriel in 1834, the former church lands were turned into private land grant ranchos. In 1837, Rancho San Jose was purchased by three partners: Ygnacio Palomares, Ricardo Vejar, and Luis Arenas (who sold his share to Henry Dalton). The ranch contained 22,340 acres of land and extended north to San Dimas, west to Covina, east to the San Bernardino County line, and south to the Chino rancho. Rancho San Jose was split roughly into thirds amongst the partners, with Dalton's land lying in San Dimas, Palomares's in Pomona/Claremont, and Vejar's in Spadra/Walnut. Much of the land was utilized for cattle and sheep grazing, providing the owners a steady stream of income. The modern-day communities of Claremont, Pomona, La Verne, San Dimas, and Glendora are all on land once contained in this massive rancho.

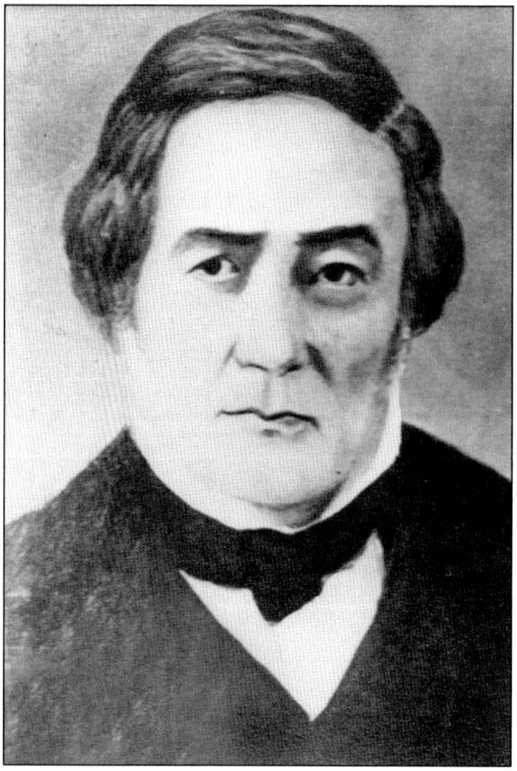

Don Ygnacio Palomares. Shown here is a portrait of Ygnacio Palomares, one of the owners of the Rancho San Jose and an early settler of the Pomona Valley. After emigrating from Mexico to Los Angeles, Palomares received a land grant in 1837 from Juan Alvarado, governor of Alta California, giving him partial ownership of the vast rancho. The Palomares family would control these lands for the next several decades.

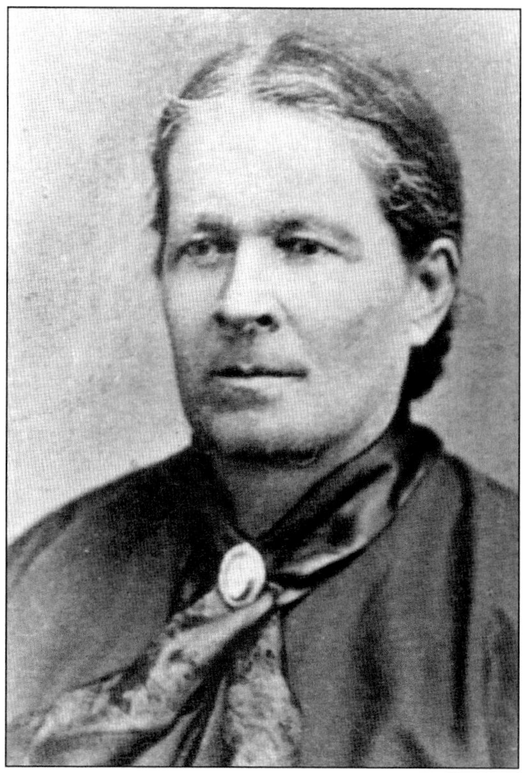

Concepcion Palomares. Pictured here is Doña Concepcion Palomares, the wife of Don Ygnacio. Affectionately known as "China" ("Curly") for her thick, curly, black hair, Concepcion oversaw the Palomares adobe. Ygnacio and Concepcion raised a large family on the rancho, with eight children, numerous grandchildren, and other relatives all living nearby. Several of the Palomares children intermarried with the Vejar family, forging a strong relationship between the rancho families.

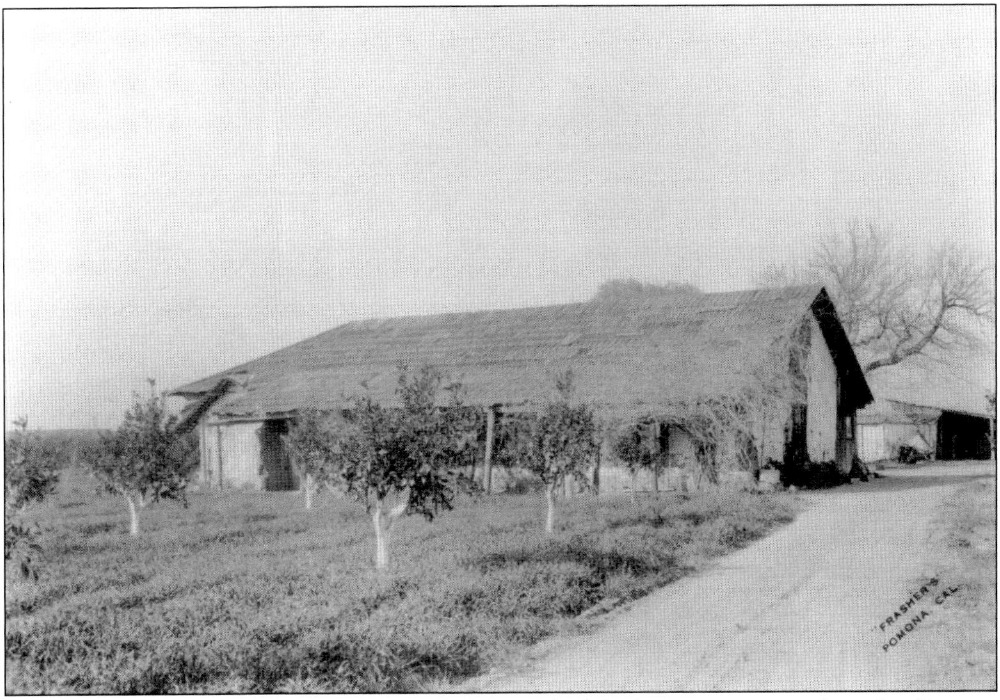

PALOMARES ADOBE. Don Ignacio Palomares's second adobe home was situated on the Camino de San Bernardino (now Arrow Highway), an important route running from Los Angeles and San Bernardino. As the house was strategically located at a midpoint between the two cities, Palomares built a small store providing shelter and basic goods to travelers. This photograph shows the home after its restoration in 1939. (Courtesy of the Judy Wright collection.)

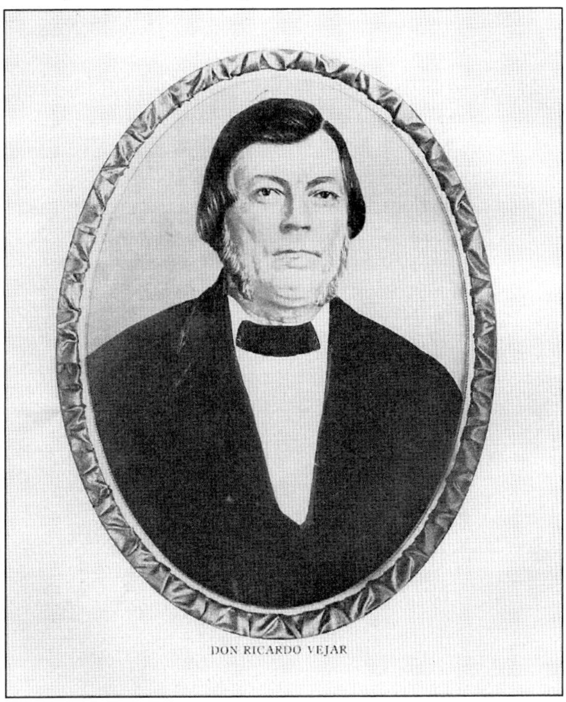

RICARDO VEJAR. Palomares's friend and partner Ricardo Vejar owned the southern portion of the Rancho San Jose lands. Vejar's home was located near present-day Walnut. Both Palomares and Vejar were important figures of the rancho, often acting as de facto government officials. The partners oversaw the land, settled disputes, and even organized rodeos for neighbors to attend.

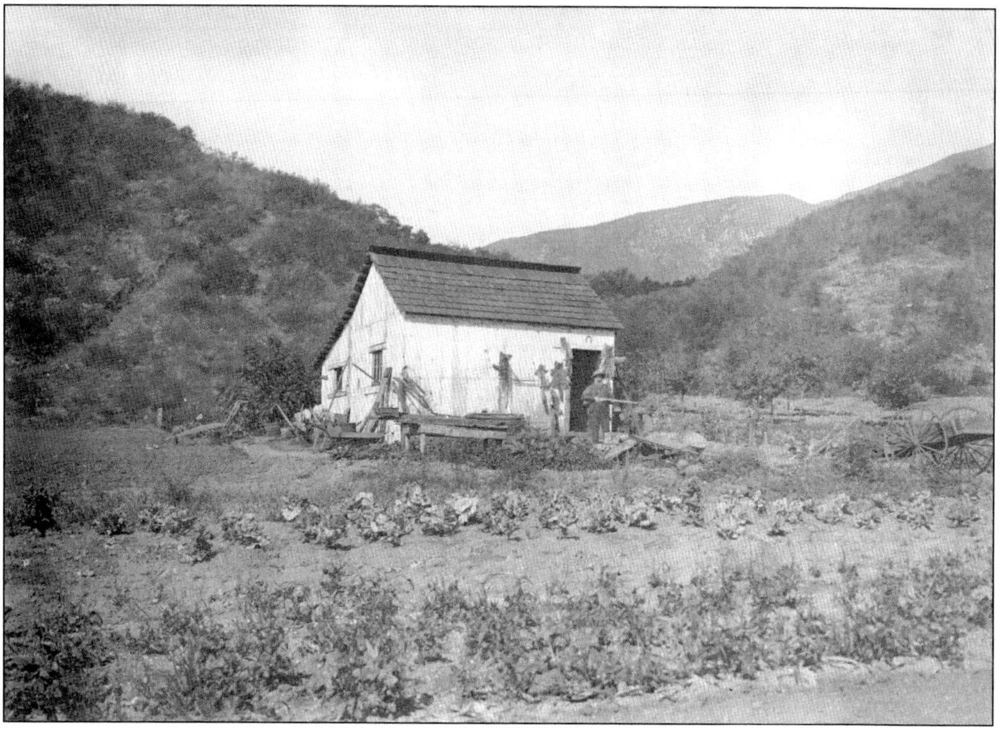

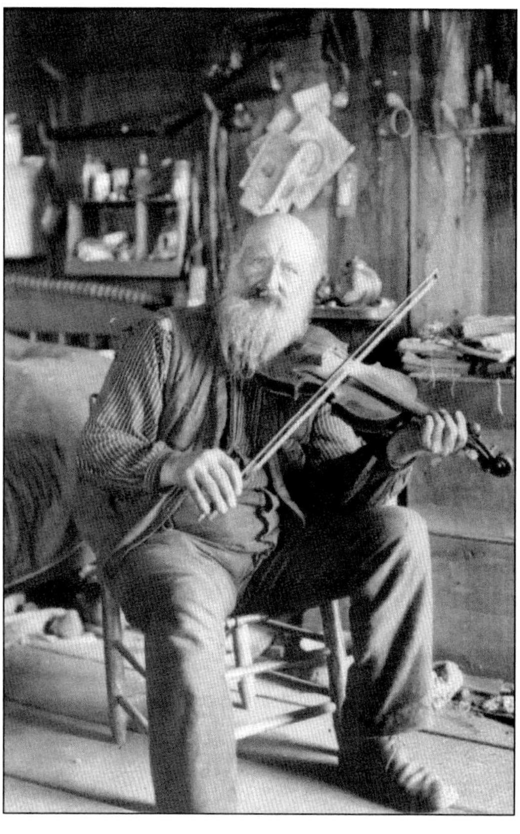

WILLIAM "TOOCH" MARTIN, C. 1909. One of Claremont's more eccentric characters, Martin has the distinction of being the town's first white settler. In 1871, he purchased 156 acres in Claremont, near what is now Eleventh Street and Indian Hill Boulevard. Martin was very involved in the community, becoming a Los Angeles County supervisor, founding the Pomona Masonic Lodge in 1877, and serving as the chairman of Pomona's school board in 1909. In his later years, Martin sought to escape the growing city, moving to a cabin in Palmer Canyon and living as a recluse. He is seen above standing in front of his cabin and at left passing time playing his beloved fiddle. (Both, courtesy of Special Collections, Honnold/Mudd Library of the Claremont Colleges.)

Two

Roads and Rails

A Development along the Lines

The expansion of railroads into Southern California, following the completion of the country's first transcontinental railroad in 1869, brought unprecedented growth to the area. New towns sprang up beside the railway lines as land-hungry easterners poured into the vast, largely unpopulated region. Between Los Angeles and San Bernardino alone, over 30 prospective towns were developed along the Southern Pacific line and the competing Santa Fe. Claremont, on the Santa Fe route, was one of these boomtowns.

Claremont was established largely due to efforts by new resident Henry Austin Palmer. A shrewd Northern Californian land buyer, Palmer had purchased 80 acres of land in Pomona at the beginning of the land boom and had then moved his family into El Alisal, the old home of the Alvarado family. When Palmer learned of the Santa Fe Railroad's interest in building a line through the area, he cleverly suggested it pass above North Pomona, thus establishing the town of Claremont.

In 1887, the Pacific Land Improvement Company, a Santa Fe Railroad subsidiary, began preparations for the planned 430-acre town. Thick brush was cleared, and a handful of buildings were constructed. "Claremont," posters advertised, "is . . . for people from the East who want a place for a home that possesses all the natural attraction that makes life worth living for." The first Claremont land auction, on April 7, was a smashing success, with about 300 lots sold.

However, by spring of the following year, the land bubble burst—land sales crashed, interest rates rose, and Claremont was left a near ghost town. The beautiful hotel sat abandoned and unfurnished, and the only sign of the town's prior success were the rows of white posts marking the purchased but empty lots. Claremont seemed destined to go the way of so many other boomtowns and fade into the dust. It was only the founding of the nearby Congregationalist Pomona College that saved it from such a fate.

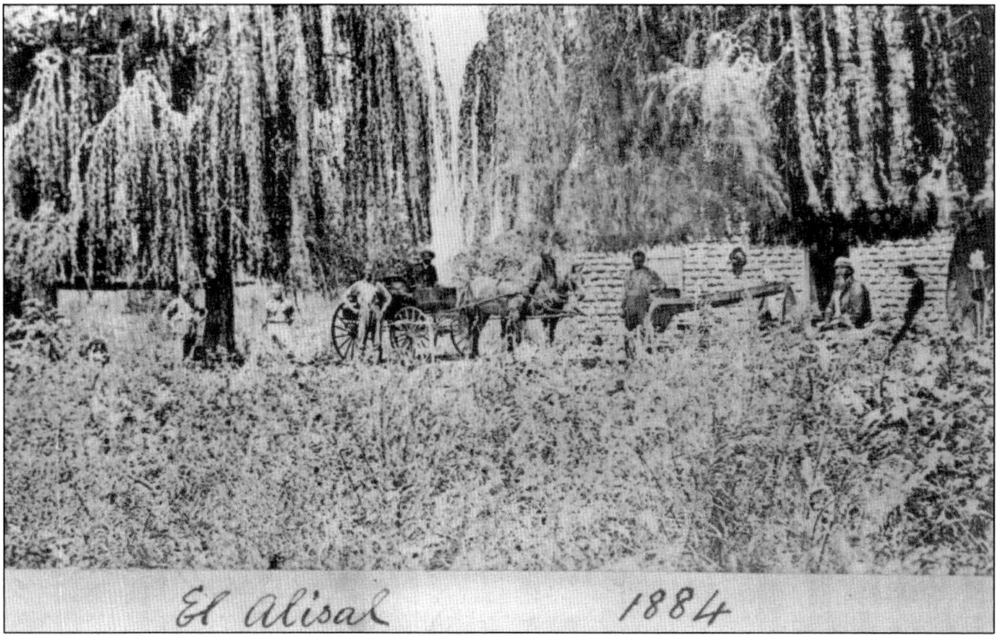

EL ALISAL, C. 1884. The original adobe El Alisal ("The Sycamore") was built by the Alvarado family in 1846 as a residence and stagecoach station. Local legend has it that a wealthy family member buried treasure under a sycamore on the property, though despite much searching, it has never been found. This photograph shows the remodeled home after it was purchased by Henry Palmer (seen standing in front of the buggy).

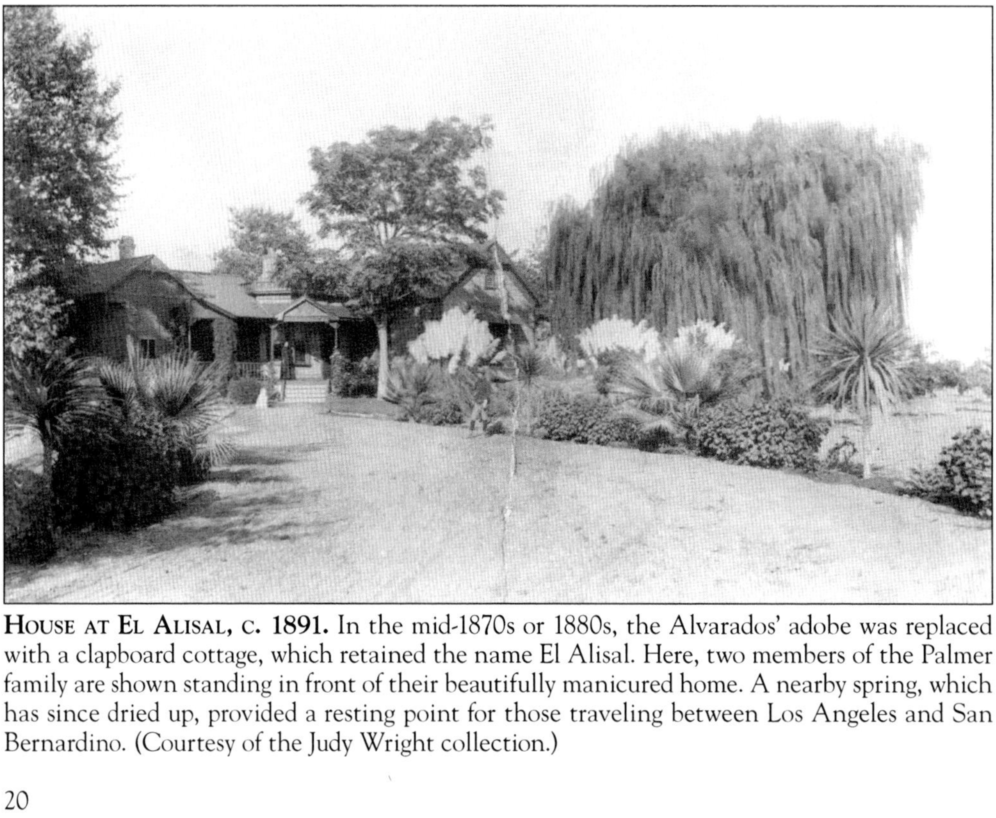

HOUSE AT EL ALISAL, C. 1891. In the mid-1870s or 1880s, the Alvarados' adobe was replaced with a clapboard cottage, which retained the name El Alisal. Here, two members of the Palmer family are shown standing in front of their beautifully manicured home. A nearby spring, which has since dried up, provided a resting point for those traveling between Los Angeles and San Bernardino. (Courtesy of the Judy Wright collection.)

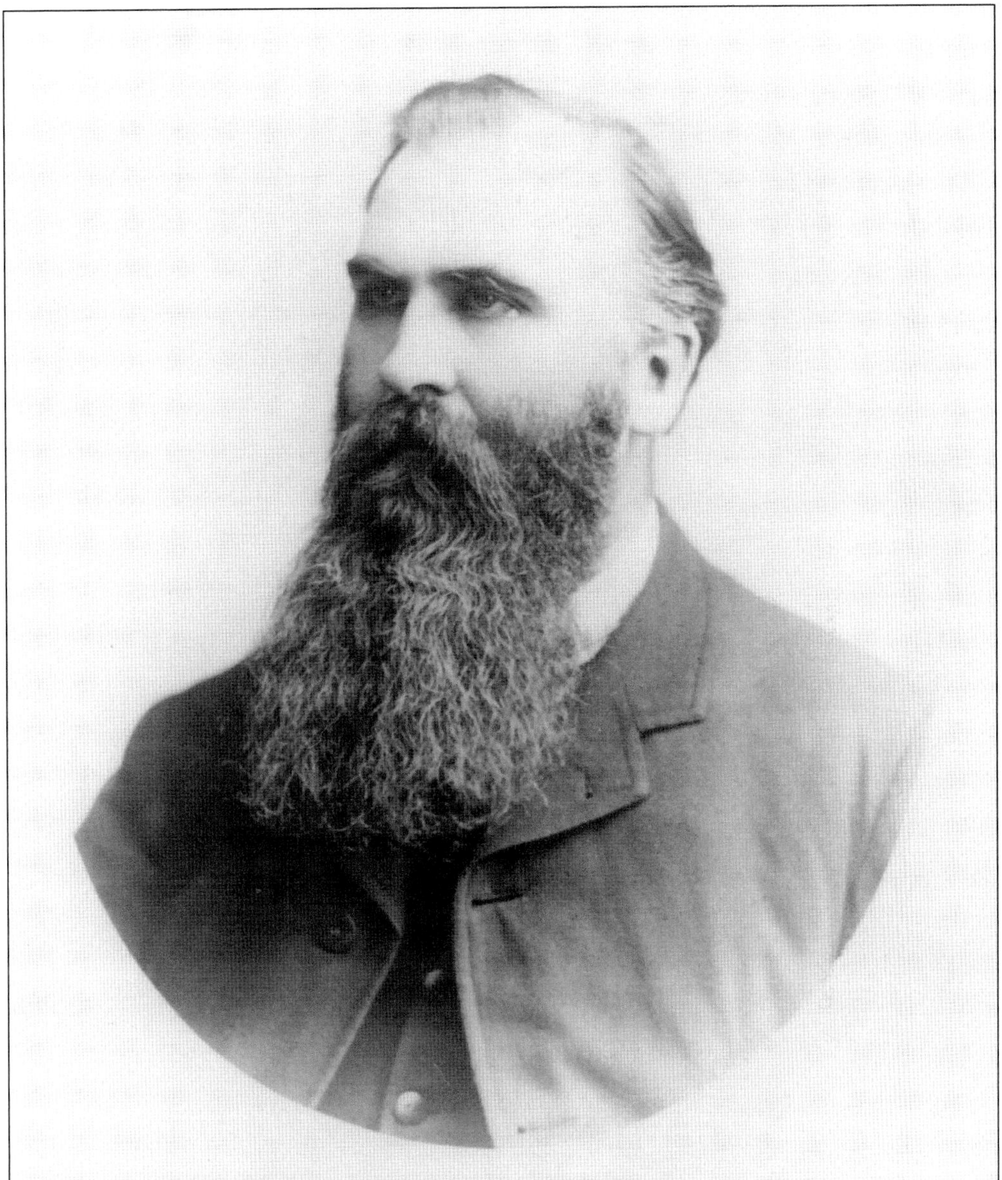

Henry Austin Palmer. A key figure in Claremont's establishment, Palmer has even been called the "father" of the town. Born in 1842 in Connecticut, Palmer moved to Oakland, California, at age 20 to work in banking and try his hand at politics. In 1882, he traveled to the Pomona Valley, where he helped incorporate the Pomona Land and Water Company and the Pomona Bank. Remarkably, he found time to serve as president of both. The achievement that earned him the title "father of Claremont," however, was his instrumental role in convincing the Santa Fe Railroad to build its line through northern Pomona, effectively siphoning off the area that would become Claremont. Palmer is also thought to have suggested the name Claremont for the newly platted town. Aside from his contributions to land development, he was involved in the Congregationalist movement and helped establish churches in both Pomona and Claremont. To top off his impressive resume, Palmer was also the first president of the Pomona College Board of Trustees. (Courtesy of the Judy Wright collection.)

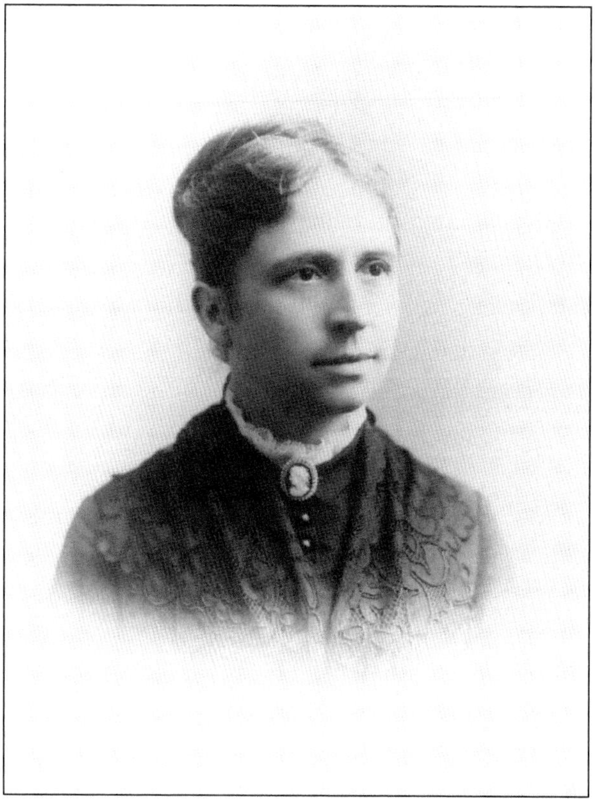

Jennie Day Palmer. In 1867, Jane Olivia "Jennie" Day married her second cousin Henry Palmer in San Francisco. She is notable for being the granddaughter of Jeremiah Day, the president of Yale in the early 1800s. Jennie lived with her family in El Alisal for many years until financial ruin following the collapse of the Pomona Bank forced the Palmers to move to Los Angeles. (Courtesy of the Judy Wright collection.)

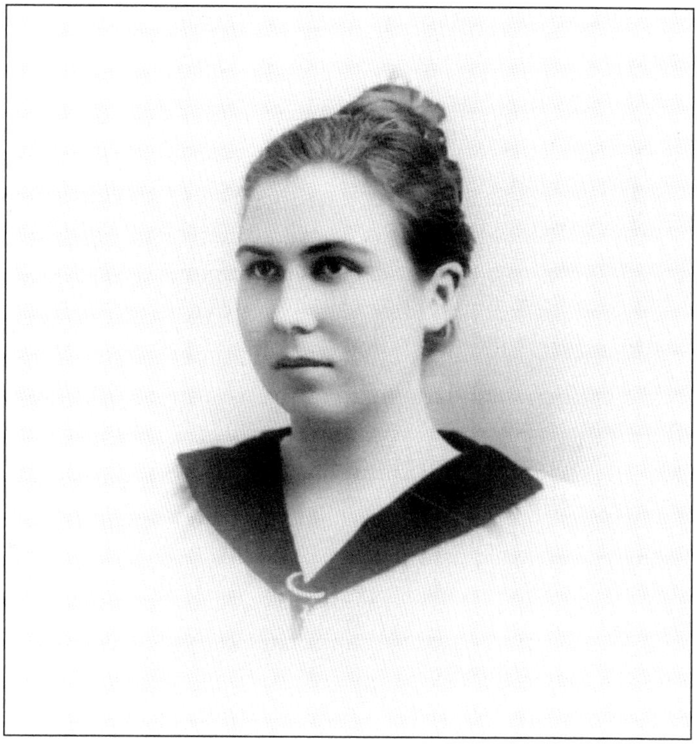

Elizabeth Day Palmer. Henry and Jennie Palmer's only daughter, Elizabeth, who was called Bessie by her family, was born in Oakland, California, in 1872. A passionate learner, she graduated from the University of California, Berkeley and taught briefly at the Claremont Grammar School before beginning her long career as a science teacher at Los Angeles High School. (Courtesy of the Judy Wright collection.)

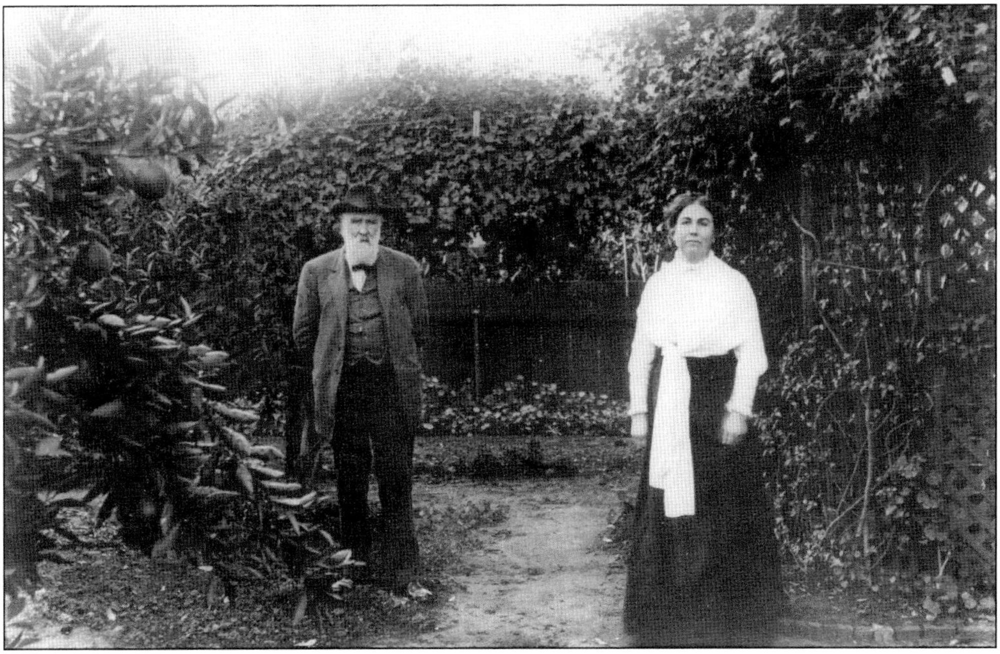

Henry and Elizabeth Palmer. Henry and Elizabeth Palmer, shown here in front of El Alisal, were especially close throughout their lives. Henry named Palmer Canyon in Claremont in honor of his beloved daughter, and Elizabeth lived with her parents after they moved from the Pomona Valley to Los Angeles. The Palmers also had two sons, Theodore Sherman Palmer and Harold King Palmer. (Courtesy of the Judy Wright collection.)

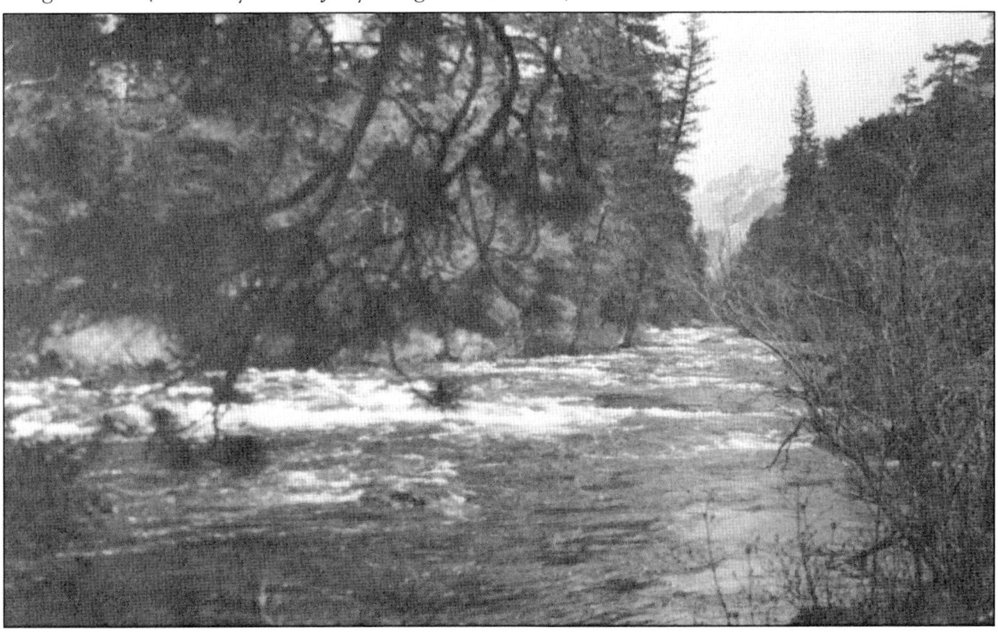

San Antonio Canyon. The lifeblood of the Pomona Valley, the water from San Antonio Canyon helped to transform arid foothills and valleys into a more lush and hospitable environment for settlers. In the 1870s, Rev. C.F. Loop and A.R. Meserve bought the water rights to the canyon from the Palomares family, marking the first of the area's many water sales.

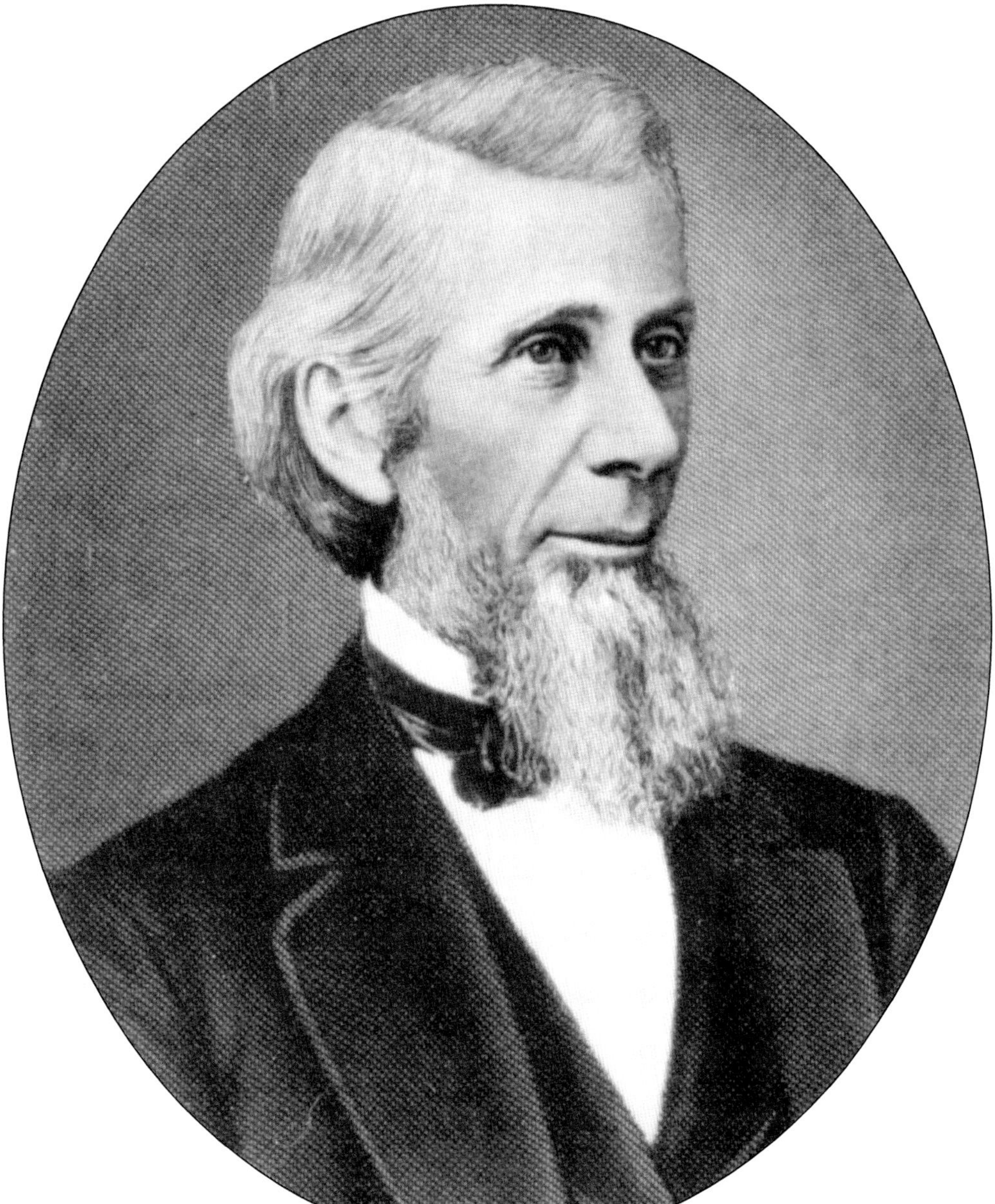

Cyrus Mills. In the all-important fight for water rights, Mills played a key role in bringing water to the Pomona Valley, markedly changing the area's landscape. Born in 1819 in New York, he spent his early life traveling the world, teaching in Ceylon and India and serving as president of Oahu College in Hawaii. He and his family came to Southern California in the 1870s to invest in land, and, in 1882, alongside Henry Palmer and M.L. Wicks, Mills incorporated the Pomona Land and Water Company. As the company's first president, Mills purchased 2,500 acres of land and water rights from the defunct Pomona Water Company to construct a pipeline to San Antonio Canyon. This project, which was finished in 1883, gave the Pomona Valley its first stable water source, with water from the canyon now reliably available to the area's settlers. (Courtesy of the Judy Wright collection.)

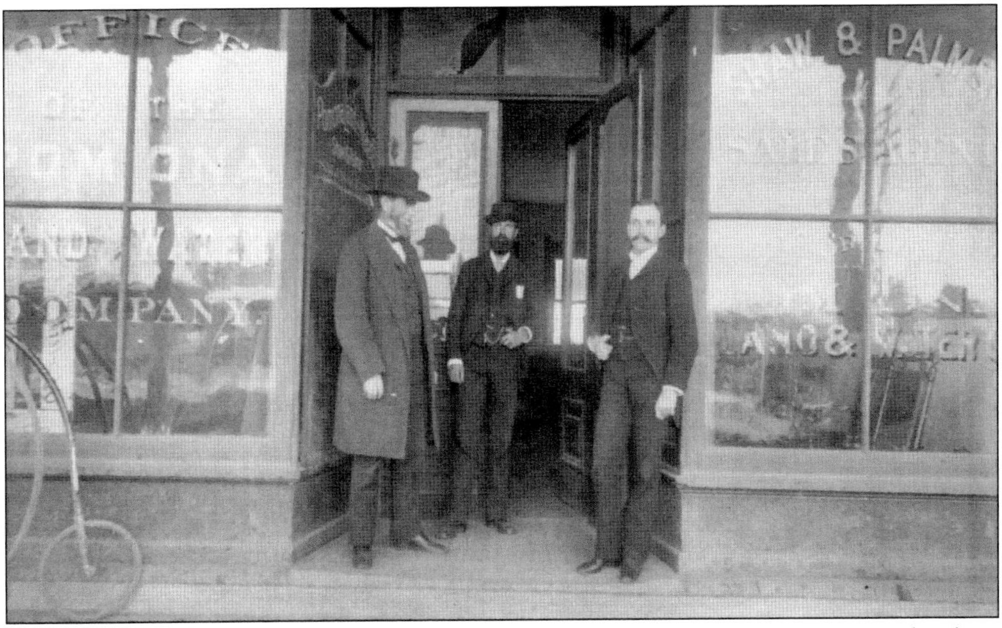

POMONA VALLEY LAND AND WATER COMPANY SALES OFFICE. Henry Palmer's nephew Frank Palmer (center) is shown here in front of the office of the Pomona Valley Land and Water Company, of which he was secretary and treasurer. The company, led first by Cyrus Mills and then by Henry Palmer, acquired water rights for the valley and was instrumental in constructing irrigation pipes and plumes.

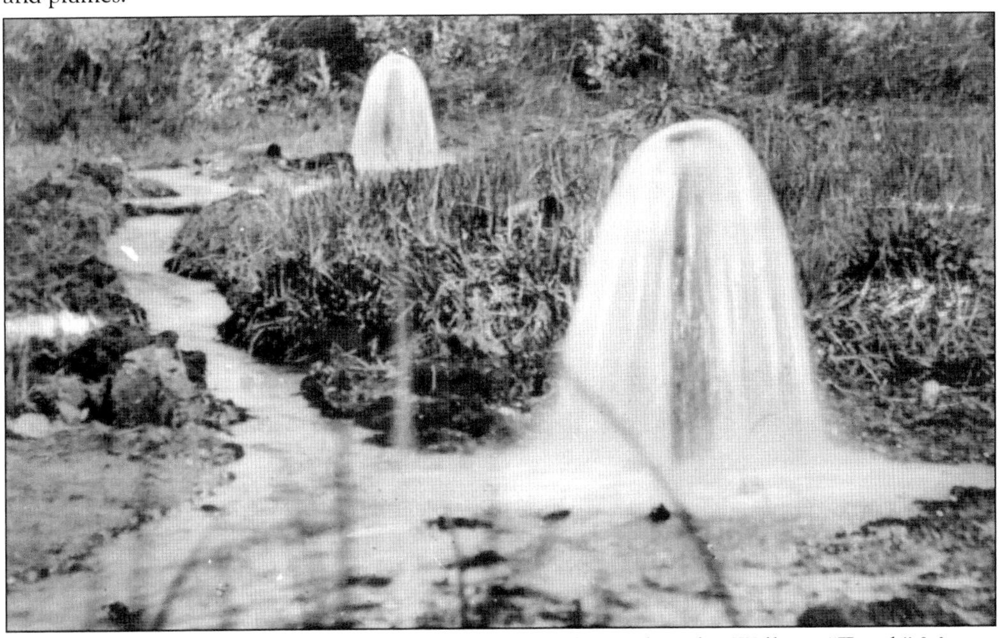

"TWIN WELLS," C. 1886. These artesian wells were located at the William "Tooch" Martin Cienega, where Pilgrim Place stands today. Such wells were once abundant in the Pomona Valley, helping provide a steady water supply to early residents. By the late 1880s, the Pomona Land and Water Company had gained ownership of most of these natural springs, which ranged in depth from 100 to 200 feet.

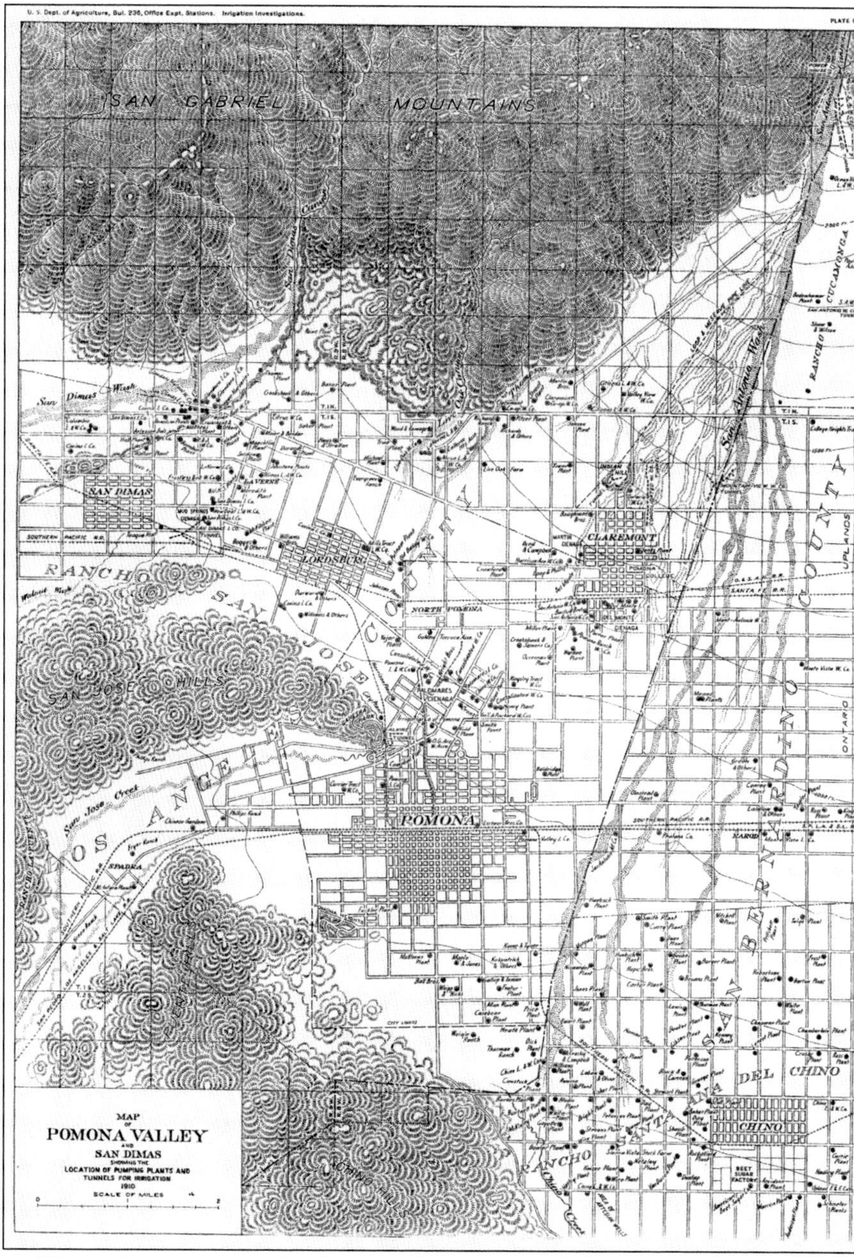

POMONA WATER MAP, C. 1910. As this map shows, natural springs were found throughout the valley, with irrigation tunnels stretching as far as the neighboring communities of La Verne, Chino, and San Dimas. The land boom of the 1870s sparked a fierce battle for control of the water in the Pomona Valley. After changing hands several times, the water rights were eventually secured by the Pomona Land and Water Company in 1882, and divided between Pomona and Ontario a few years later. The Pomona Land and Water Company's aqueduct, completed in 1883, brought water from San Antonio Canyon through Claremont and into Pomona. Construction of this massive undertaking was completed in only 18 months, at a cost of $65,000. Its completion helped provide the area with a reliable source of water, which would be important in the creation of Claremont just a few years later.

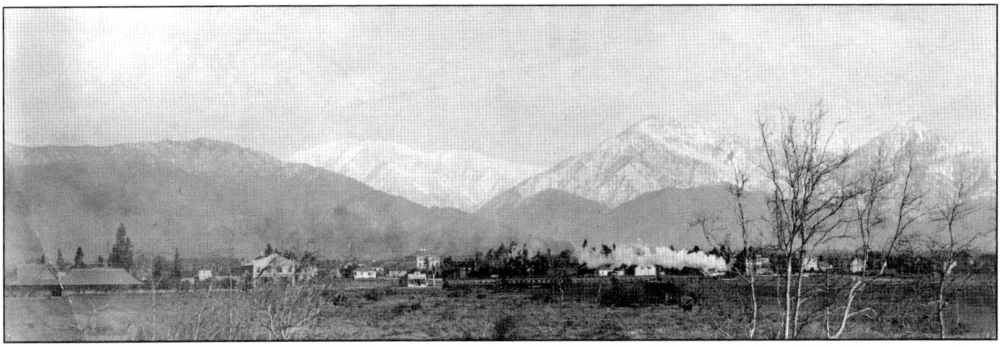

Santa Fe Railroad. In the midst of the land boom of the 1870s and 1880s, a railroad rate war raged between the monopolistic Southern Pacific and the newcomer Santa Fe Railroad. Each wanted greater control of the underserved Southern California area, which in 1885 had only one local train line running between Los Angeles and Pomona. In 1887, the Santa Fe Railroad Company built its own line along the route, making travel to the valley markedly more efficient and laying the groundwork for the establishment of numerous towns along the way. Henry Palmer worked with the railroad agents to arrange for the line to run through northern Pomona, thus creating the boomtown of Claremont. Below, a Santa Fe train is seen in Claremont. (Both, courtesy of Special Collections, Honnold/Mudd Library of the Claremont Colleges.)

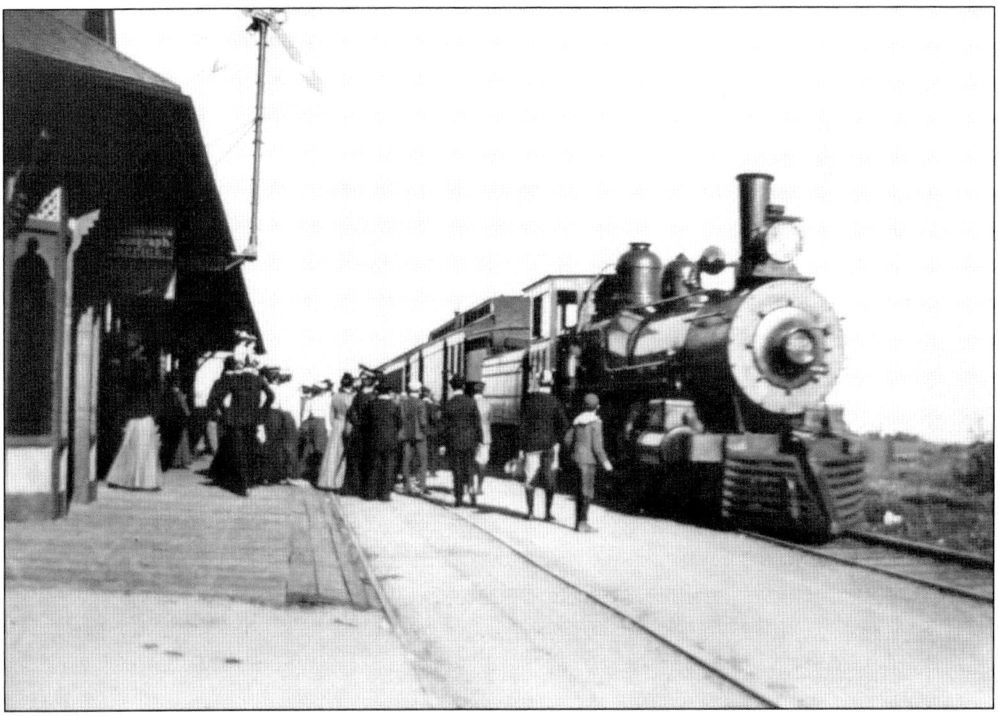

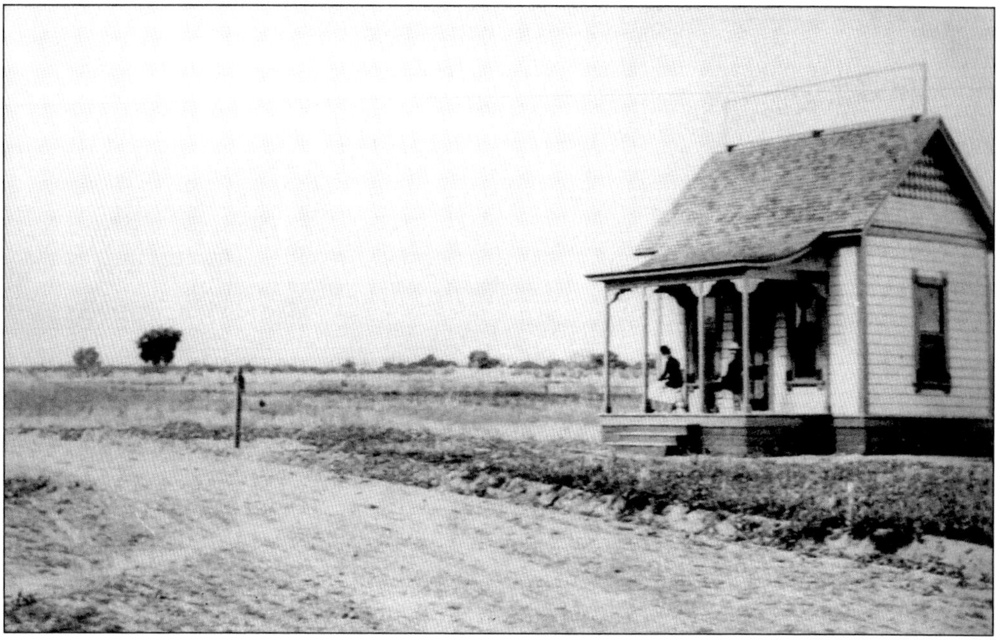

Pacific Land Improvement Company Sales Office. After the Santa Fe had selected the route for its Los Angeles–San Bernardino line, a syndicate, the Pacific Land Improvement Company, was formed to manage and sell lots in the new railroad town above Pomona. The name Claremont was selected by company agents, and efforts to "improve" the wilderness by removing bushes and rocks, laying streets, and constructing a hotel were soon under way. (Courtesy of Special Collections, Honnold/Mudd Library of the Claremont Colleges.)

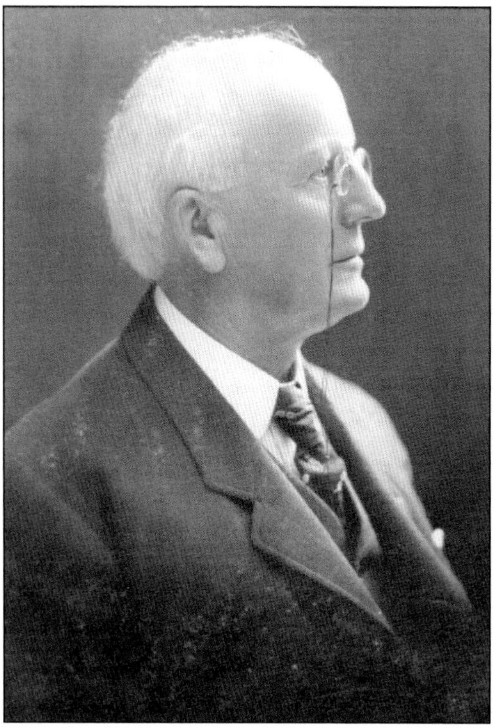

Col. William Holabird. A Civil War veteran turned land developer, Holabird served as the Claremont overseer and chief land auctioneer for the Pacific Land Improvement Company. After moving to town in 1887, he built Claremont up from the dust, constructing a number of houses and laying out the streets with the help of hired Chinese workers. His painstaking effort helped sell hundreds of lots. (Courtesy of Special Collections, Honnold/Mudd Library of the Claremont Colleges.)

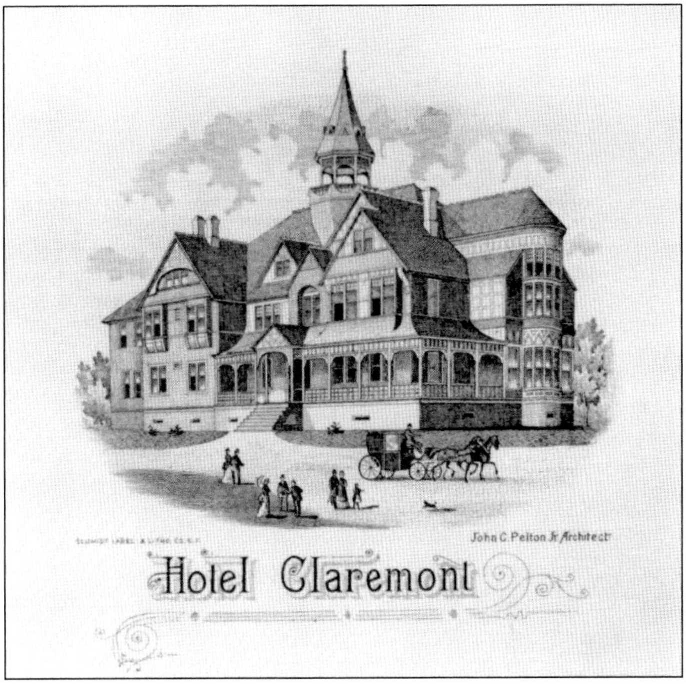

HOTEL CLAREMONT SKETCH. To give Claremont the appearance of a thriving city, the Pacific Land Improvement Company constructed the grand Hotel Claremont. Designed by San Francisco architect John C. Pelton Jr., it was meant to serve as the hub of the burgeoning new community. This beautiful sketch, intended to illustrate the hotel's potential, reveals the grandiose dreams the overly optimistic Claremont developers had at the height of the land boom. (Courtesy of Special Collections, Honnold/Mudd Library of the Claremont Colleges.)

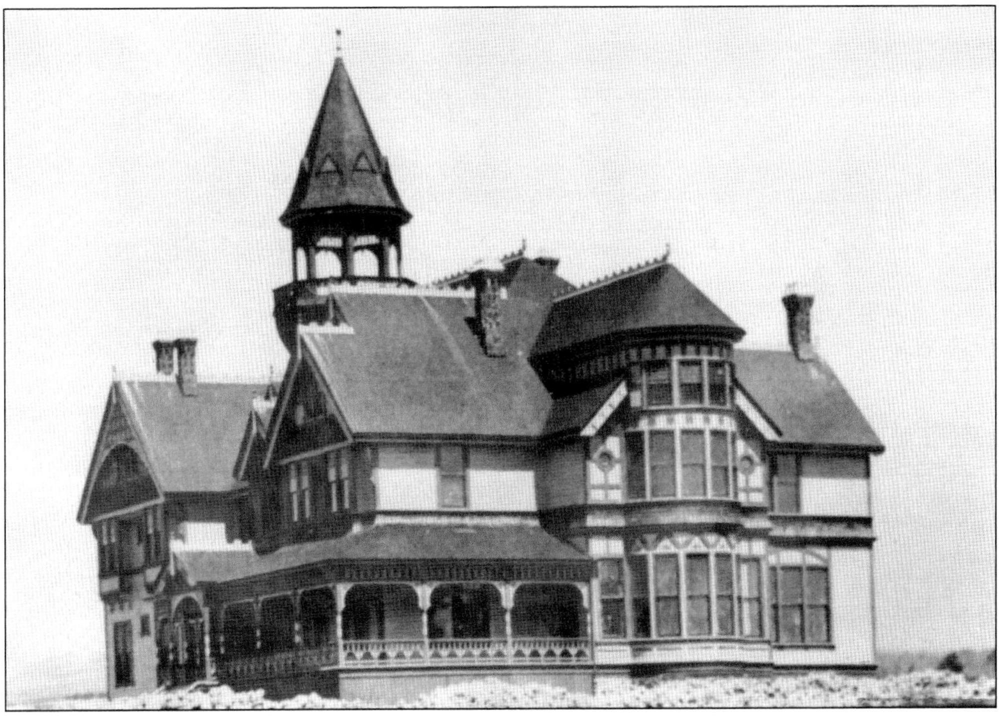

HOTEL CLAREMONT, C. 1887. Town developers hoped that the lavish Hotel Claremont would entice buyers to purchase lots in Claremont. Unfortunately, however, the building was largely unfinished by the time of the final land auction, with only the lobby and dining rooms completed. The hotel never served a single guest, but it would later get a second chance at life as the home of Pomona College.

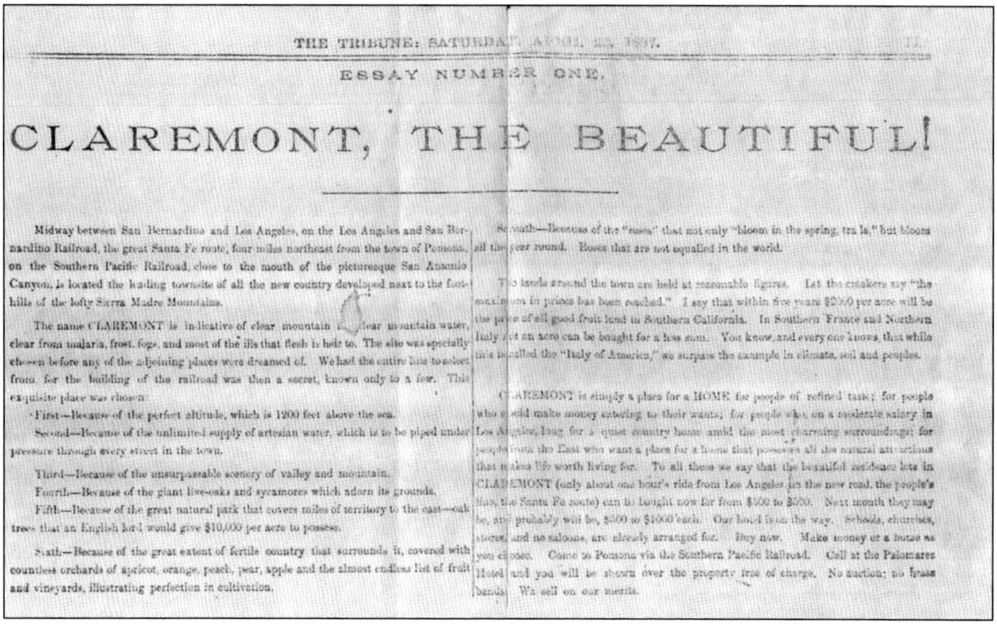

THE TRIBUNE: SATURDAY, [illegible] 1887.

ESSAY NUMBER ONE.

CLAREMONT, THE BEAUTIFUL!

Midway between San Bernardino and Los Angeles, on the Los Angeles and San Bernardino Railroad, the great Santa Fe route, four miles northeast from the town of Pomona, on the Southern Pacific Railroad, close to the mouth of the picturesque San Antonio Canyon, is located the leading townsite of all the new country developed next to the foothills of the lofty Sierra Madre Mountains.

The name CLAREMONT is indicative of clear mountain [illegible] clear mountain water, clear from malaria, frost, fogs, and most of the ills that flesh is heir to. The site was specially chosen before any of the adjoining places were dreamed of. We had the entire line to select from, for the building of the railroad was then a secret, known only to a few. This exquisite place was chosen:

First—Because of the perfect altitude, which is 1200 feet above the sea.

Second—Because of the unlimited supply of artesian water, which is to be piped under pressure through every street in the town.

Third—Because of the unsurpassable scenery of valley and mountain.

Fourth—Because of the giant live-oaks and sycamores which adorn its grounds.

Fifth—Because of the great natural park that covers miles of territory to the east—oak trees that an English lord would give $10,000 per acre to possess.

Sixth—Because of the great extent of fertile country that surrounds it, covered with countless orchards of apricot, orange, peach, pear, apple and the almost endless list of fruit and vineyards, illustrating perfection in cultivation.

Seventh—Because of the "roses" that not only "bloom in the spring, tra la," but bloom all the year round. Roses that are not equalled in the world.

The lands around the town are held at reasonable figures. Let the croakers say "the maximum in prices has been reached." I say that within five years $2000 per acre will be the price of all good fruit land in Southern California. In Southern France and Northern Italy not an acre can be bought for a less sum. You know, and every one knows, that while this is called the "Italy of America," we surpass the example in climate, soil and peoples.

CLAREMONT is simply a place for a HOME for people of refined taste; for people who would make money catering to their wants; for people who, on a moderate salary in Los Angeles, long for a quiet country home amid the most charming surroundings; for people from the East who want a place for a home that possesses all the natural attractions that makes life worth living for. To all these we say that the beautiful residence lots in CLAREMONT (only about one hour's ride from Los Angeles on the new road, the people's line, the Santa Fe route) can be bought now for from $300 to $500. Next month they may be, and probably will be, $500 to $1000 each. Our hotel is on the way. Schools, churches, stores, and no saloons, are already arranged for. Buy now. Make money or a home as you choose. Come to Pomona via the Southern Pacific Railroad. Call at the Palomares Hotel and you will be shown over the property free of charge. No auction; no brass bands. We sell on our merits.

"CLAREMONT, THE BEAUTIFUL," 1887. "Claremont, The Beautiful!" is one of three descriptive essays written in early 1887 to attract settlers to Claremont. The city's clear mountain air and water were used as key selling points. The author is generally thought to be one of the three primary men involved in the development of Claremont: Henry Palmer, William Holabird, or Frank Miller, the town's sales agent.

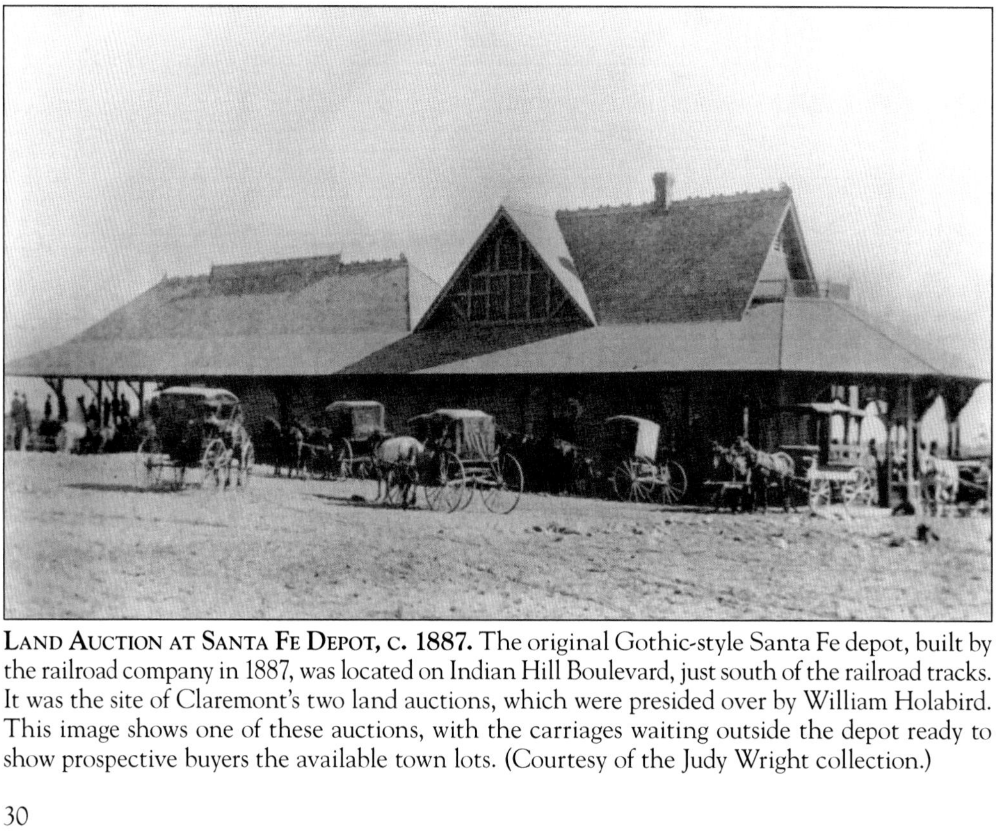

LAND AUCTION AT SANTA FE DEPOT, C. 1887. The original Gothic-style Santa Fe depot, built by the railroad company in 1887, was located on Indian Hill Boulevard, just south of the railroad tracks. It was the site of Claremont's two land auctions, which were presided over by William Holabird. This image shows one of these auctions, with the carriages waiting outside the depot ready to show prospective buyers the available town lots. (Courtesy of the Judy Wright collection.)

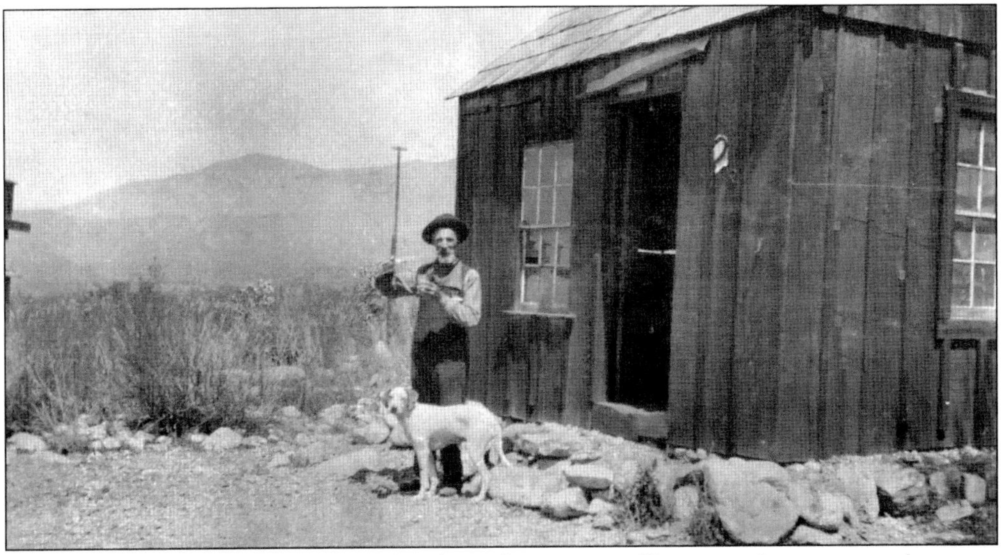

Gale Goat Ranch. During the land rush, settlers came to Claremont for a variety of reasons. Stephen Gale (above) arrived in the Pomona Valley in 1884 to prospect for gold and homestead. After more than 10 years of isolated existence, Gale was joined by his business-savvy nephew Warren Gale, who set about making the homestead profitable. Eventually, Gale Ranch boasted a flock of over 3,000 goats and Angora sheep. Warren, in addition to being a dedicated rancher, gained a reputation for throwing raucous parties that attracted people from as far away as Los Angeles. The ranch closed around 1920, after a nearby fire forced the Gales to set their animals free into the foothills. Descendants of Gale's Angora sheep are still rumored to live on Mount Baldy today.

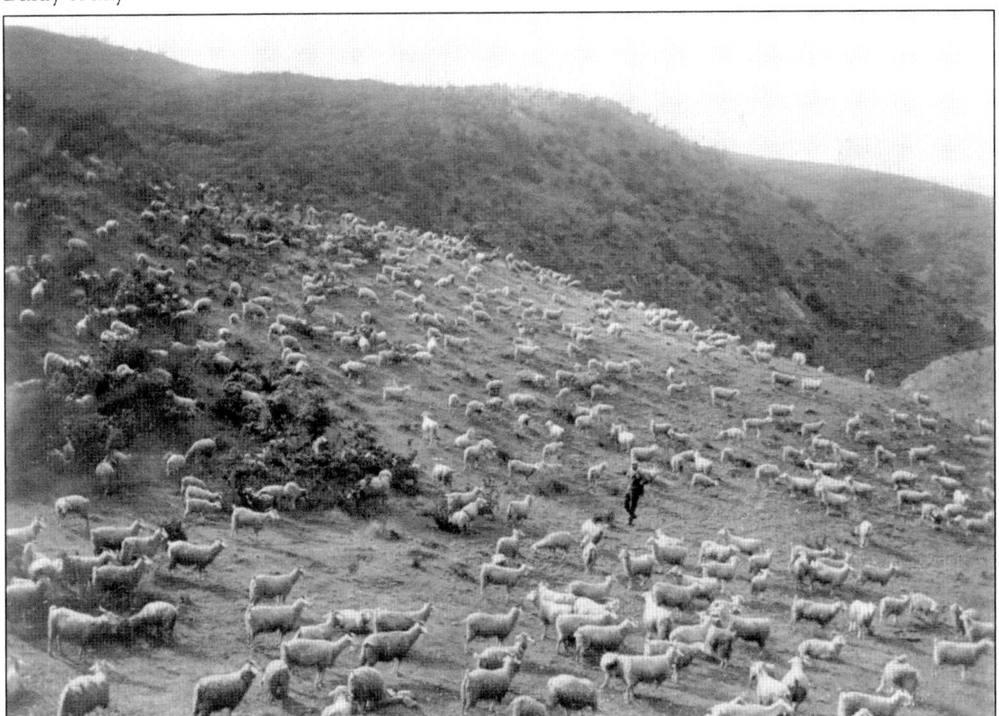

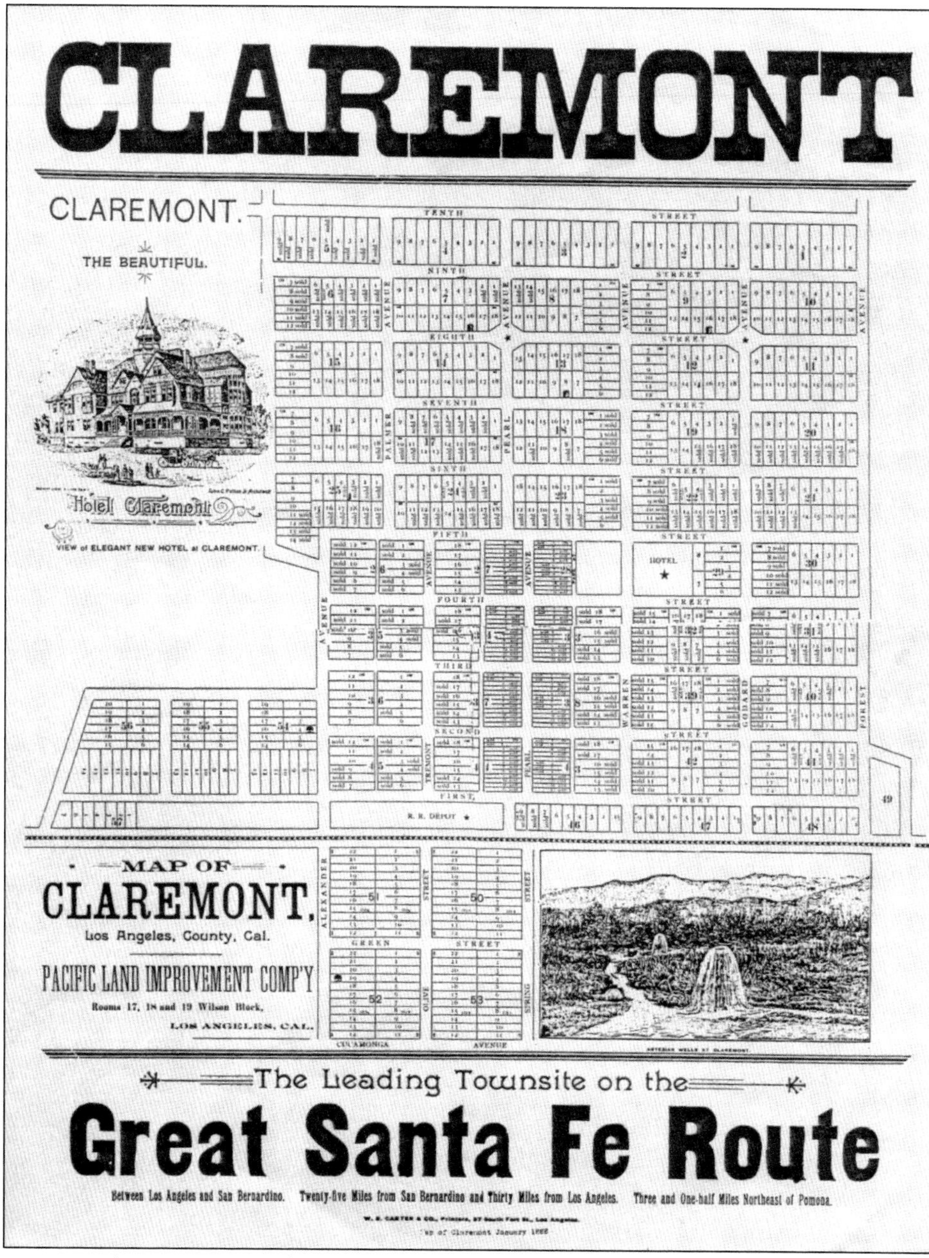

Claremont Auction Map. This auction map from the April 1887 land sale shows the planned town of Claremont, which, at the time, was made up of little more than a hotel, a railroad depot, and a handful of houses. The Pacific Land Improvement Company divided the land into a business section, which had lots 20 feet by 100 feet, and a residential section, which had lots of 50 feet by 100 feet. The company intentionally created these rather small lots as a way to sell as many landholdings in the boom as possible. The first Claremont auction, in April, sold around 300 lots, while the second, held in January 1888, sold slightly fewer. Combined, the two sales made over $80,000. However, by mid-1880, before nearly any of Claremont's buyers had actually moved to town, the land boom busted. As interest rates rose and land values plummeted, Claremont, like so many other boom communities, became a veritable ghost town.

Three

Church, Town, and Gown
A College Community

Claremont's saving grace was the recently founded Pomona College, which was itself struggling in the post-boom years. In the frenzy of the land rush, plans had been made for the Congregationalist school to be built in the proposed town of Piedmont on Scanlon Mesa, at the mouth of Live Oak Canyon. The cornerstones were laid at that location in September 1888, but when the bubble burst and funds became tight, the college was forced to hold classes in a small cottage in Pomona.

It was then that a brilliant plan was engineered to ensure the future of both the town and the college: the school could move into the abandoned hotel in Claremont, at least temporarily. Over the Christmas break of 1888–1889, Pomona College relocated to the large, unfurnished Claremont Hall, as the hotel was called. This proved successful, and, by the winter of 1892, the college's board had made the decision to remain permanently in Claremont.

In those early years, church, town, and gown were inextricably linked. Pomona College had breathed new life into Claremont, and the town gradually began to attract new residents, mostly Congregationalist New Englanders drawn by the promise of free land and a good education for their children. In the spirit of community, residents and college students alike would gather together on holidays to plant trees, smooth roads, and otherwise improve their town. New England–style town meetings, which served as the main form of government for the tight-knit community, were held regularly for residents to discuss and vote on issues. With the support of its devoted and enthusiastic early residents, Claremont had made a full recovery from its ghost town days.

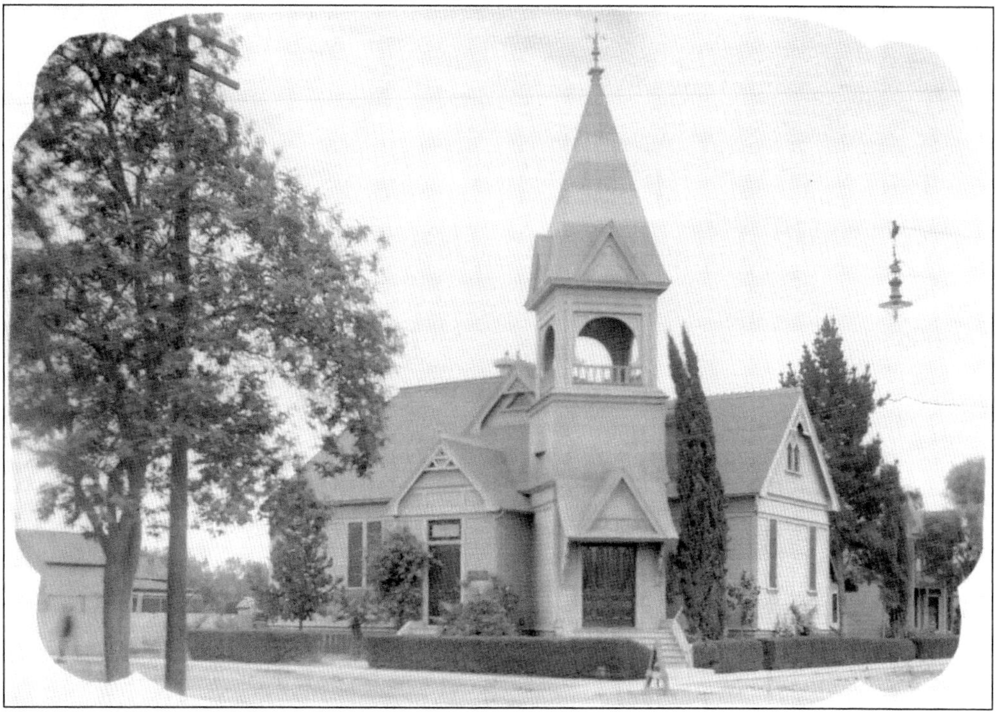

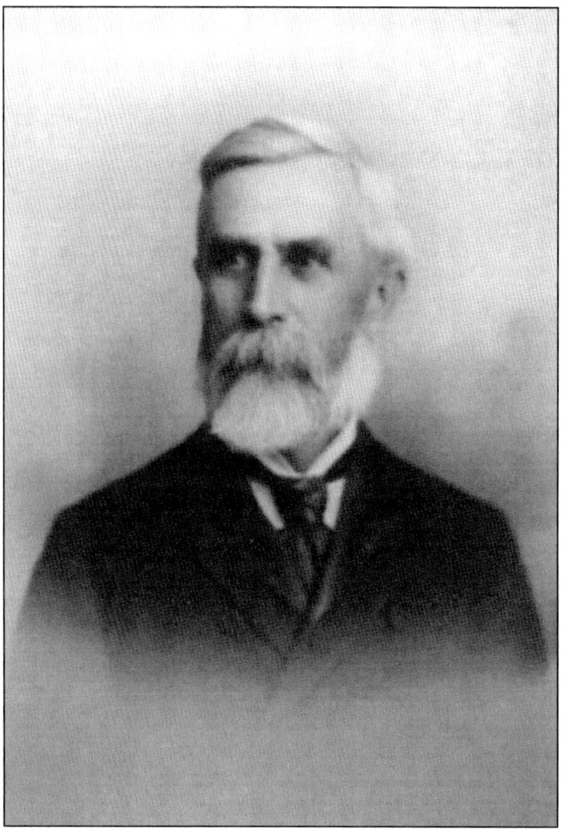

PILGRIM CONGREGATIONAL CHURCH, 1903. The Pilgrim Congregational Church of Pomona was founded in 1887 by Rev. Charles B. Sumner. The following January, the young choir leader, Frank P. Brackett, began teaching preparatory school courses to a dozen or so students inside the church. This small church school would eventually develop into the Congregationalist Pomona College. (Courtesy of the Judy Wright collection.)

REV. CHARLES BURT SUMNER. As the founder of Pilgrim Congregational Church, Reverend Sumner was deeply involved in Pomona College's growth. He served as the financial officer and secretary of the board of trustees and worked tirelessly to raise funds for the school. Even after his death in 1927, Sumner's legacy lived on: his son George was a professor at Pomona, and his grandson George Sumner Charles Benson eventually became the founding president of Claremont Men's College.

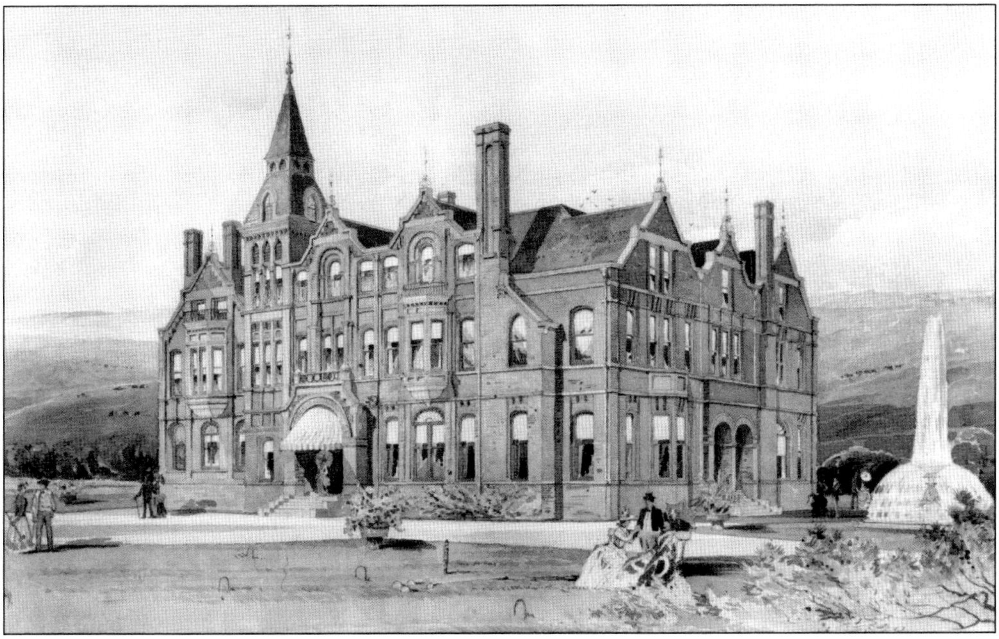

PROPOSED PIEDMONT CAMPUS, c. 1888. In May 1888, the newly formed board of trustees made the decision to relocate Pomona College, as Frank Brackett's fledgling school was now called, to the proposed town of Piedmont, on Scanlon Mesa. The chairman of the board, Henry Palmer, donated 120 acres of Mesa land, and a grand building, seen here in an artist's rendering, was designed by architect Clinton Day. (Courtesy of the Judy Wright collection.)

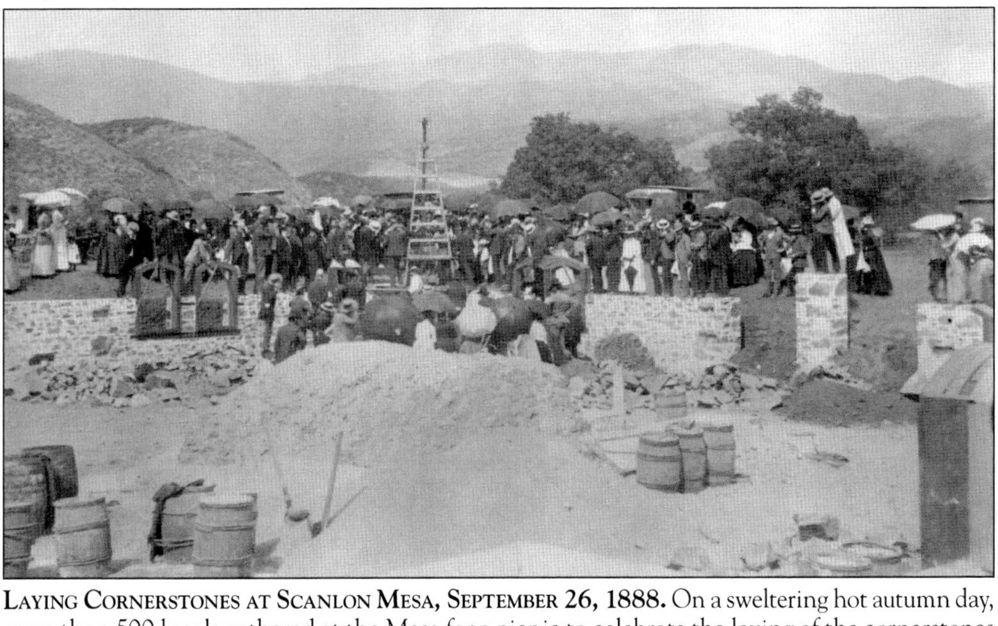

LAYING CORNERSTONES AT SCANLON MESA, SEPTEMBER 26, 1888. On a sweltering hot autumn day, more than 500 locals gathered at the Mesa for a picnic to celebrate the laying of the cornerstones of the new Piedmont campus. That same evening, however, the Pomona College Board of Trustees met to acknowledge that, with the ending of the land rush, there was not enough money left to continue construction. (Courtesy of Special Collections, Honnold/Mudd Library of the Claremont Colleges.)

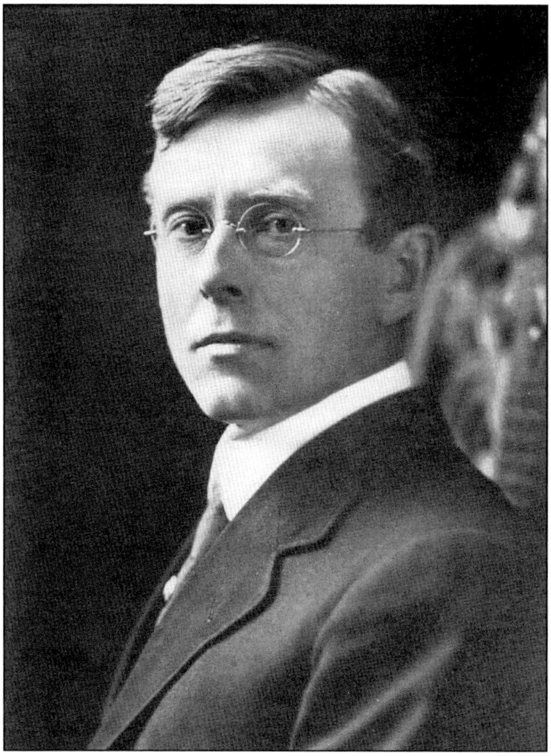

Frank Parkhurst Brackett. Only 23 years old when he was hired as the first faculty member of Pomona College, Brackett was known as a "shatteringly handsome" and highly intelligent man. He was a Dartmouth graduate who was trained as a mathematician, though he also taught French, Latin, and astronomy. Brackett later married Lucretia Burdick, the daughter of one of the first California pioneers.

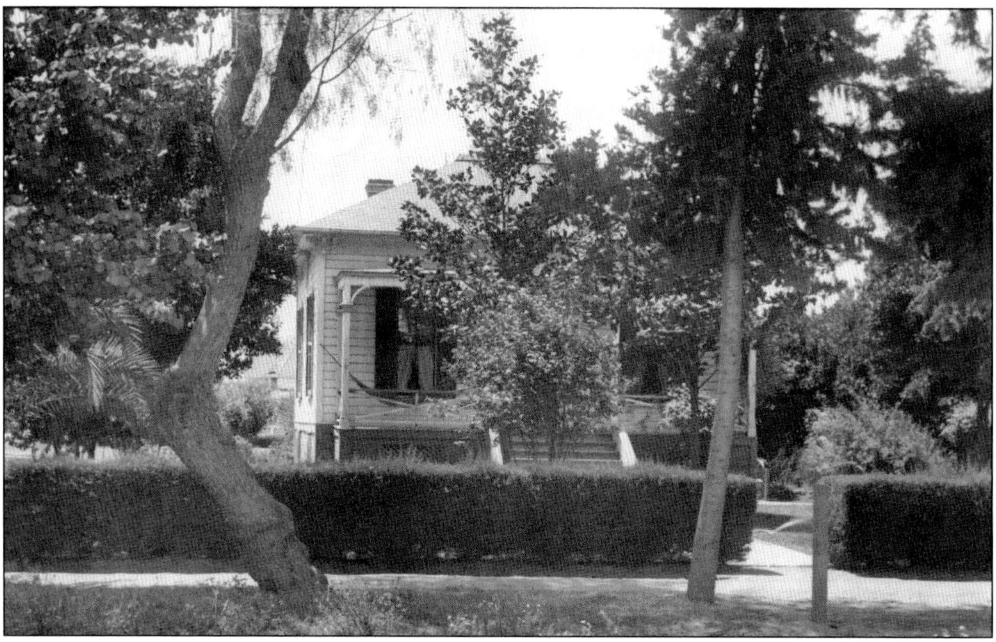

Ayer Cottage, c. 1890. While waiting for the completion of the ill-fated Piedmont campus, Brackett moved his growing school into this four-room cottage, located at the corner of White Avenue and Fifth Street in Pomona. Classes began in September, with 30 pupils, two additional teachers, and a handful of rattlesnakes, which were known to crawl in through the windows. (Courtesy of Special Collections, Honnold/Mudd Library of the Claremont Colleges.)

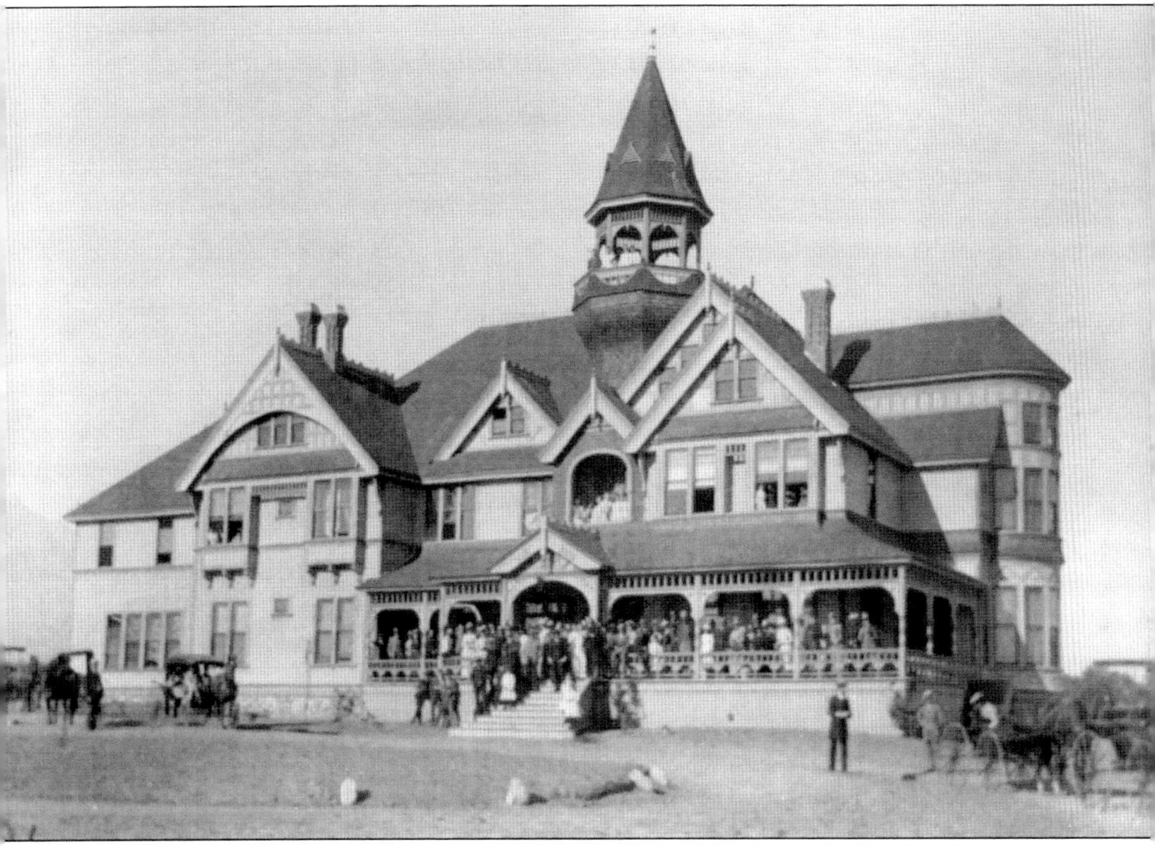

SUMNER HALL, C. 1894. Construction on this grand hotel began at the height of the land boom. By the fall of 1888, it was completed, but it sat empty and abandoned. Fortunately for its investors, Pomona College's financial troubles and search for a new home gave the hotel, and the city, a second chance. A clever deal orchestrated between Claremont's investors and the college's board of trustees allowed the school to move into the hotel, renamed Claremont Hall, over the Christmas break of 1888–1889. The building had failed as a hotel, but it proved perfect for the tiny Pomona College. In January, classes began in Claremont on what was supposed to be a temporary basis. By 1892, plans to move back to the Piedmont campus were finally abandoned. In 1893, the building was renamed Mary L. Sumner Hall in honor of the ailing wife of faculty member Charles Sumner. (Courtesy of the Judy Wright collection.)

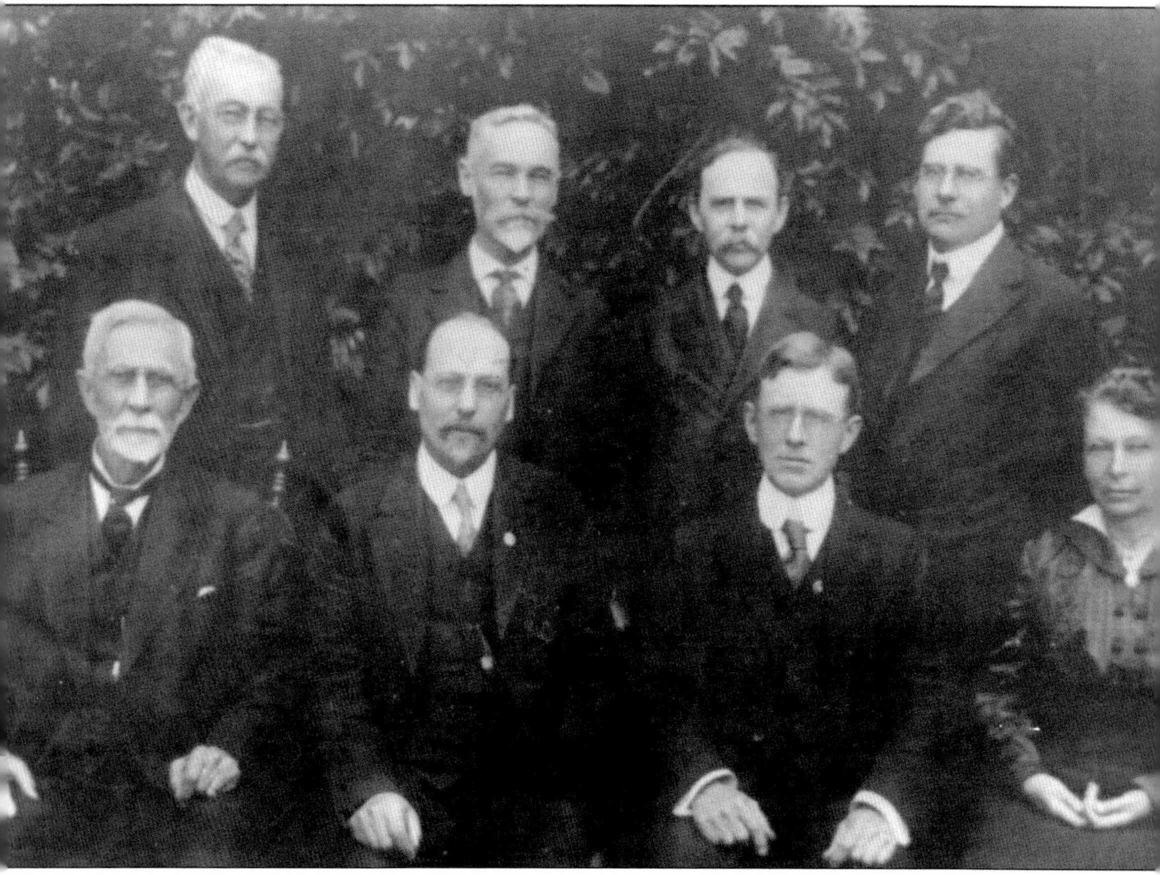

Early Town Life, 1888–1900. Shown here are the "old guard"—early faculty of Pomona and some of Claremont's earliest residents. From left to right are (seated) Charles Sumner, Edwin Norton, Frank Brackett, and Phebe Estelle Spalding; (standing) Daniel Colcord, Arthur Bissell, George Hitchcock, and George Sumner. Faculty members, their families, and college students all lived together in Claremont Hall, which, despite its imposing exterior, was far less impressive inside, with no furnishings, window shades, or lights. Claremont's business district was comprised of one small general store, and the nearest developed town, Pomona, was six miles of bumpy wagon road away. Frances Norton, one of the original Claremont residents, recalled years later in the Claremont history book *This is Claremont*, "One by one, families began to move to the place and new houses were built, and as the newcomers appeared we welcomed them heartily, wondering, with secret misgivings, why they came and how they dared to come!" (Courtesy of Special Collections, Honnold/Mudd Library of the Claremont Colleges.)

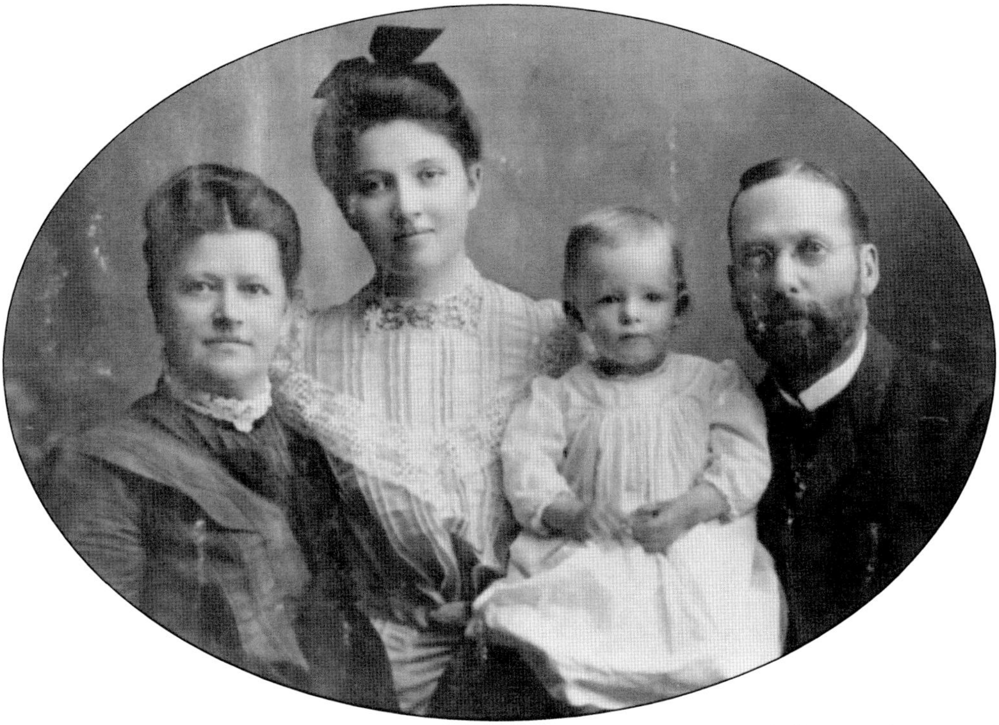

NORTON FAMILY, C. 1903. Frances and Edwin Norton, pictured with their children Katharine and Theodore, were two of the original Pomona College faculty members. Edwin served as a professor of Greek and Sanskrit, while Frances taught German language and literature. Before coming to Claremont, the couple had helped found the Congregationalist Yankton College in the Dakota Territories and was thus well prepared for the wilderness of Southern California.

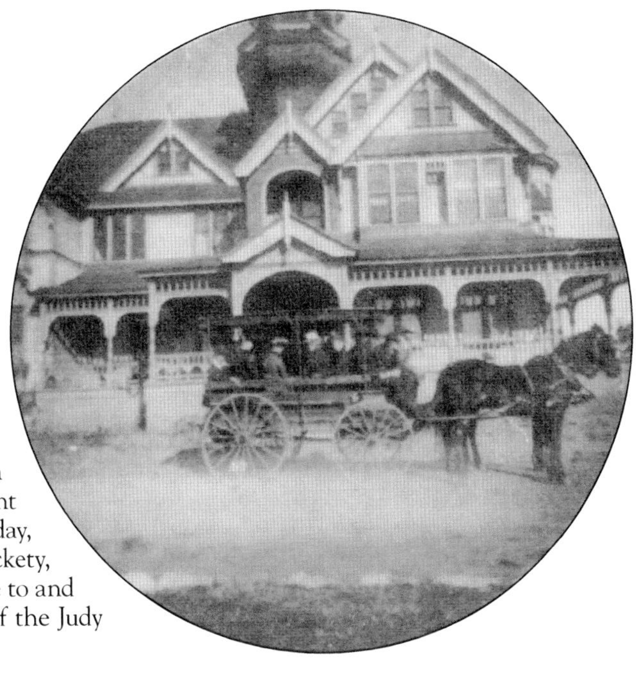

POMONA COLLEGE SCHOOL BUS, C. 1889. Although their school had moved to Claremont, the early Pomona College faculty and students were still very closely tied to the town of Pomona. Nearly the entire Claremont population still attended Pomona's Pilgrim Congregational Church, as Claremont had no church of its own. Each Sunday, Claremonters would pile into this rickety, horse-drawn "school bus" for a ride to and from the larger town. (Courtesy of the Judy Wright collection.)

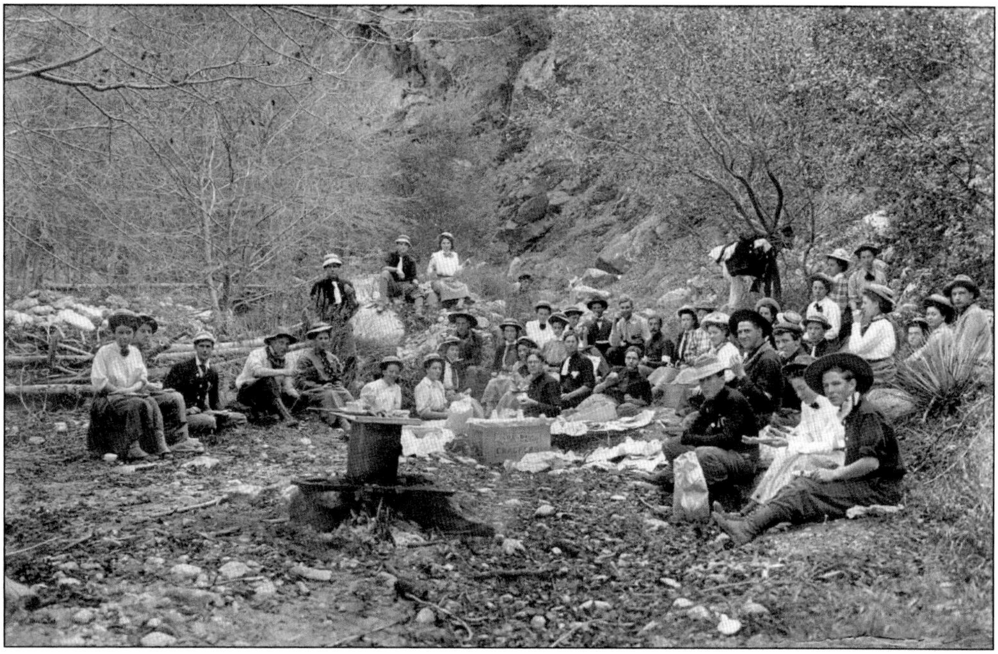

POMONA COLLEGE STUDENTS, C. 1910. As a Congregationalist school, Pomona College forbid many typical forms of recreation, such as dancing or card-playing. Of course, this did not stop students from finding ways to entertain themselves. Regular hiking trips and horse rides into the foothills and mountains allowed the students to fully enjoy the untainted natural beauty around them. Above, a group of young men and women enjoy a picnic in San Antonio Canyon. The college also organized sporting events, at which students could show off their athletic prowess and their school spirit, as seen below. Football and running were especially popular. (Both, courtesy of the Judy Wright collection.)

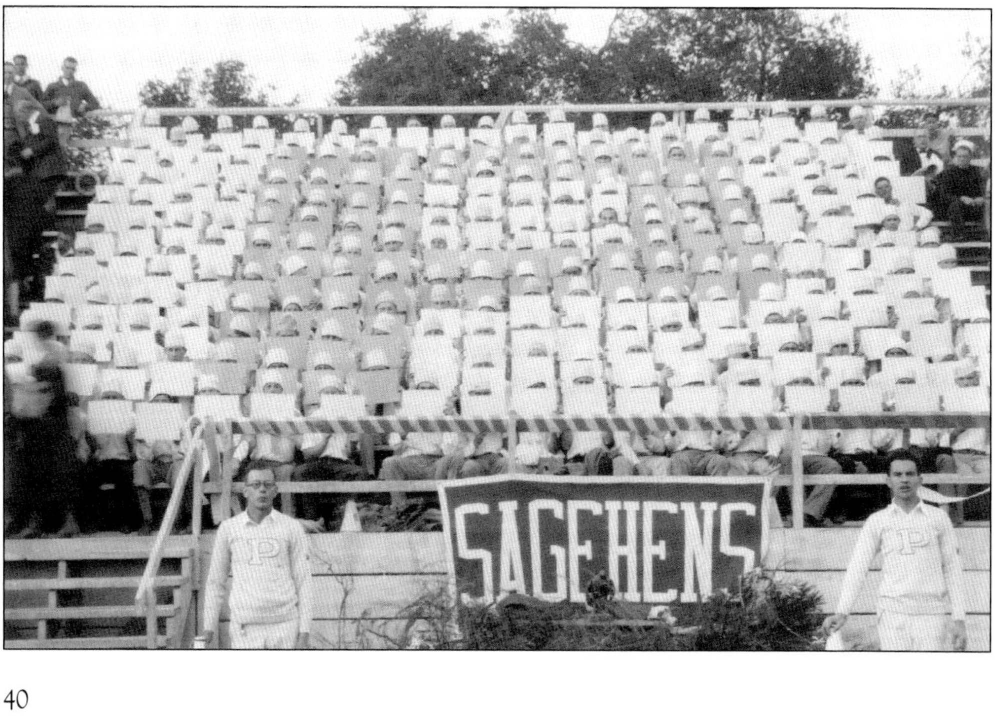

CYRUS GRANDISON BALDWIN. In 1890, Baldwin was hired to serve as Pomona College's first president. Though only 38 at the time, he was already a well-known Congregational clergyman thanks to his remarkable charisma, which kept him popular with the faculty and the student body. His presidency saw the addition of several significant buildings to campus, including Holmes Hall. However, in 1897, Baldwin resigned, citing difficulties with financial leadership. (Courtesy of the Judy Wright collection.)

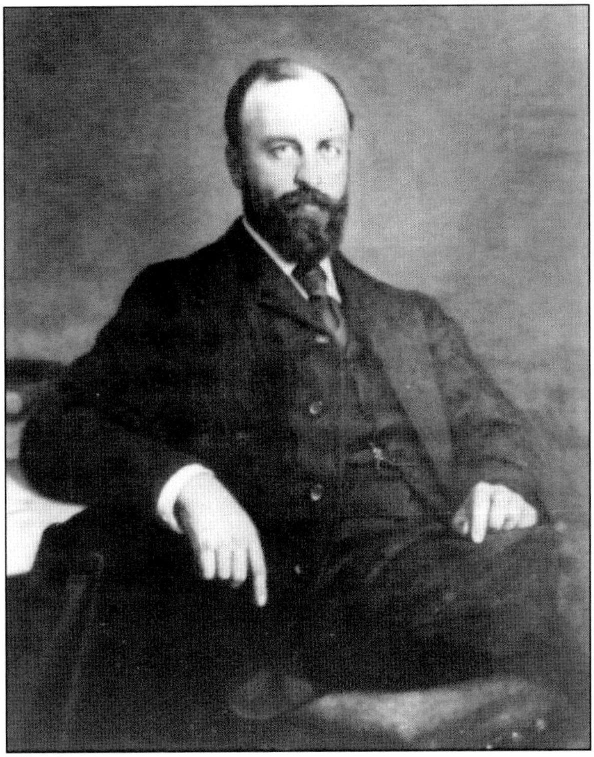

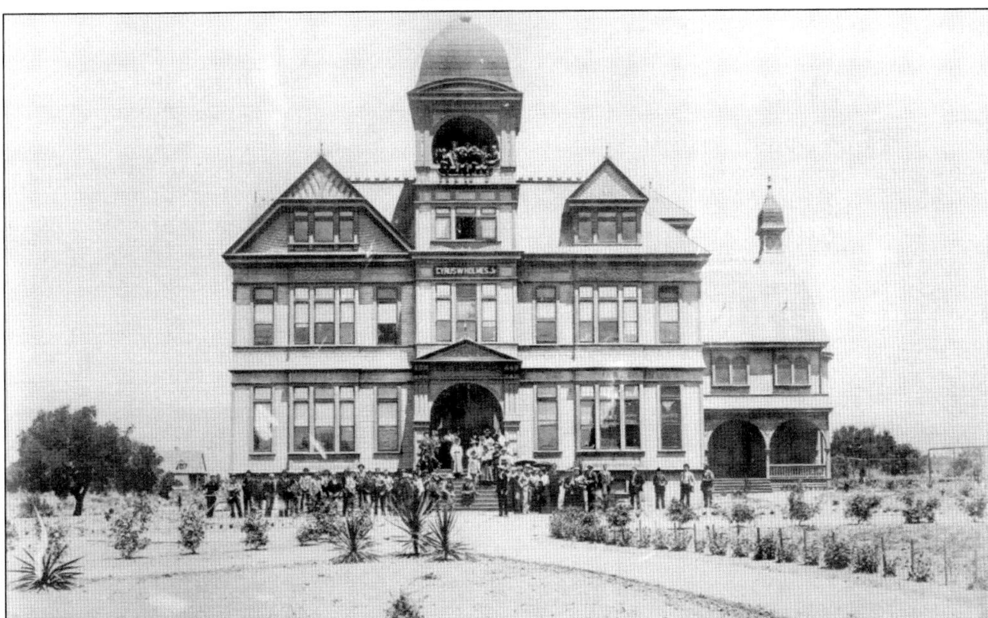

HOLMES HALL. In 1891, Pomona College was facing financial problems, having never fully recovered from the land bust. Fortunately, in that year, Charles Sumner was able to secure a donation of $25,000 from a wealthy Massachusetts woman in honor of her father, Cyrus W. Holmes. This was, at the time, the college's largest single donation, and it was enough to fund the construction of the campus's second building, Holmes Hall. (Courtesy of the Judy Wright collection.)

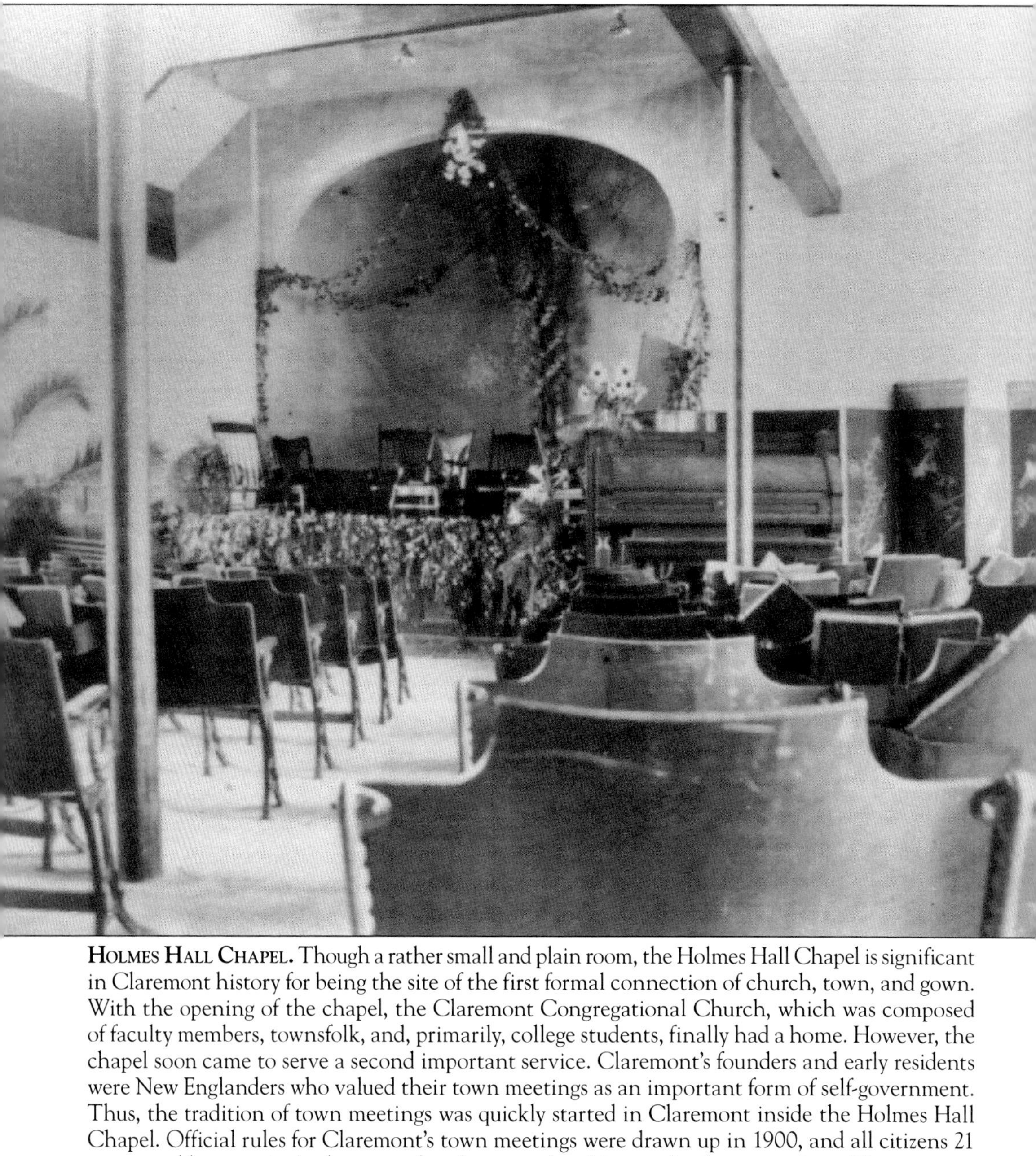

HOLMES HALL CHAPEL. Though a rather small and plain room, the Holmes Hall Chapel is significant in Claremont history for being the site of the first formal connection of church, town, and gown. With the opening of the chapel, the Claremont Congregational Church, which was composed of faculty members, townsfolk, and, primarily, college students, finally had a home. However, the chapel soon came to serve a second important service. Claremont's founders and early residents were New Englanders who valued their town meetings as an important form of self-government. Thus, the tradition of town meetings was quickly started in Claremont inside the Holmes Hall Chapel. Official rules for Claremont's town meetings were drawn up in 1900, and all citizens 21 years or older were invited to attend and vote on local issues. At these meetings, Claremonters showed their devotion to their little village, often voting in favor of mandatory labor and self-imposed taxes to beautify and maintain city property. (Courtesy of the Judy Wright collection.)

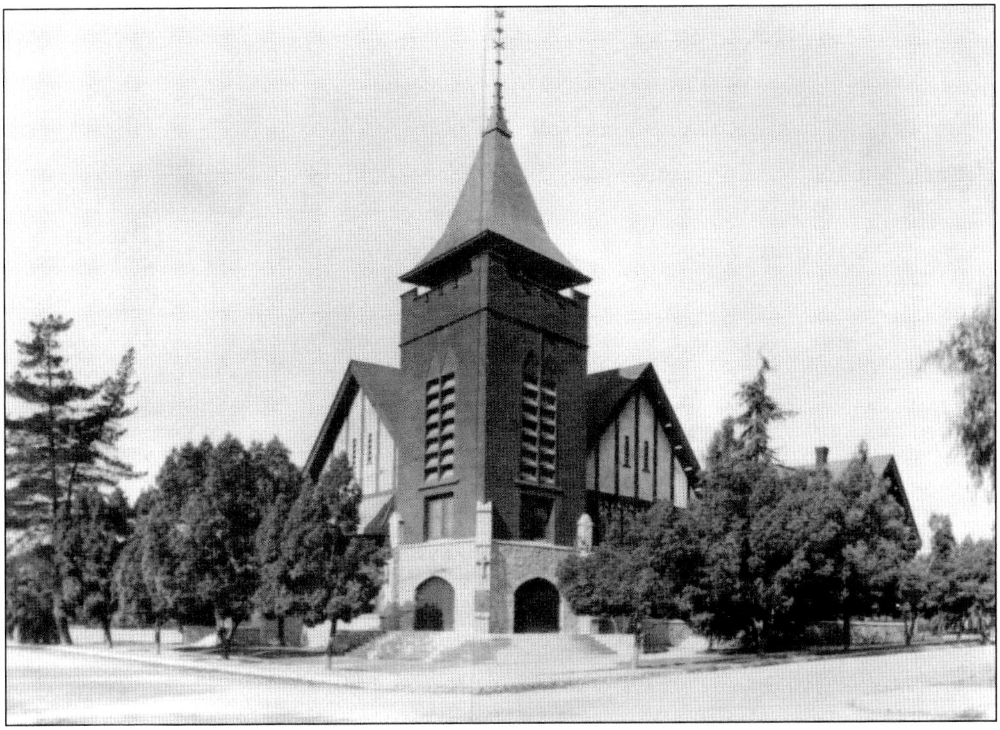

CLAREMONT CONGREGATIONAL CHURCH, C. 1910. The Claremont Congregational Church was founded in June 1891 by 49 charter members and held its first meetings in the cramped Sumner Hall dining room. Later, the resilient congregation moved into the more suitable Holmes Hall Chapel, and, finally, in 1906, into its own building (above), located at the corner of Harrison and Harvard Avenues. (Courtesy of the Judy Wright collection.)

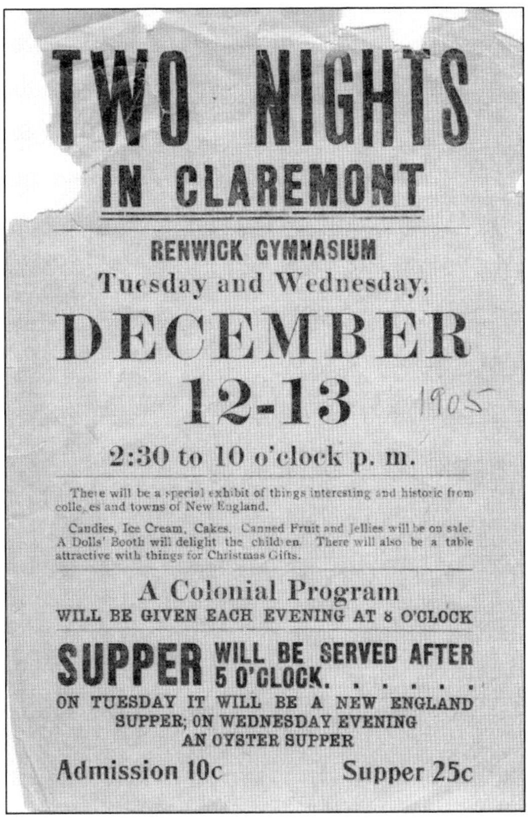

TWO NIGHTS
IN CLAREMONT

RENWICK GYMNASIUM
Tuesday and Wednesday,
DECEMBER
12-13
1905
2:30 to 10 o'clock p. m.

There will be a special exhibit of things interesting and historic from colleges and towns of New England.

Candies, Ice Cream, Cakes, Canned Fruit and Jellies will be on sale. A Dolls' Booth will delight the children. There will also be a table attractive with things for Christmas Gifts.

A Colonial Program
WILL BE GIVEN EACH EVENING AT 8 O'CLOCK

SUPPER WILL BE SERVED AFTER 5 O'CLOCK. . . . . .
ON TUESDAY IT WILL BE A NEW ENGLAND SUPPER; ON WEDNESDAY EVENING AN OYSTER SUPPER

Admission 10c Supper 25c

CHRISTMAS BAZAAR, 1905. The Claremont Congregational Church cost $25,000 to build—no small sum in a town of less than 1,000 people. To raise money for its construction, the women of Claremont hosted a Christmas bazaar at the Pomona College gymnasium. Later, the industrious townswomen successfully published their own cookbook in order to help pay for a church sidewalk.

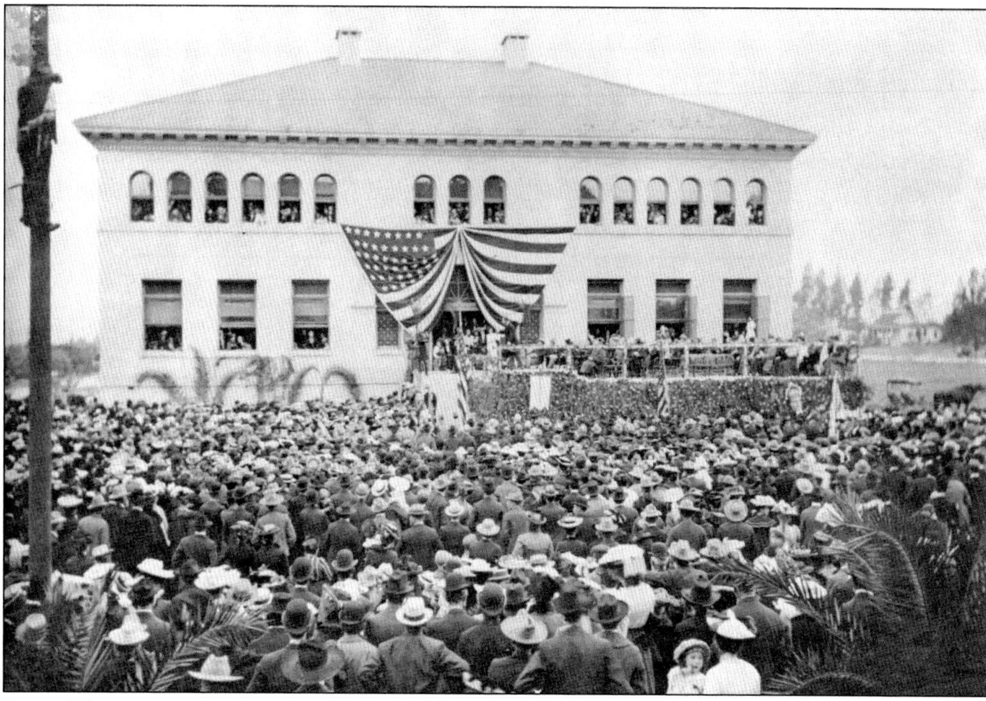

PRES. THEODORE ROOSEVELT, 1903. Pomona College's third president, George A. Gates, was particularly successful in bringing many notable speakers to Claremont. Here, Pres. Theodore Roosevelt speaks to a crowd of over 10,000 spectators in front of Pearsons Hall on May 3, 1903. The president spoke for 25 minutes about the development of California before planting an oak sapling in front of the building.

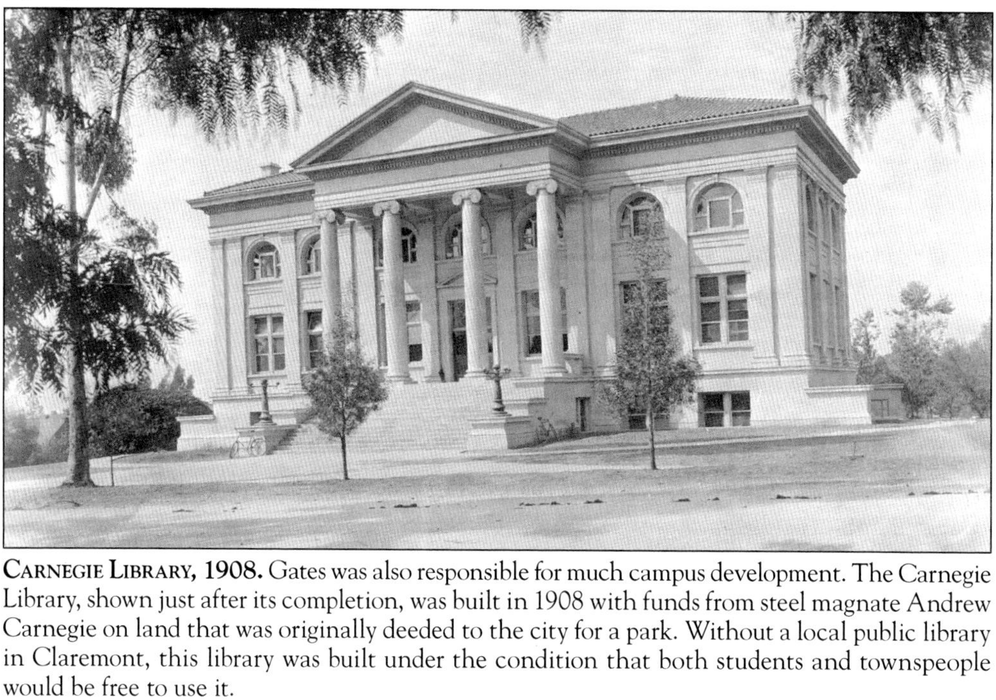

CARNEGIE LIBRARY, 1908. Gates was also responsible for much campus development. The Carnegie Library, shown just after its completion, was built in 1908 with funds from steel magnate Andrew Carnegie on land that was originally deeded to the city for a park. Without a local public library in Claremont, this library was built under the condition that both students and townspeople would be free to use it.

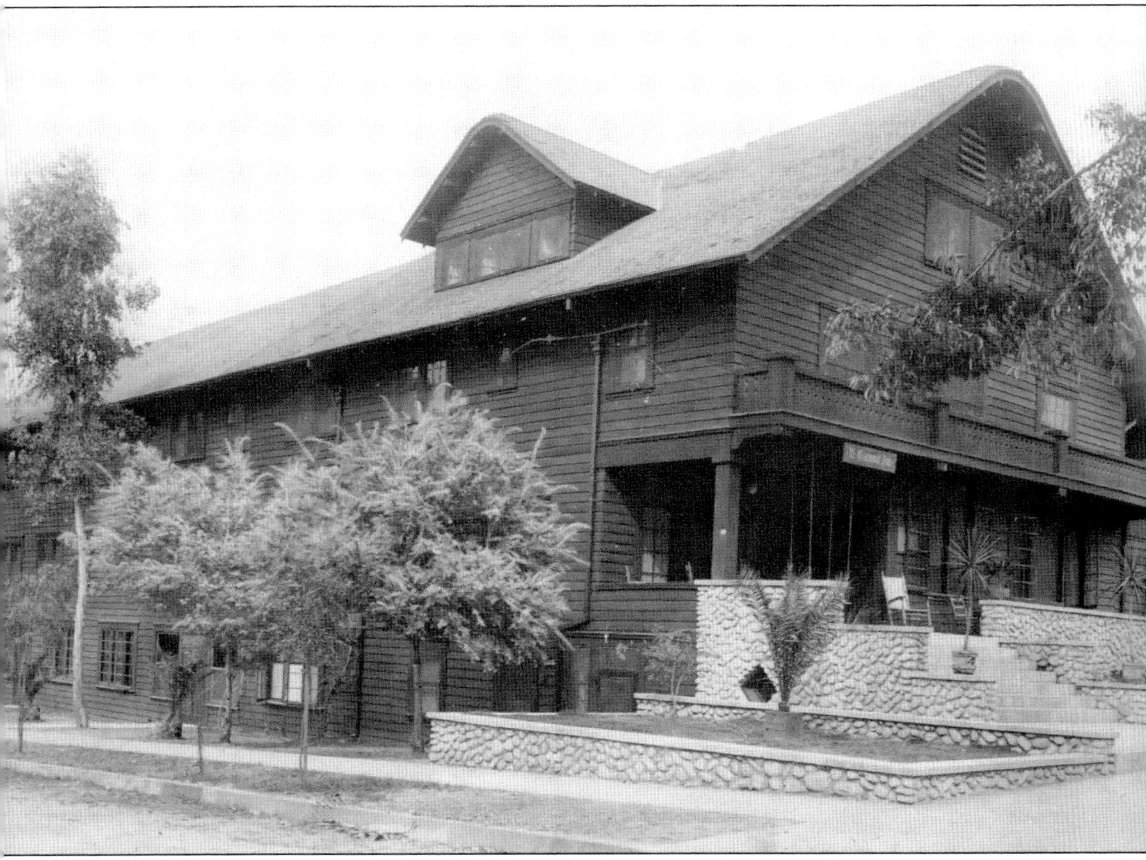

Claremont Inn. In Claremont's early years, town and gown relations were exceptionally good, as exemplified through the story of the Claremont Inn. At a town meeting in 1905, the town's citizens decided that Claremont ought to have a hotel. At the same time, Pomona College was in need of a new dining room, as the student body was quickly outgrowing Sumner Hall. These two goals combined into a single project, and the Claremont Inn Company, a joint venture between private citizens and the college, was born. The beautiful, Craftsman-style Claremont Inn was opened in 1906 with 12 guest rooms and a common room, which could be used as a dining room for the college. A few years later, the college bought out the private investors, but, in a goodwill gesture, it kept the main part of the inn open as a hotel to serve the city. Over the years, the inn became a community center where residents would gather to eat and talk. Sadly, it was declared a fire hazard and demolished in 1968. (Courtesy of the Judy Wright collection.)

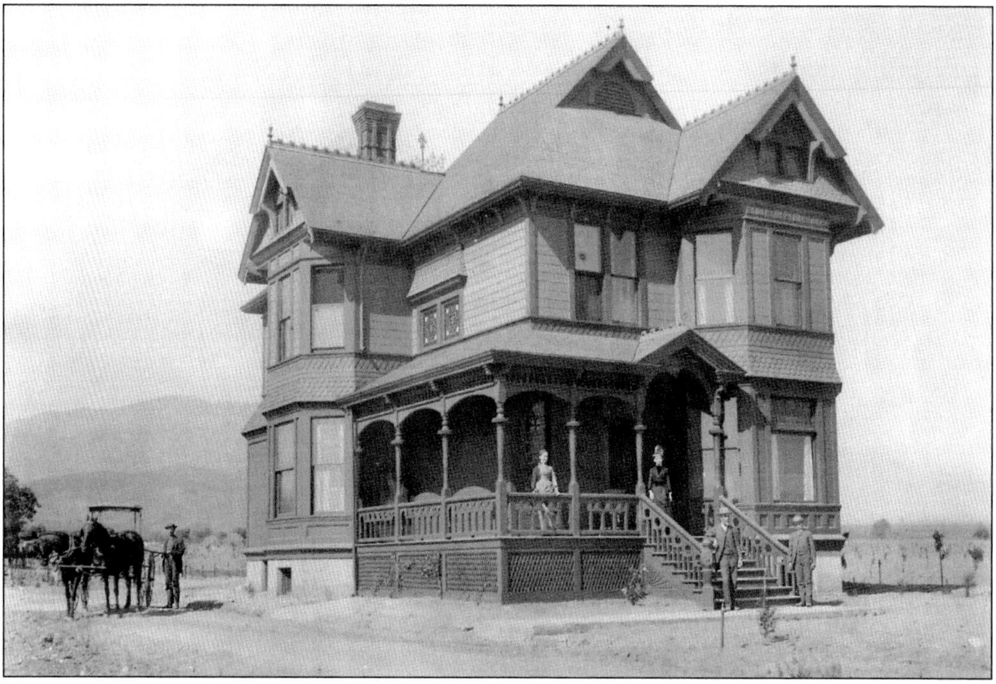

Sumner House. This beautiful Queen Anne Victorian house, called Twin Oaks for two trees in its yard, was home to the Sumner family. It was originally built on Scanlon Mesa in anticipation of the campus that was to be constructed there. Later, Charles Sumner had the house moved into Claremont. Remarkably, Sumner and his son lived in the house through the entire moving process. (Courtesy of the Judy Wright collection.)

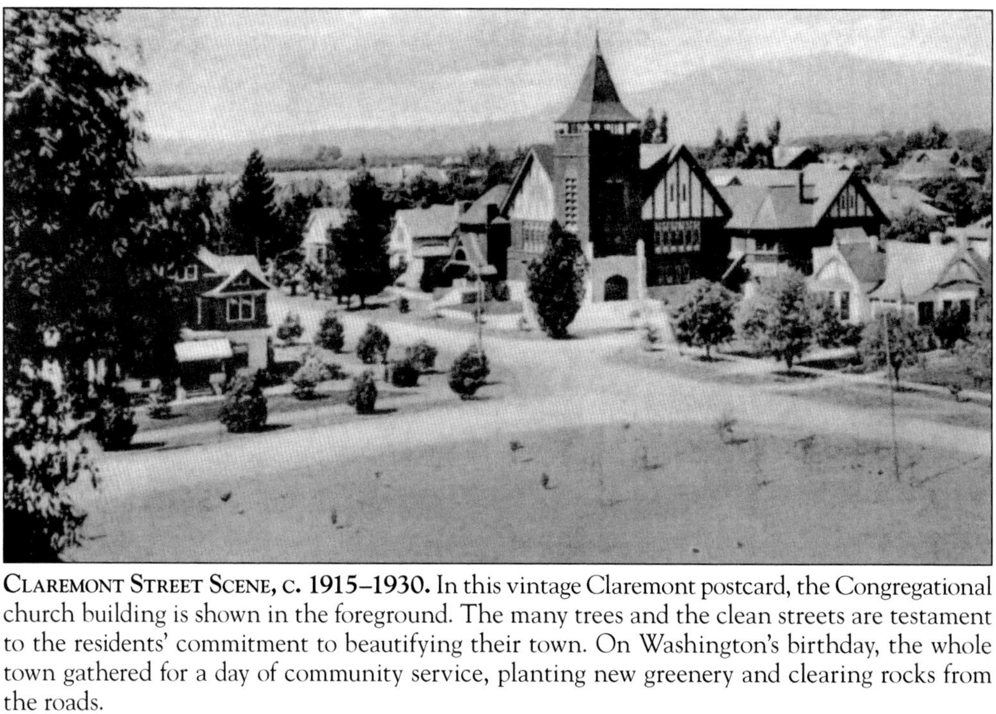

Claremont Street Scene, c. 1915–1930. In this vintage Claremont postcard, the Congregational church building is shown in the foreground. The many trees and the clean streets are testament to the residents' commitment to beautifying their town. On Washington's birthday, the whole town gathered for a day of community service, planting new greenery and clearing rocks from the roads.

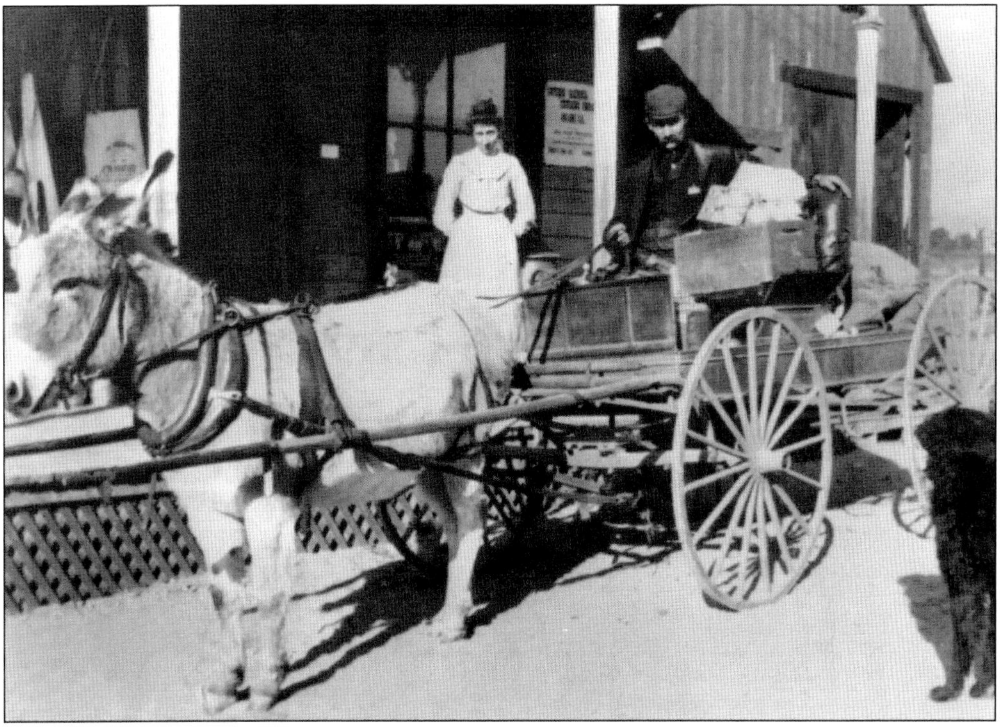

GROWTH OF A TOWN, 1890–1910. Shown above is Claremont's first store, the Urbanus General Store, which was built in 1888. For a long time Claremont's only business, the general store also served as the town post office. By 1900, however, more stores appeared and it became a bustling little town. The business district developed mainly along Yale Avenue and First Street, where the old San Antonio Hotel housed the popular Duvall's College Book and Drug Store, seen below in an early postcard. In 1908, there were enough businesses—among them the Claremont Feed and Fuel, a cobbling shop, a meat market, and a town newspaper—for a chamber of commerce to be established. (Both, courtesy of Special Collections, Honnold/Mudd Library of the Claremont Colleges.)

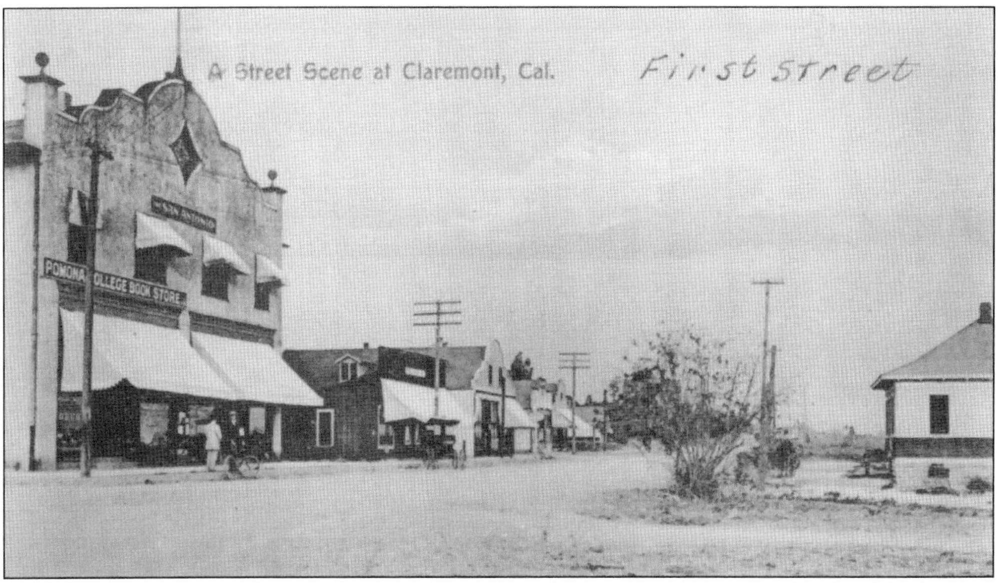

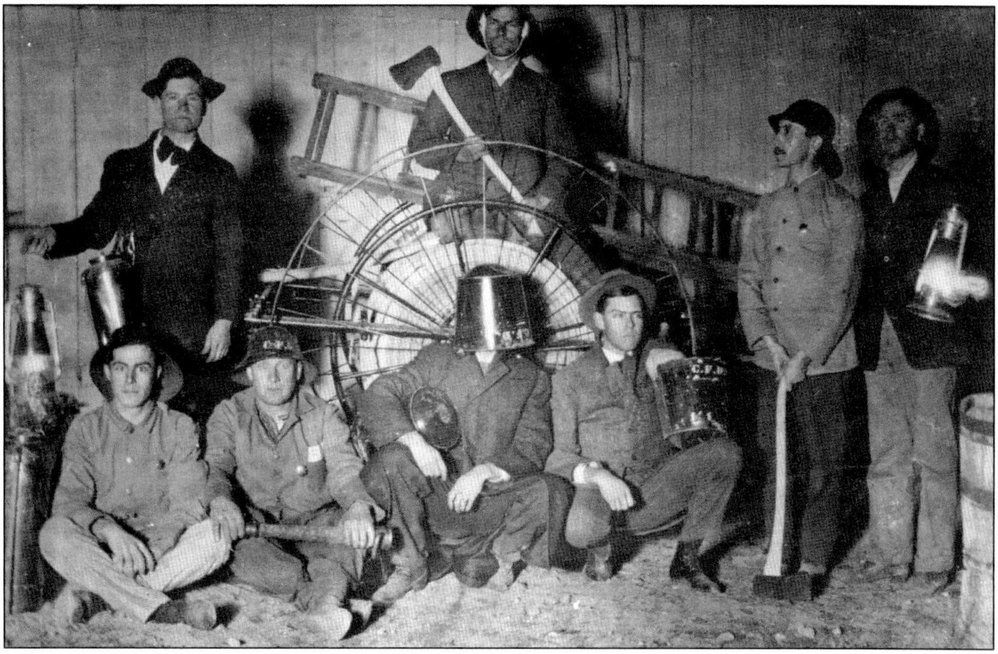

CLAREMONT VOLUNTEER FIRE COMPANY, 1906. These men represented Claremont's first official volunteer fire company, which was formed in 1906 with the city's purchase of a hand-drawn hose cart and other assorted firefighting equipment. The Holmes Hall Chapel bell served as the fire bell for the headquarters-less company. The fire department was not alone in its simplicity, however; as late as 1921, the tiny police force patrolled the town on bicycle. (Courtesy of Special Collections, Honnold/Mudd Library of the Claremont Colleges.)

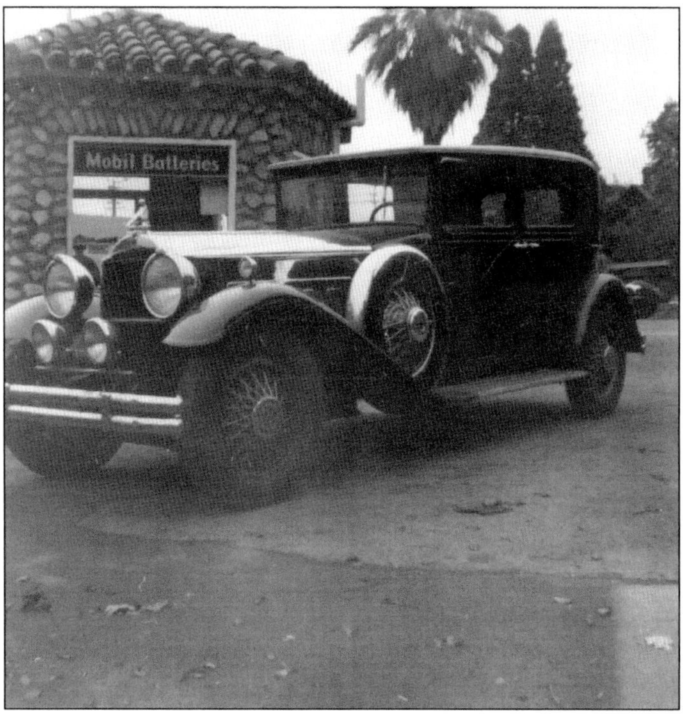

CAR. In 1907, when Claremont had a grand total of four cars, residents decided in a town meeting that traffic was becoming a major issue in their little town. Thus began Claremont's long-standing reputation as an automobile-unfriendly town. Police marshal James Johnson was so enthusiastic in his enforcement of the 12-mile-per-hour speed limit that the Claremont "speed trap" warranted its own cartoon in the *Los Angeles Examiner.*

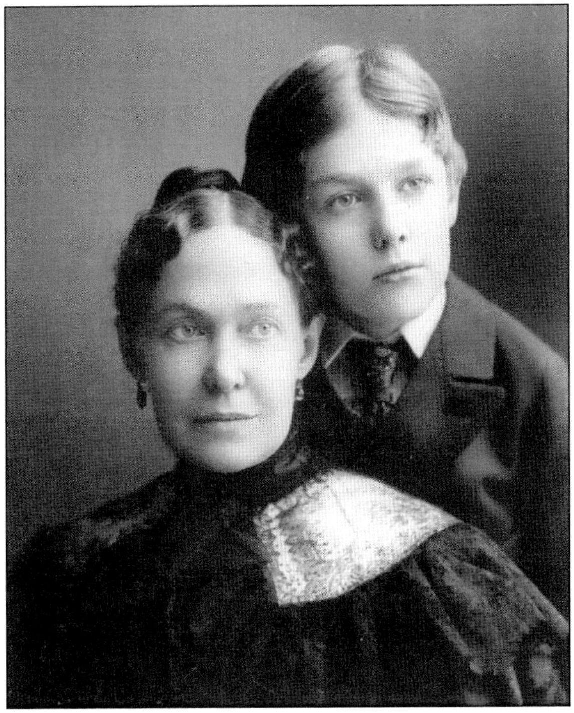

HELEN AND WILLIAM RENWICK. Helen Goodwin Renwick, shown here with her son William, was one of Claremont's first philanthropists. The widow of a wealthy lumber mill developer and a graduate of Oberlin College, Renwick contributed to many local organizations, including Pilgrim Place and the public library. She also funded the construction of Renwick Gymnasium and the Rembrandt House at Pomona College. (Courtesy of the Judy Wright collection.)

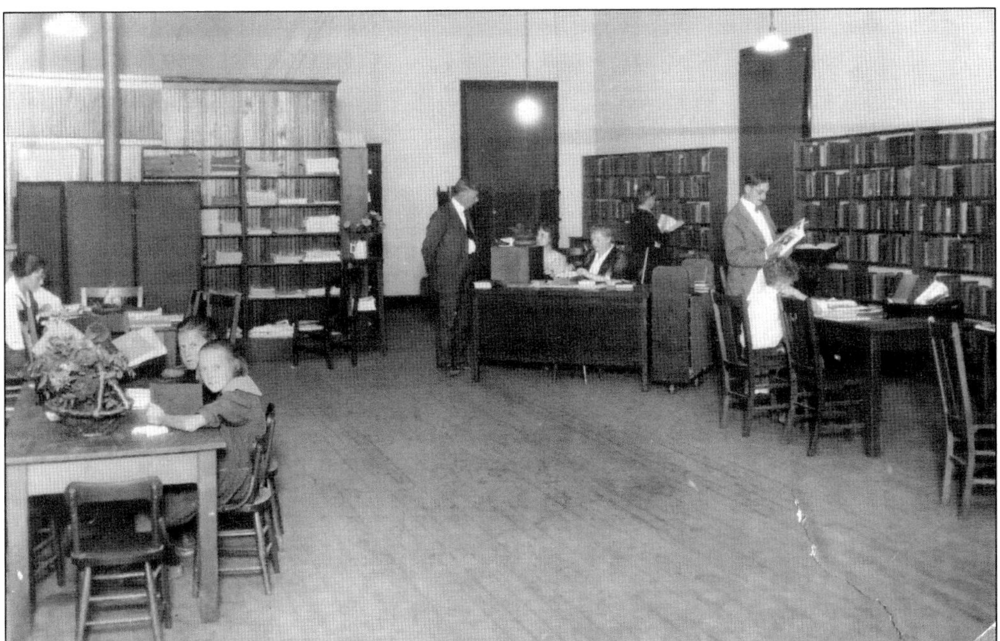

CLAREMONT LIBRARY, 1914. Pomona College professor Phebe Estelle Spalding established the first Claremont library in 1889 with 200 of her own books. However, this library generally served only faculty and students. Thus, in 1914, Anna M. Robinson successfully spearheaded a movement for a public county library branch in Claremont. The room shown here was rented to house Claremont's collection, which included a special children's section. (Courtesy of the Judy Wright collection.)

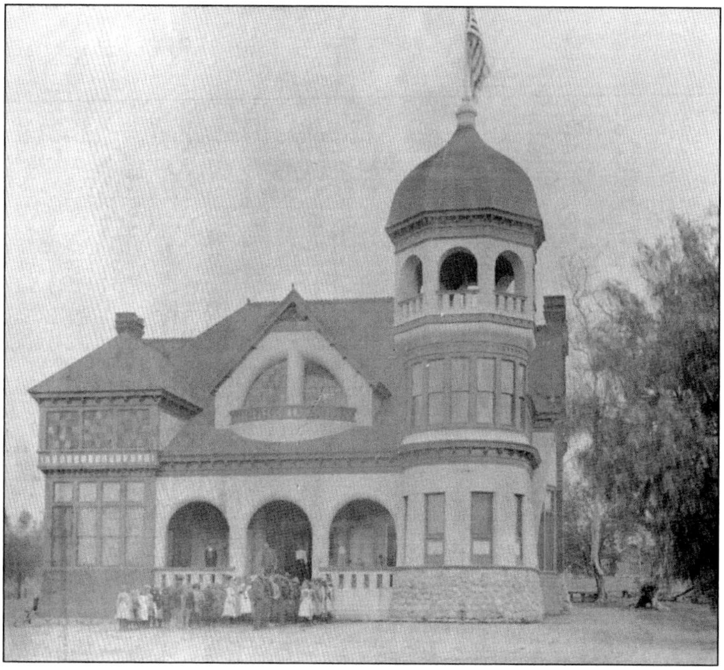

CLAREMONT GRAMMAR SCHOOL, C. 1900. The original grammar school was built in 1890, complete with a turret and colored glass windows. Despite its charming appearance, the school struggled to retain teachers for more than a year due to a high student turnover rate; the 1892–1893 school inventory included "two very tired teachers, much in need of repair." The building later became city hall, after a new school was completed in 1907.

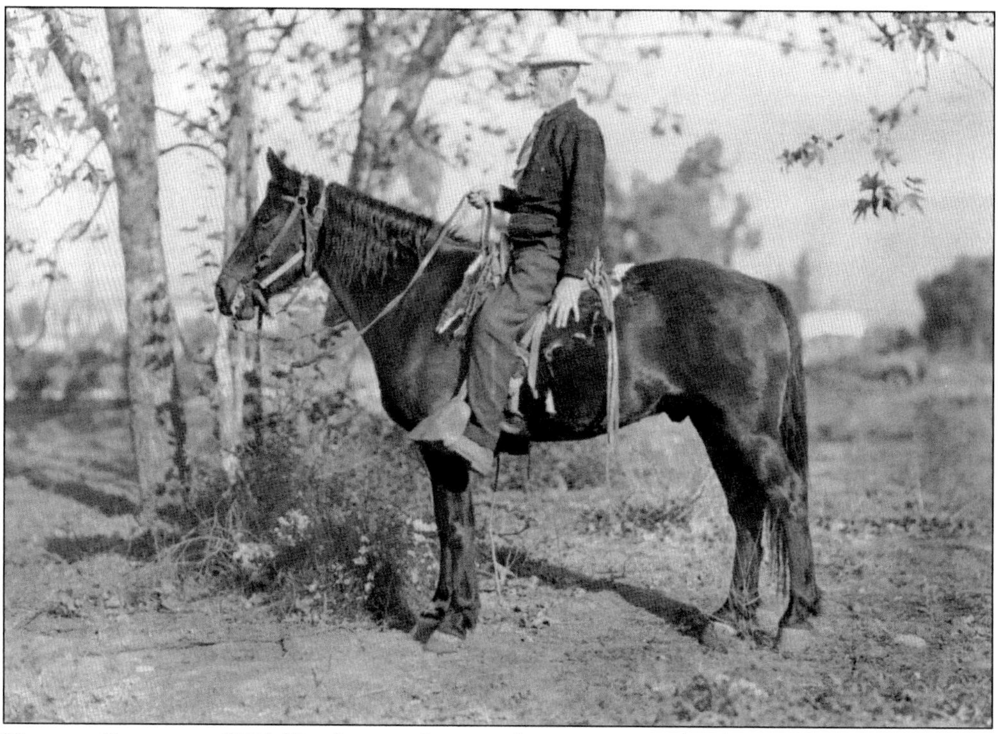

HERBERT PATTEN, C. 1915. Hired to run the struggling grammar school in 1895, Patten, seen here on his horse Brownie, was a remarkable principal. His revolutionary belief that students should change rooms between classes put the school far ahead of its time. Over his 20-year career, Patten added more than 3,000 books to the school library, organized a student garden, hired over 10 new teachers, and established special art, music, and exercise classes.

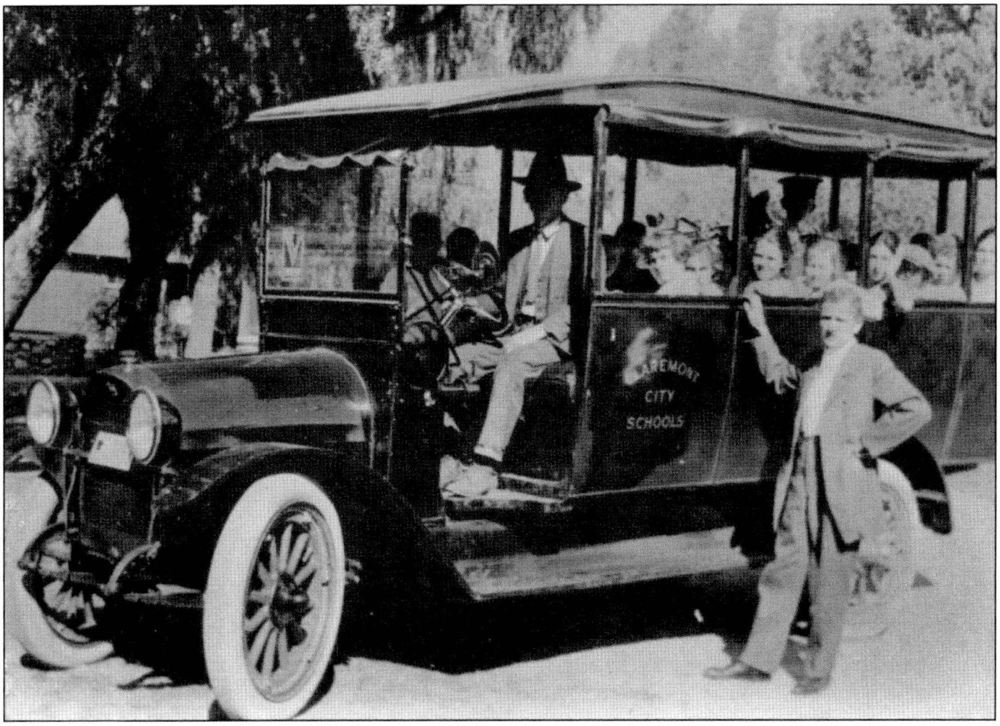

CLAREMONT SCHOOL BUS. By 1910, enrollment at Claremont Grammar School had soared to 269 students, many of whom rode this bus from the citrus ranches to town every day. However, Spanish-speaking Mexican American children from citrus industry families were not permitted to attend the grammar school. Segregation of Claremont's public schools continued until the mid-1940s. (Courtesy of the Judy Wright collection.)

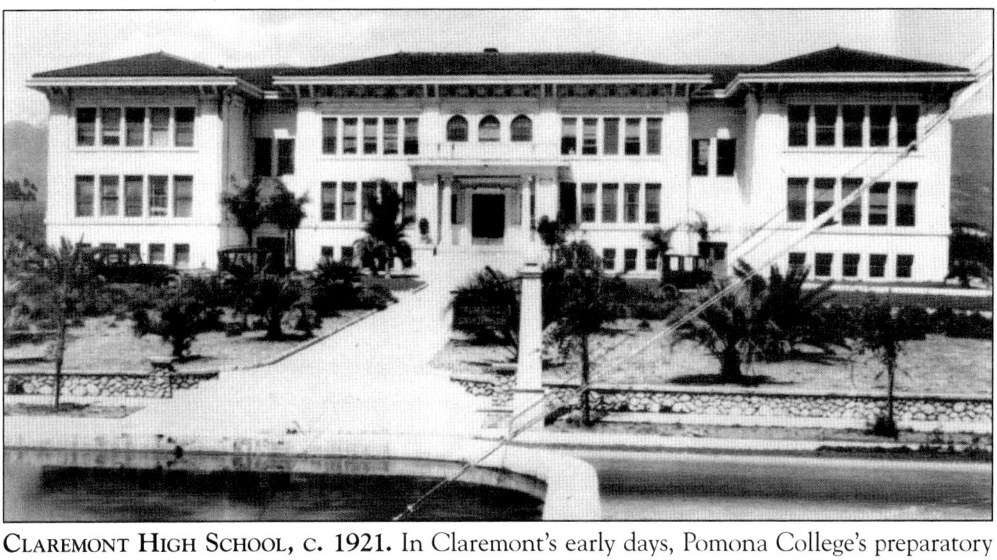

CLAREMONT HIGH SCHOOL, C. 1921. In Claremont's early days, Pomona College's preparatory program served local high school students. However, when the program ended in 1911, the city quickly established a public high school, which opened that September in the home of resident Thomas Barrows. The grand Claremont High School building, shown here, was constructed in 1921. Today, the Old School House is a shopping center and office complex.

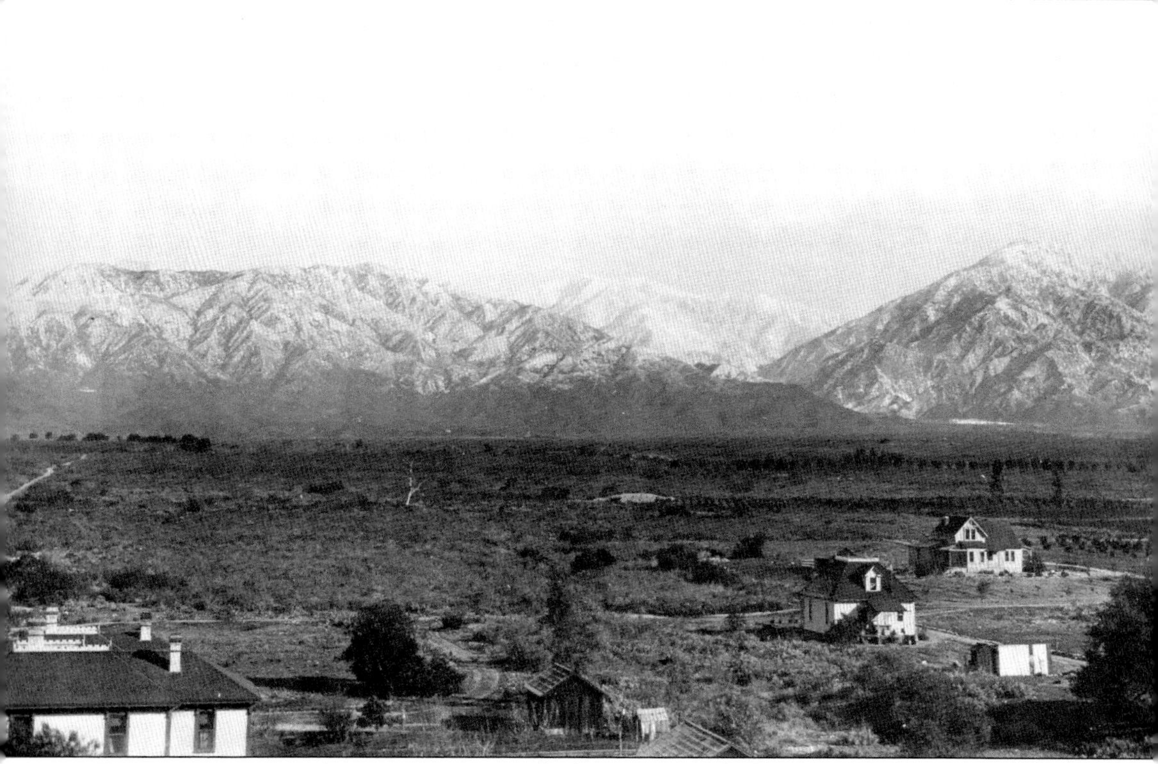

Panoramic View of Claremont, 1896. The late 1800s marked a time of change in Claremont's history. With the demise of the ranchos and the extension of the Santa Fe Railroad through Pomona, new settlers slowly began to populate the towns of the Pomona Valley. While the growth of Claremont was slow in the beginning, the advent of an efficient transportation line had sown the seeds of Claremont's development into a city. This panoramic photograph gives a great sense of what sparsely populated Claremont's early days were like. Pomona College professor George G. Hitchcock took this collection of three photographs in 1896, looking north from the Holmes Hall bell tower. Sixth Street can be seen on the far left, running near the base of the photograph.

Four

Culture and Commerce

Citrus and More

With its Congregational college and close-knit community, Claremont was in many ways a New England village transplanted into the western wilderness. Nonetheless, the town did have one key element that made it distinctly Californian—citrus.

In the same year that Pomona College moved to Claremont, Peter Dreher planted his first orange trees in town. The climate and soil proved ideal for the fruit, but profits were slim. Convinced that citrus could prove lucrative, Dreher joined with other local growers to form a cooperative, the Claremont Fruit Growers Association, which worked directly with eastern brokers, not through commercial shippers, thus increasing growers' returns. This venture was highly successful, and by 1916–1917, Claremont was shipping over two million boxes of fruit east.

The 1940s was the true citrus heyday. Northern Claremont especially was overtaken by vast groves, with their neat rows of trees tended to by crews of Mexican American workers. Interestingly, in the midst of World War II, these crews were reportedly assisted by German prisoners from the nearby labor camps. After the fruit was picked, it had to be sorted for quality, labeled by brand, and shipped. In the industry's early days, the fruit had been packed at the small, clapboard Santa Fe depot. The Santa Fe Railroad constructed a new, larger Spanish Colonial Revival depot in 1927. By that time, citrus packing had been moved into the large packinghouses that lined the railroad tracks.

With the strong involvement of the Mexican American community in the citrus industry, it is unsurprising that distinctly Latino districts developed. Claremont had two barrios, as they were called: the East Barrio, now commonly known as Arbol Verde, and the West Barrio. The East Barrio, where Claremont's primary Catholic church was located, was home to a thriving community for many decades. The West Barrio, which was constructed specifically for citrus packinghouse families, contained Claremont's first school for Mexican American children.

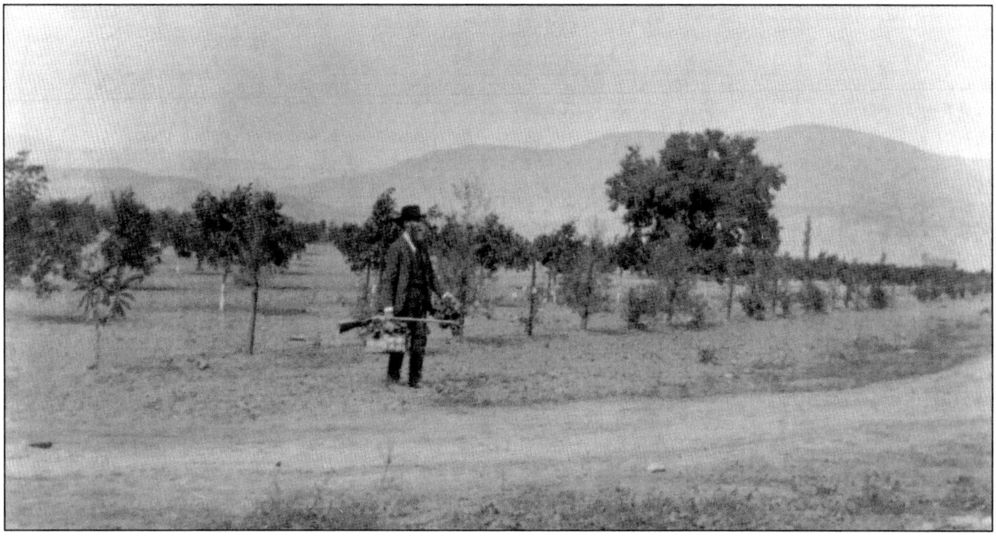

Shaw Ranch, c. 1910. Citrus was introduced to the region during the Rancho period, but it would not become a booming industry in Claremont until the beginning of the next century. In 1888, Peter Dreher became the first person to plant orange trees in Claremont, with other townspeople soon following suit. Residents like Edward Shaw, seen here, tended to their trees themselves but made little profit. (Courtesy of the Judy Wright collection.)

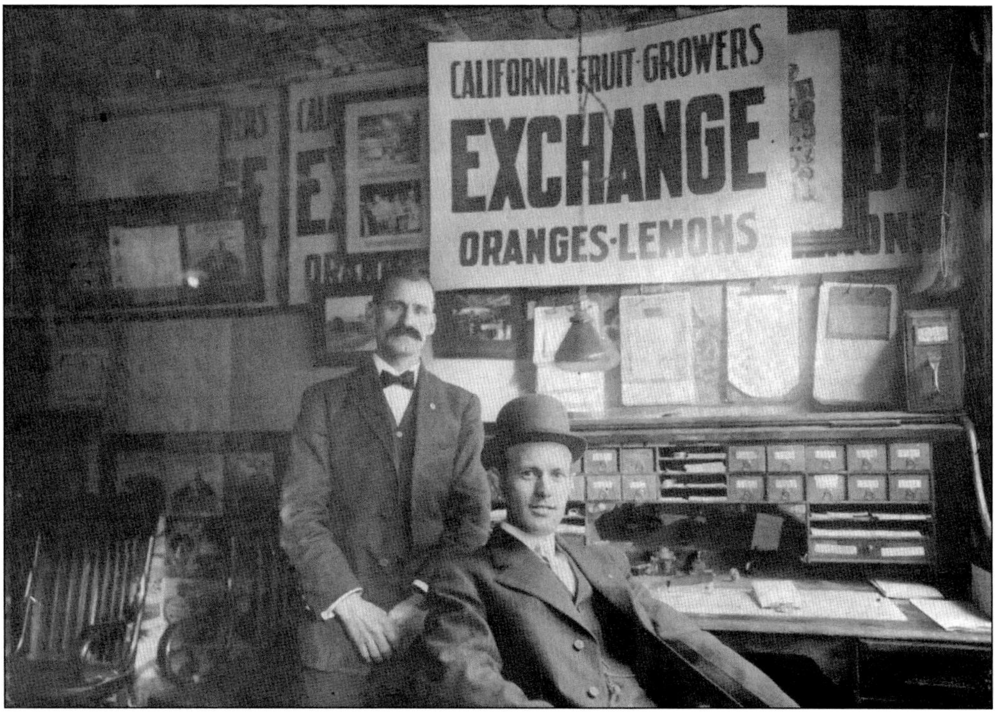

California Fruit Growers Exchange. In 1893, tired of marginal profits selling citrus fruit, Dreher brought together local citrus growers into a cooperative, the Claremont Fruit Growers Exchange. The co-op sought to bring about greater profits for farmers by uniting the city's major growers. The offices of the exchange, seen here, handled business from local growers, aligning them with larger associations for packaging. All products were shipped and distributed by the co-op.

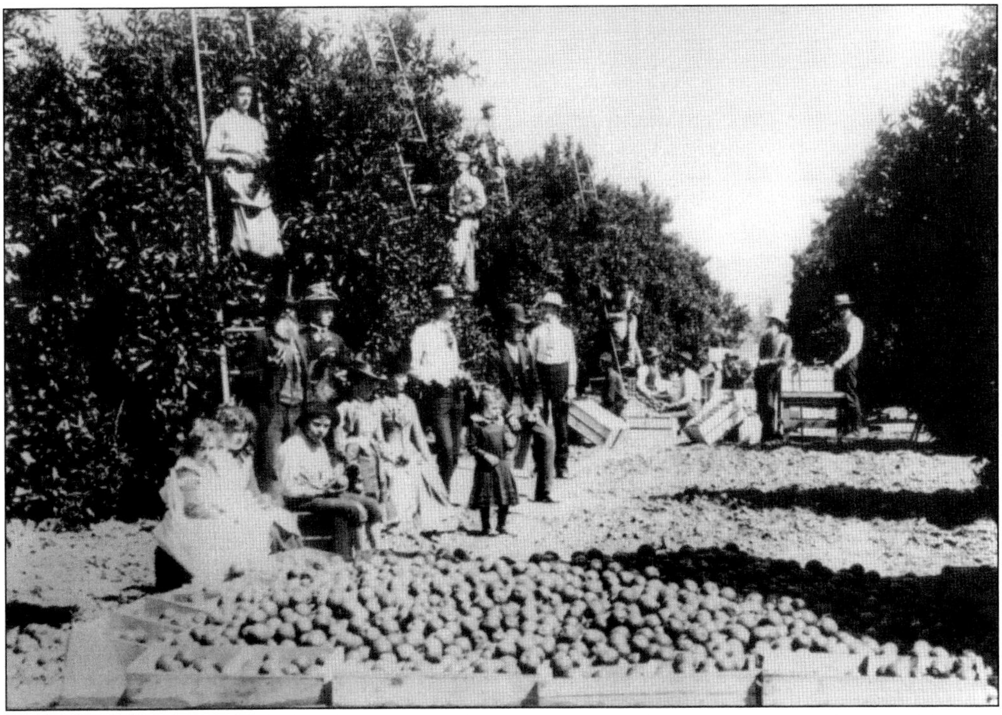

Citrus Picking Crews. Before the citrus industry became big business, citrus pickers would move throughout agricultural areas of the Southwest looking for work. Picking crews were generally made up of about 15 to 30 men, who were usually paid by the hour, with a bonus for each box picked. A single worker could pick anywhere from 60 to 100 boxes a day. By 1913, general wages were 30¢ an hour and 2¢ a box, which was comparable to the average farm worker's salary and made picking desirable work for unskilled laborers. As the labor force grew, so too did Claremont's citrus industry, which saw the Fruit Growers Association shipments increase from 6,300 boxes a year in 1892–1893 to over two million boxes by 1916–1917. (Both, courtesy of the Judy Wright collection.)

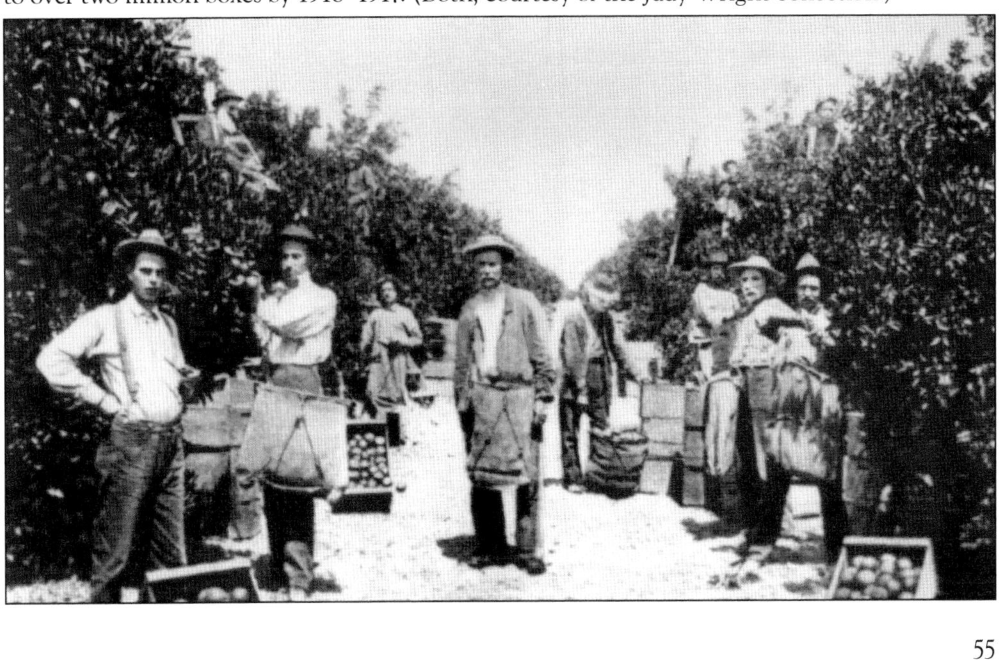

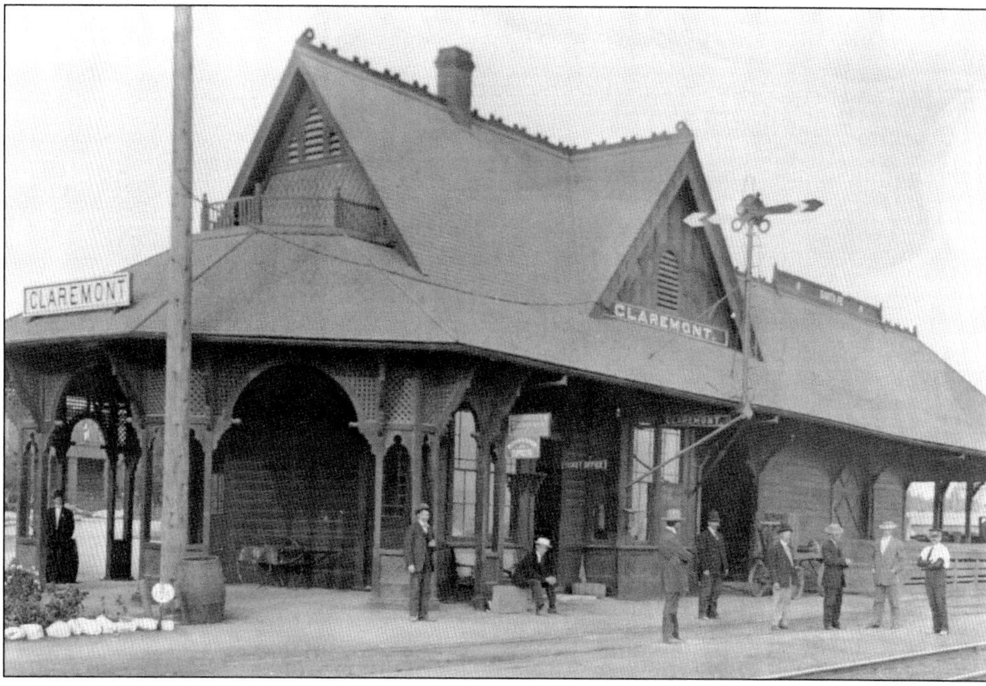

Santa Fe Depot, 1887. Claremont's original Gothic-style train depot, built by the Santa Fe Railroad in 1887, served as a makeshift citrus packinghouse in the citrus industry's early years. Workers would gather to sort the fruit by size, label it by brand, and then load it onto railroad cars. The depot was demolished in 1927.

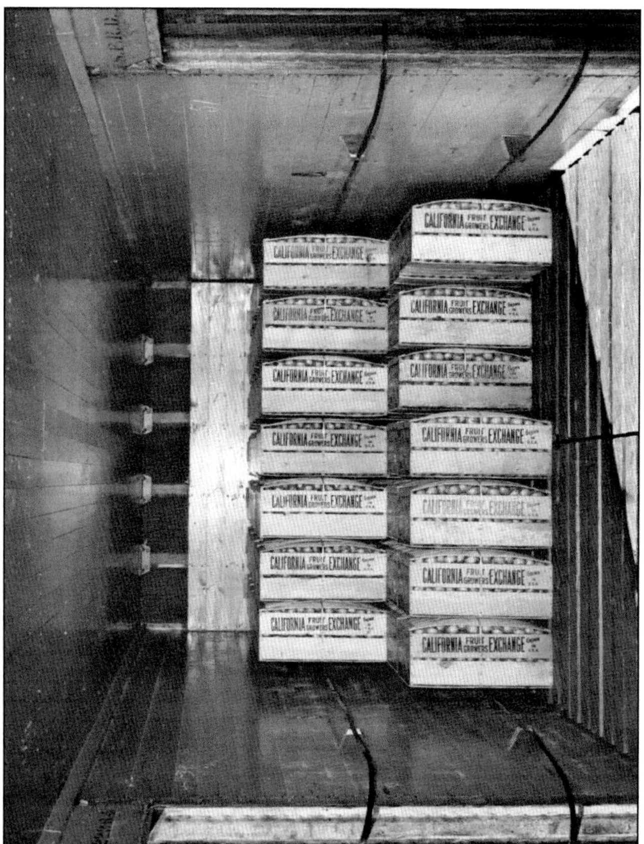

Citrus Boxcar. The proximity of the Santa Fe depot to the groves allowed for efficient shipping of citrus products all over the country. Crates of oranges or lemons could be packed, stored, labeled, and loaded onto a train for shipment across the country in a matter of hours. Here, crates of oranges from the Claremont Fruit Growers Exchange are loaded into a waiting boxcar.

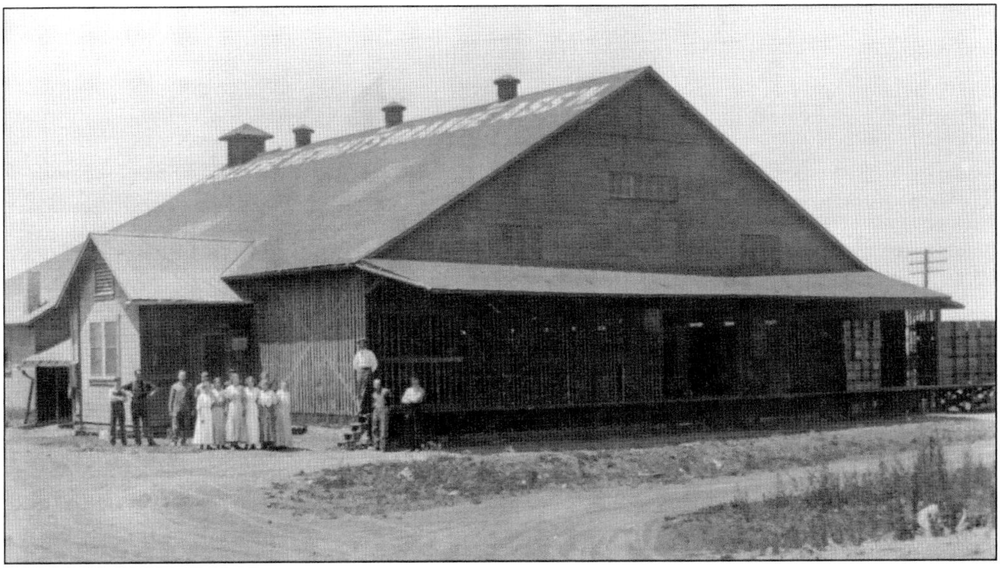

College Heights Packinghouse. The College Heights Orange and Lemon Association, which opened shortly after the Claremont Fruit Growers Exchange was established, was one of Claremont's first citrus packinghouses. The new, cavernous packinghouses that lined the railway line provided a protected indoor area where citrus fruit could be properly organized and prepared for shipping. (Courtesy of Special Collections, Honnold/Mudd Library of the Claremont Colleges.)

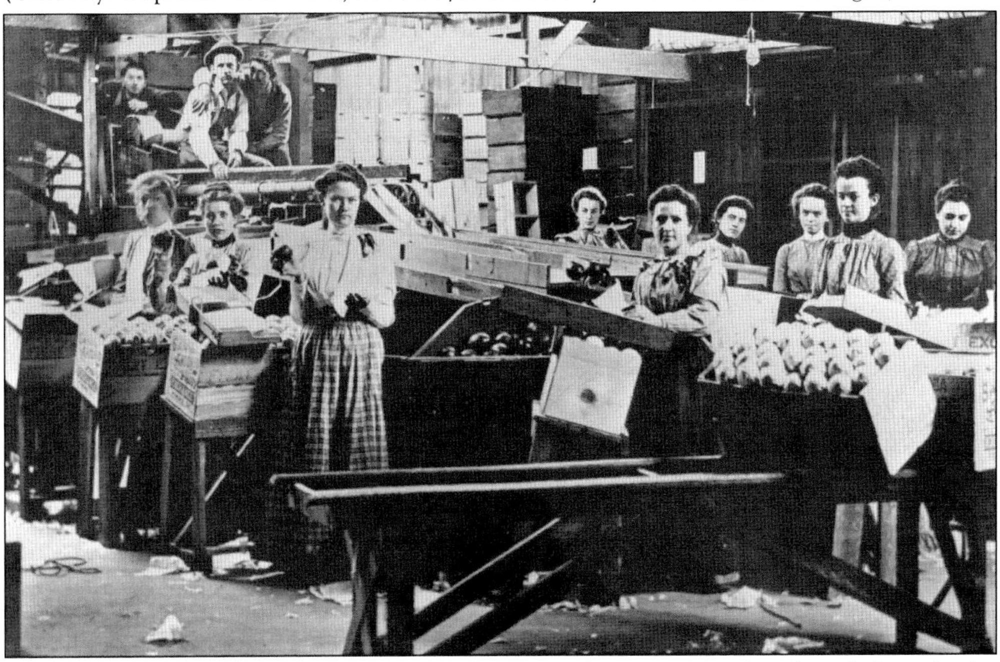

Claremont Citrus Association, c. 1893. Citrus fruit was sorted and graded inside the packinghouses based on quality and size of the fruit. Labels would then be assigned to the crates, allowing the consumer to see the quality of the product they were purchasing. Female workers in particular played an important part of the packaging of citrus fruit, providing the backbone of labor in the packinghouses well into the next century. (Courtesy of Special Collections, Honnold/Mudd Library of the Claremont Colleges.)

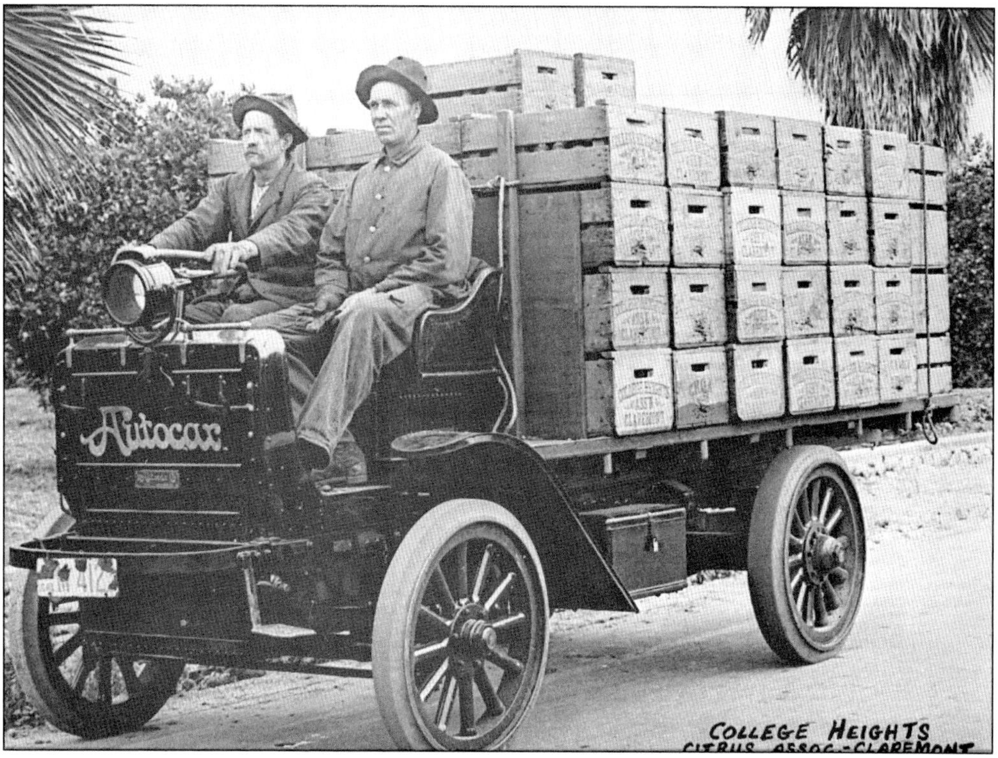

COLLEGE HEIGHTS CITRUS TRUCK, C. 1900S. In this photograph, a College Heights truck delivers crates of freshly picked oranges to the packinghouse. As the 20th century arrived, citrus farming was rapidly becoming Claremont's chief industry. The favorable climate and availability of water allowed citrus trees to flourish, eventually leading the industry to become a big business enterprise after World War I.

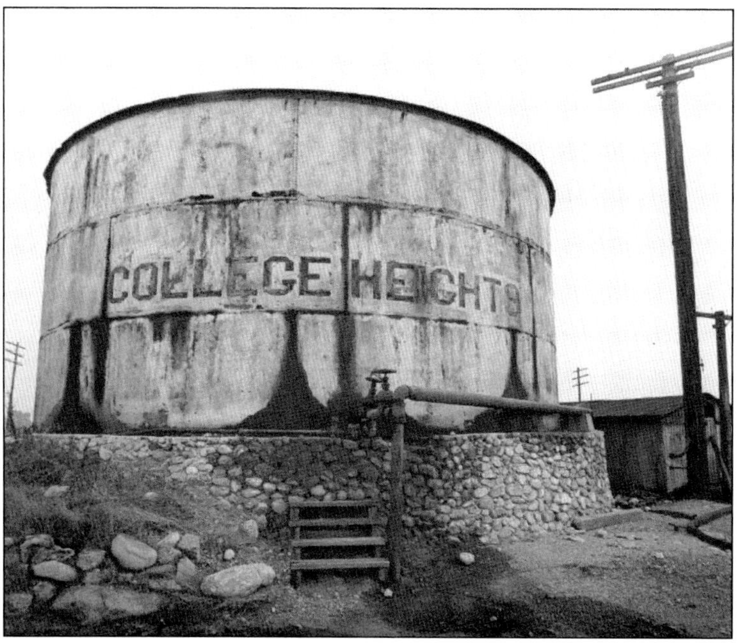

COLLEGE HEIGHTS CITRUS WATER TANK. The availability of water was key to the success of the citrus industry. Irrigation work by the Pomona Land and Water Company in the San Antonio Canyon and an abundance of artesian wells transformed the once desertlike Claremont into a fertile valley for citrus farming. Seen here in the 1970s is a derelict College Heights water tank once used for citrus irrigation.

Smudge Pots. Despite Claremont's typically ideal climate for citrus agriculture, the winter months proved dangerous, as cold weather and frost could damage or kill trees, even wiping out a whole grove. To combat this, oil-burning devices known as smudge pots were placed underneath the trees to generate heat and artificial smog to prevent frost from forming. While effective, they severely polluted the air and were later outlawed.

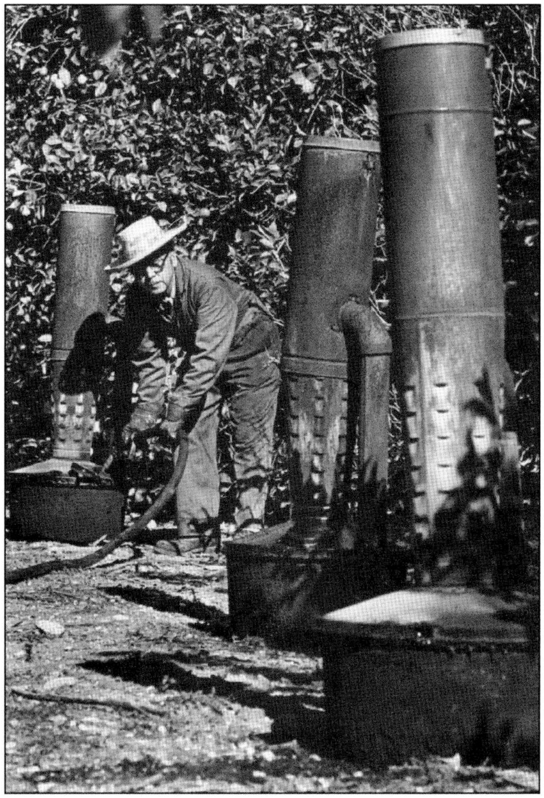

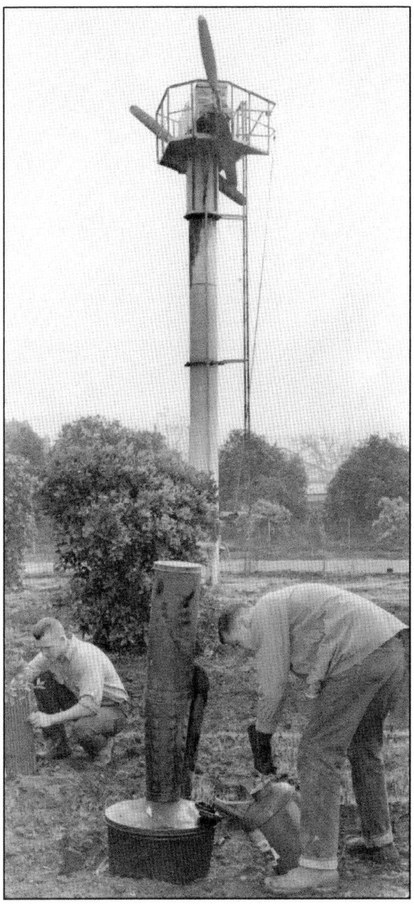

Wind Machine. Wind machines provided citrus growers with another method of warming groves during cold spells. A machine consisted of a large propeller placed above a group of trees. When a freezing temperature was forecast, the machine would be activated, warming the trees to a safe temperature. However, wind machines were more effective when used with smudge pots, somewhat hindering their benefits. (Courtesy of the Judy Wright collection.)

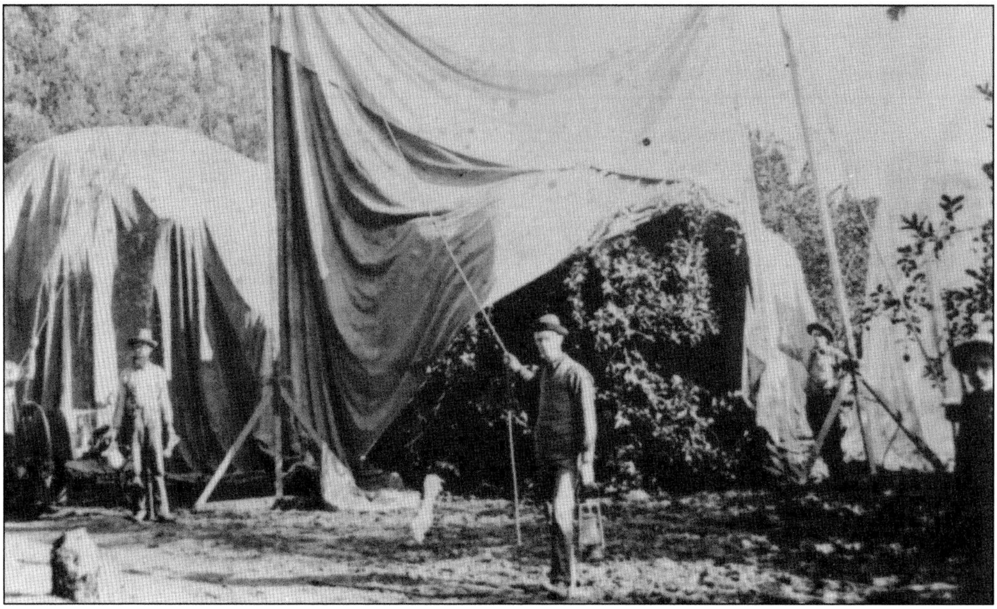

FUMIGATION. In addition to frost and cold weather, citrus growers had to contend with insects and disease. Fumigation was early farmers' preferred method of eradicating common pests like red and black scale insects and white flies. When fumigating, as illustrated above, citrus workers would put a canvas tent over the tree, place a pot of cyanide or sulfuric acid underneath, and let the gas generate inside the tent. Often done under the cover of darkness, this process was both dangerous and expensive for growers. A welcome change occurred in the 1920s, when spray rigs were implemented. These rigs, shown below, would spray insecticides on the trees and were much safer and more efficient. (Both, courtesy of the Judy Wright collection.)

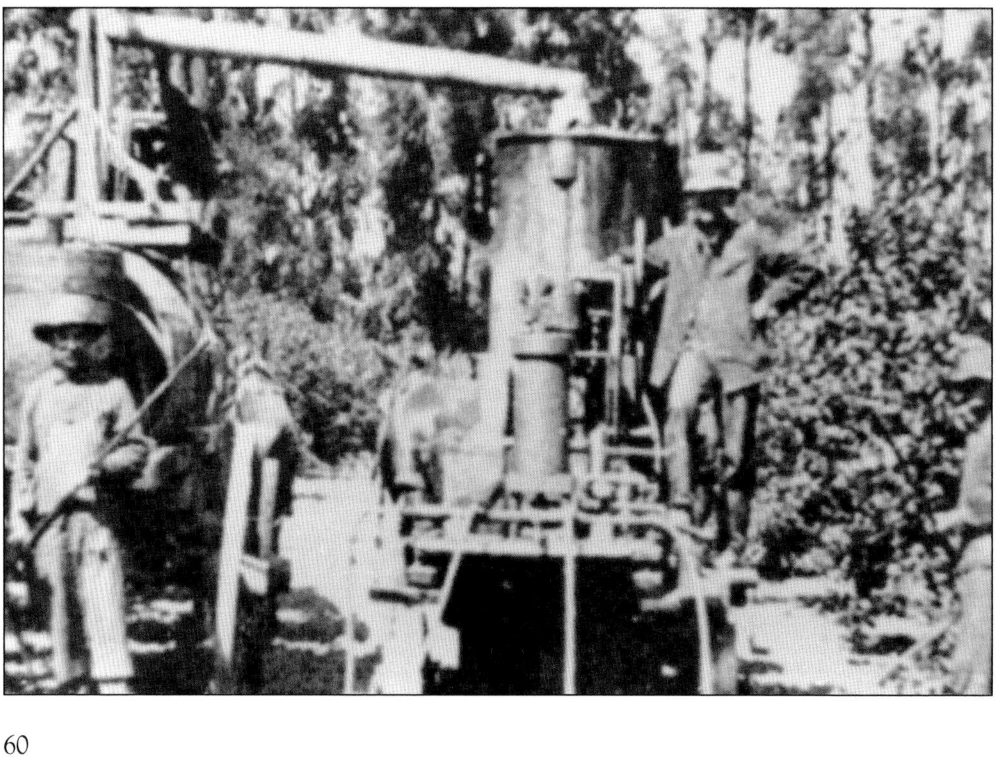

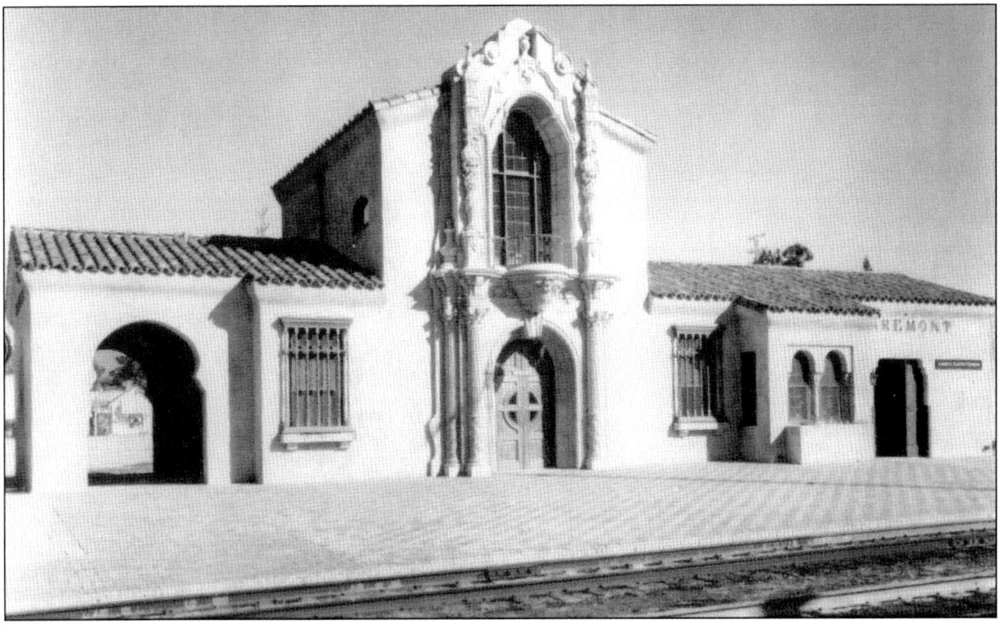

SANTA FE DEPOT, 1927. As the citrus industry grew, the constant flow of citrus-laden railroad cars in and out of Claremont warranted the construction of a larger Santa Fe depot in 1927. The new Spanish Colonial depot, built in the same location as the original, provided an excellent backdrop for citrus products leaving Claremont. (Courtesy of the Judy Wright collection.)

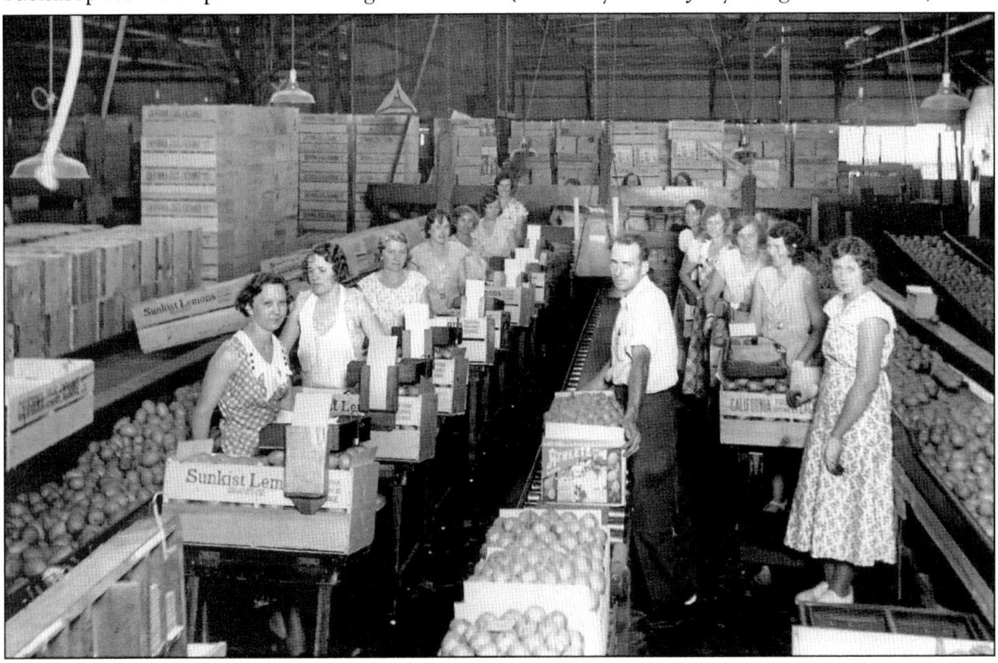

PACKINGHOUSE WORKERS, C. 1930S. Duties in the packinghouse were divided between men and women, with women mostly working as packers and men as box makers and loaders. By the 1930s, the citrus industry was a huge enterprise in Southern California. One former College Heights worker, Glenn Thompson, recalled that during a peak year, the packinghouse would hire upwards of 200 workers at any given time.

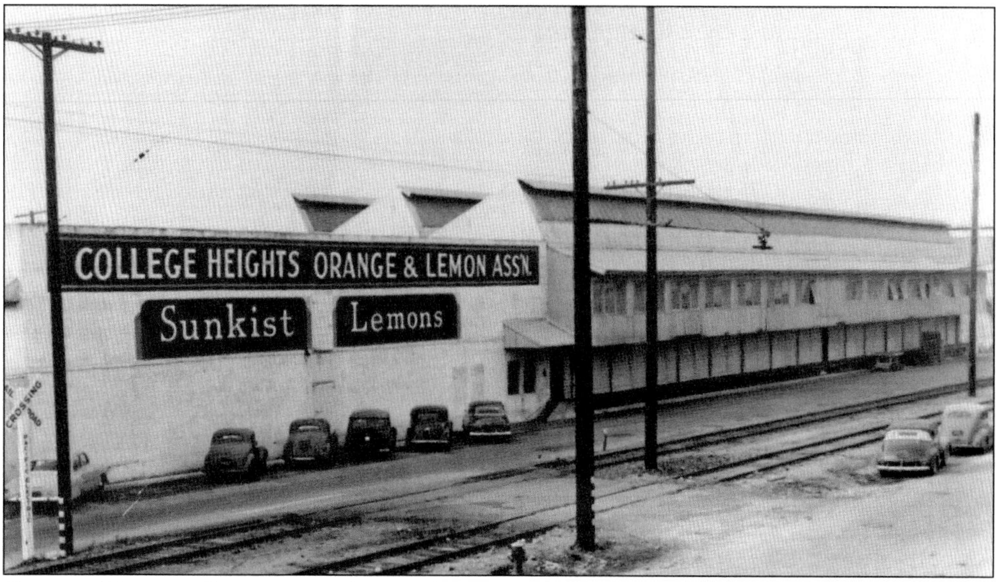

College Heights Orange and Lemon Association, c. 1940s. The 1930s and 1940s saw the citrus industry develop into an enormous business. Gone were the days of the local growers; they were replaced by large co-ops generating millions of dollars a year. College Heights became Claremont's largest packinghouse and was well known nationwide for the quality of its citrus fruit. An influx of immigrant labor and new farming technology kept College Heights profitable and running efficiently through the 1960s. (Courtesy of the Judy Wright collection; photograph by Robert C. Frampton.)

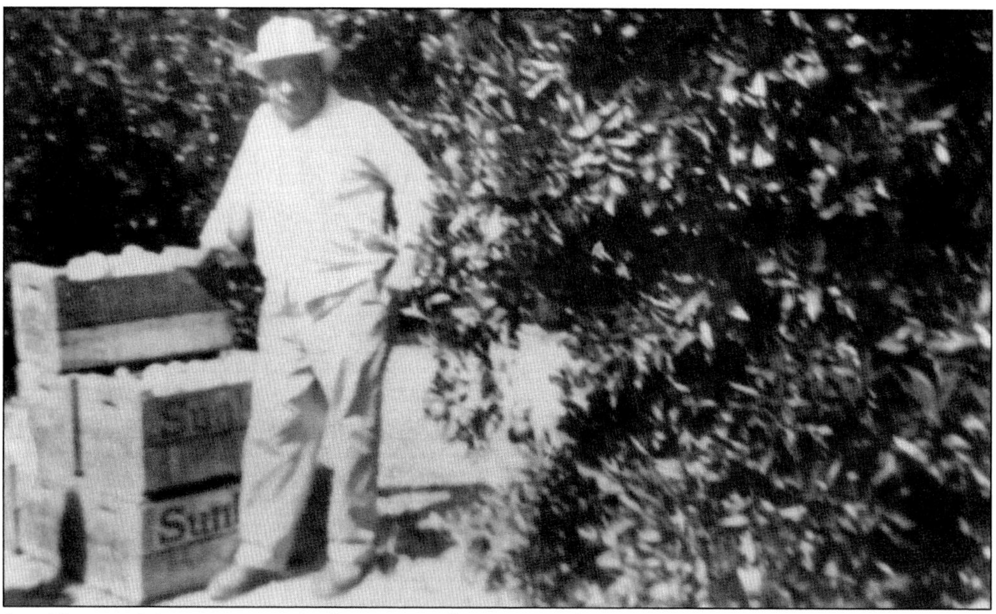

Jose Torrez, Mayordorno. As the citrus industry grew, the demand for cheap labor also increased, marking a shift towards a reliance on immigrant labor in the 1940s. The vast majority of the citrus workers of this era came from Mexico, and many would later settle in Claremont or Pomona. Claremont resident Jose Torrez worked as a "mayordorno," or field boss, for Sunkist, overseeing a crew of hardworking men and boys. (Courtesy of the Judy Wright collection.)

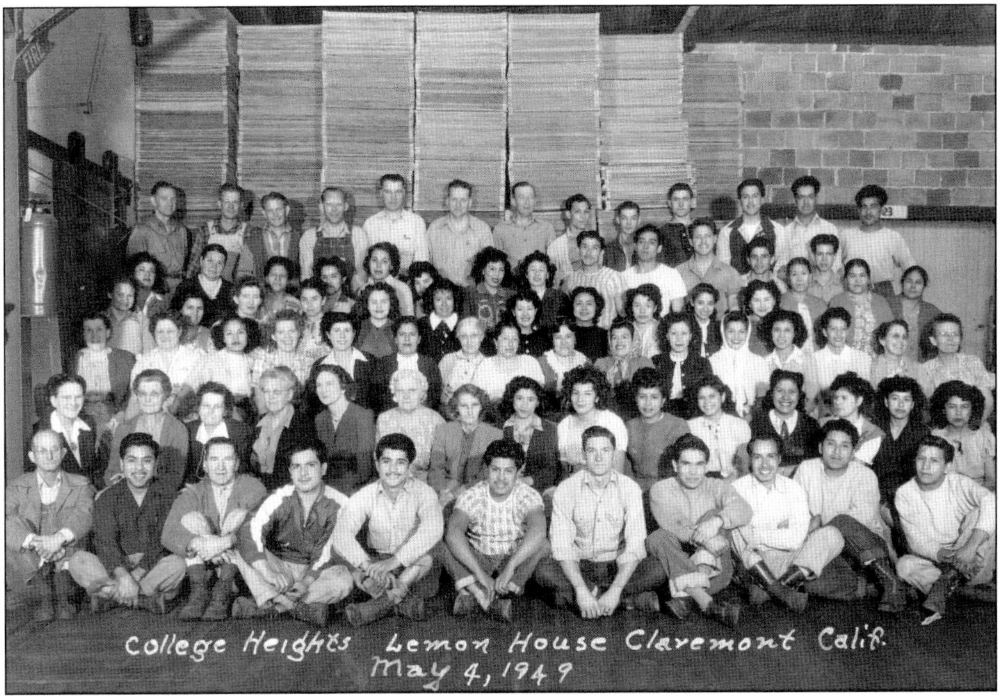

COLLEGE HEIGHTS LEMON HOUSE, MAY 4, 1949. Following World War II, growers favored a bracero program, which bused in immigrant workers to the packinghouses. The growers felt that the program would keep prices down while allowing the workers to make decent money to better their lives in Mexico. This photograph of College Heights workers in 1949 shows the predominance of Mexican laborers, leading to a unique blending of cultures in Claremont.

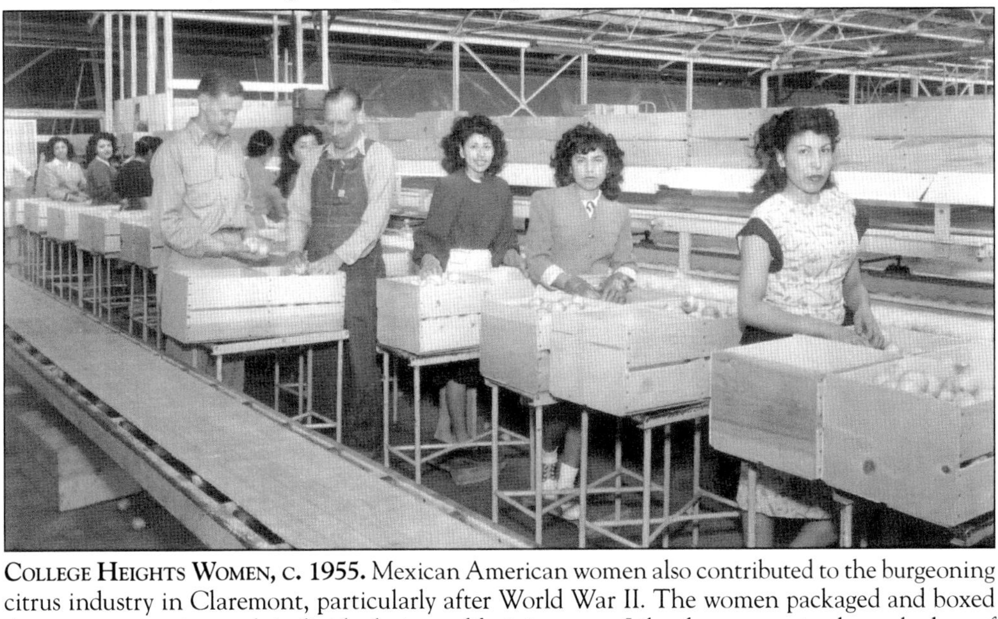

COLLEGE HEIGHTS WOMEN, C. 1955. Mexican American women also contributed to the burgeoning citrus industry in Claremont, particularly after World War II. The women packaged and boxed the citrus, wrapping each individual piece of fruit in paper. Like the women in the early days of the packinghouses, Mexican American women provided an invaluable resource to Claremont's citrus industry and provided much of the labor that made the co-ops profitable.

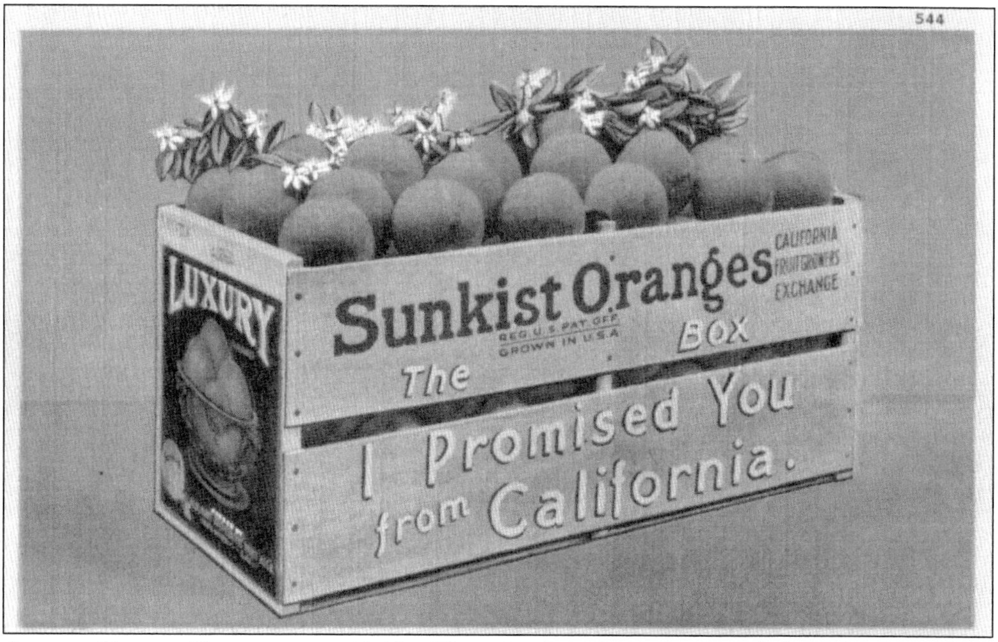

Sunkist Orange Postcards, c. 1940s. These Sunkist Orange postcards from the 1940s show the marketing strategy of the citrus companies at the time. Oranges from Southern California were particularly famous on the East Coast for their great quality, and they were often used as gifts around the holidays. These postcards, most likely sent to an envious relative, not only advertised the area's citrus products, but also emphasized the near perfect weather all year-round. The back of the postcard above contains a poem: "Here is the box I promised you filled with gold. Golden fruit; ripe and luscious from Nature's mold." Below is a beautiful image of an orange orchard with the snowcapped Mount Baldy in the background.

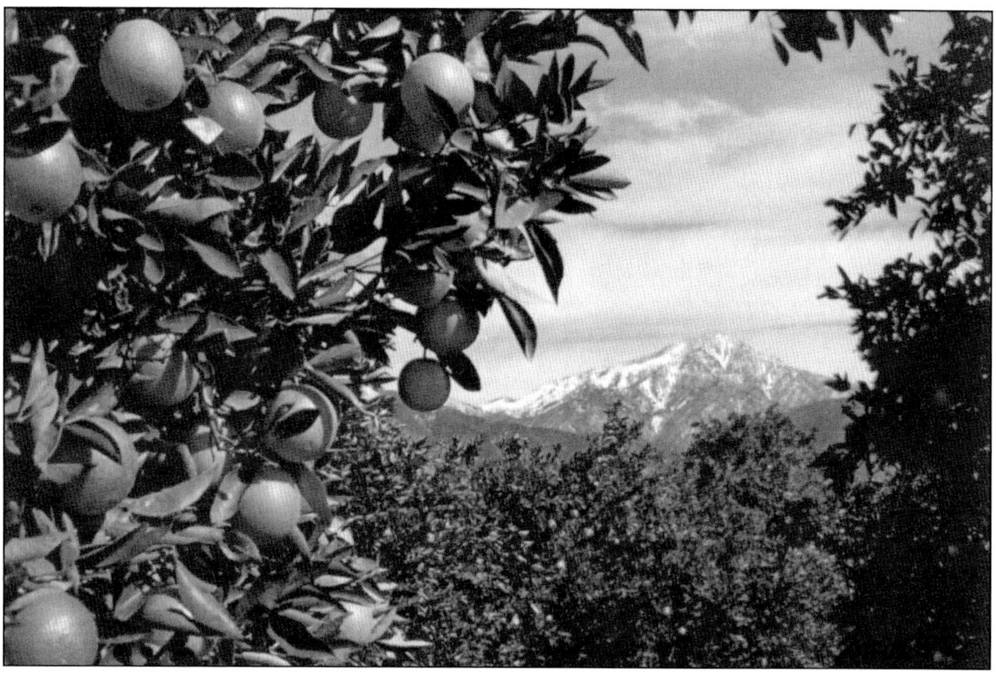

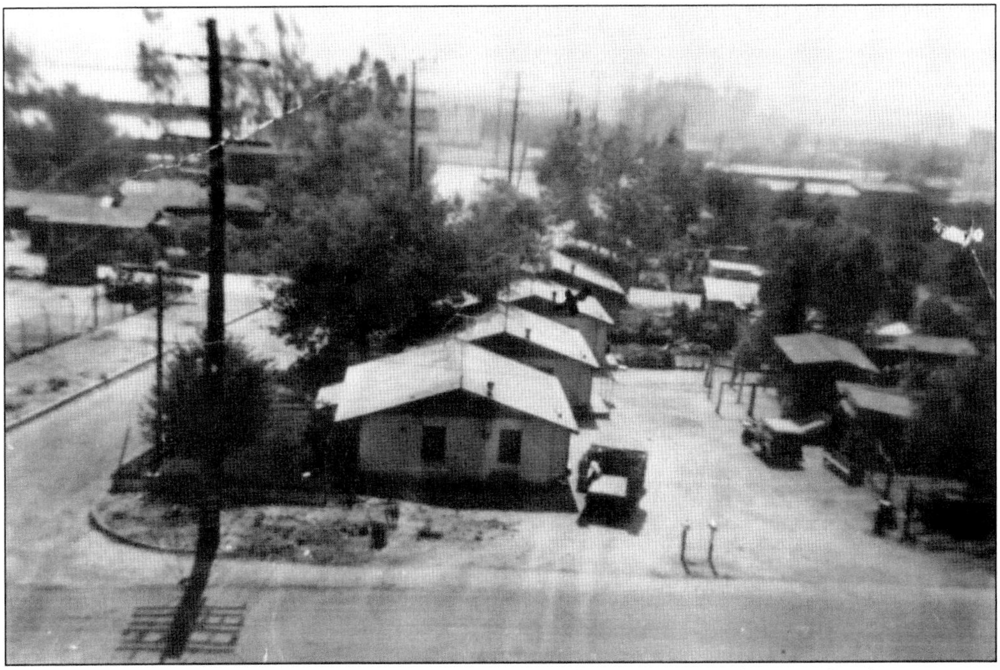

WEST BARRIO AERIAL, c. 1951. This photograph, taken from the tower of Our Lady of Assumption Church, shows the West Barrio area, running along Berkeley Avenue. The West Barrio area was developed by the College Heights Orange and Lemon Association to provide housing for its many immigrant workers. As such, the majority of residents in the West Barrio were involved in Claremont's citrus industry, and the barrio quickly became a thriving community. (Courtesy of the Judy Wright collection.)

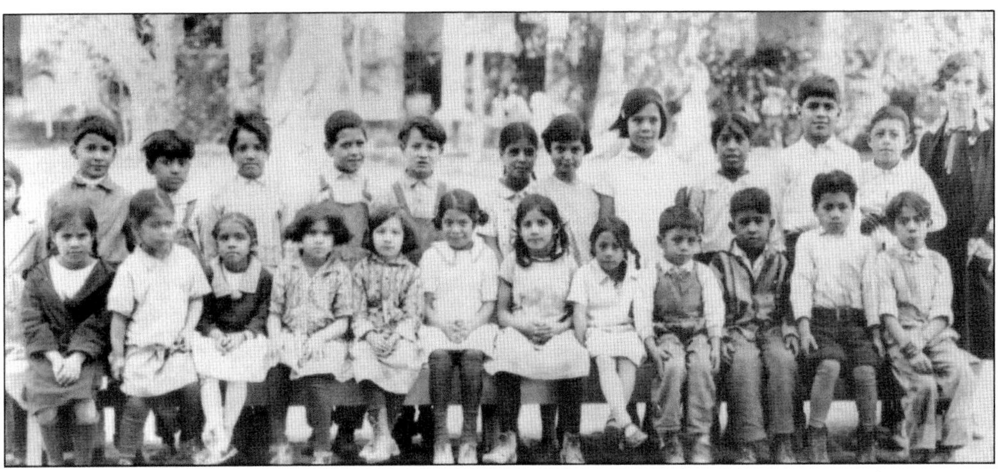

WEST BARRIO SCHOOL, 1925. The West Barrio contained Claremont's first school for Mexican children, although the first teacher spoke no Spanish, which made the learning process somewhat difficult. School was first held at a house in the West Barrio, later moving to a community house known as Su Casa, and finally settling in a location on Ninth Street. This photograph shows the third-grade class. (Courtesy of the Judy Wright collection.)

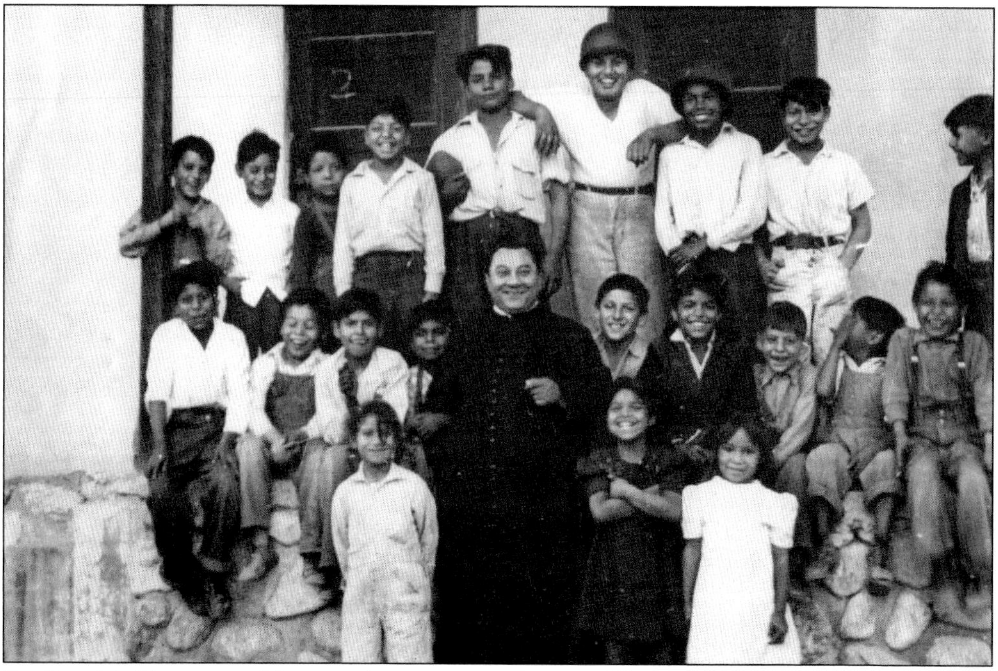

FR. JOSE M. GARGALLO. Mexican Americans working in Claremont's citrus industry generally lived in either the East or West Barrio. The East Barrio was a close-knit community located on the Arbol Verde tract of Claremont from the 1920s until 1973, when it was razed for the construction of Claremont Boulevard. Here, Father Gargallo, a priest from the East Barrio's Church of the Sacred Heart, visits with a group of local children. (Courtesy of the Judy Wright collection and Natalie Gomez.)

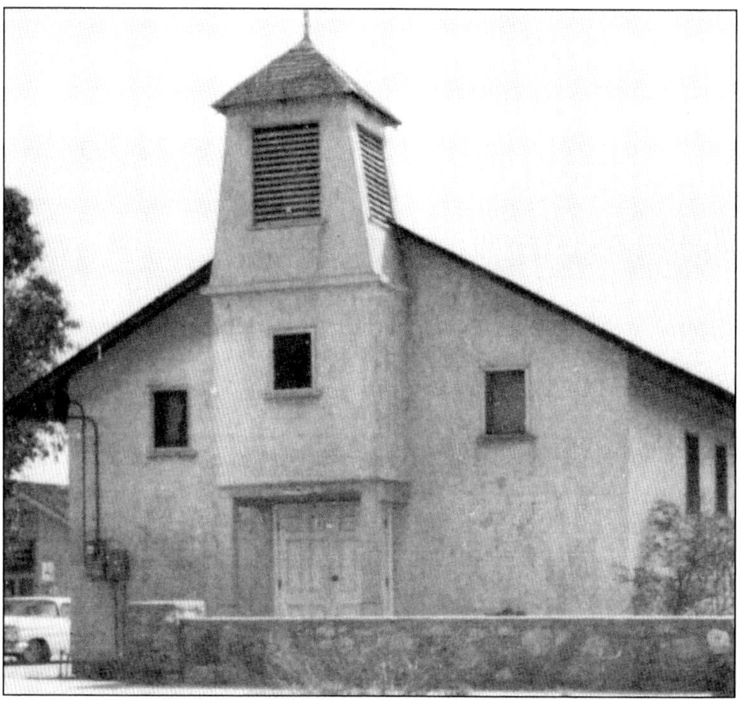

CHURCH OF THE SACRED HEART. Constructed by East Barrio residents with donations from the Claremont Congregational Church, the Church of the Sacred Heart provided a place of worship for residents of the community. Located on First Street, the chapel helped forge a strong community bond among the East Barrio residents. Sadly, it was destroyed in 1973 to make way for the construction of Claremont Boulevard.

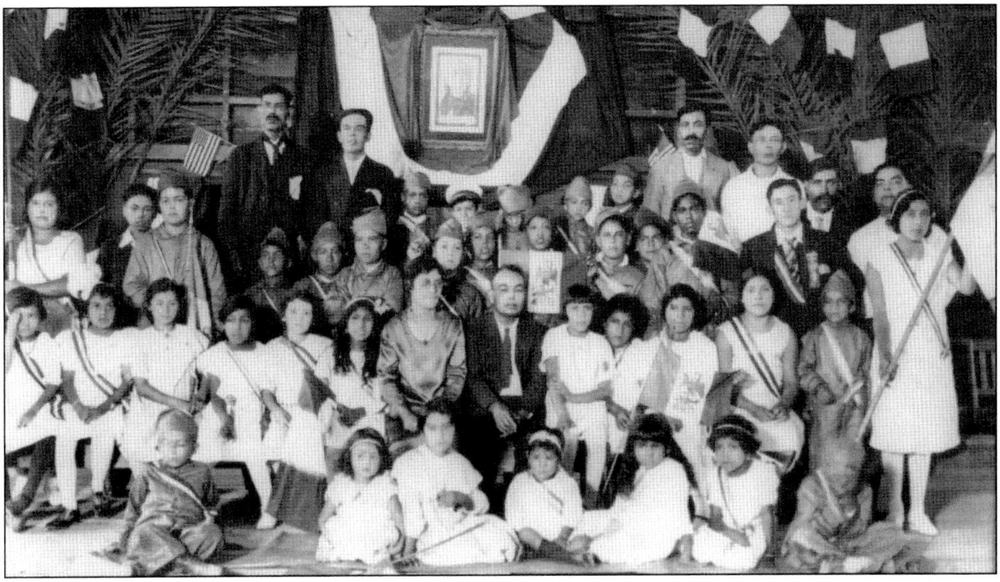

EAST BARRIO SCHOOL, 1928. The Escuela Mexicana, seen here in the Pomona College Gymnasium, provided a unique education for children of the East Barrio. Unlike the West Barrio's school, the Escuela Mexicana employed Spanish-speaking teachers, allowing for its students to learn through common language and maintain their own cultural identities. It was not until the 1940s that most Mexican American students began attending school with the general population of children in Claremont.

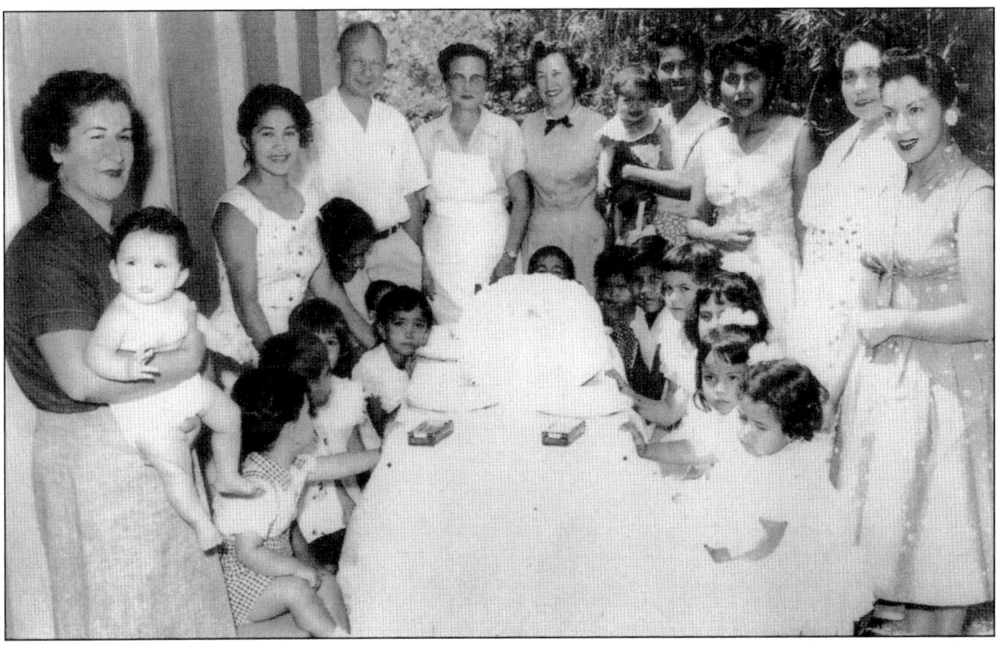

CLUB DE DAMAS, C. 1950S. During the 1940s and 1950s, there was a large push to bring together the different ethnic communities of Claremont. This was done through the establishment of social organizations like Claremont's Intercultural Council and the Club de Damas. Seen here, the Club de Damas, or "Well-Baby Clinic," allowed mothers from both communities to come and receive care for their children. (Courtesy of the Judy Wright collection.)

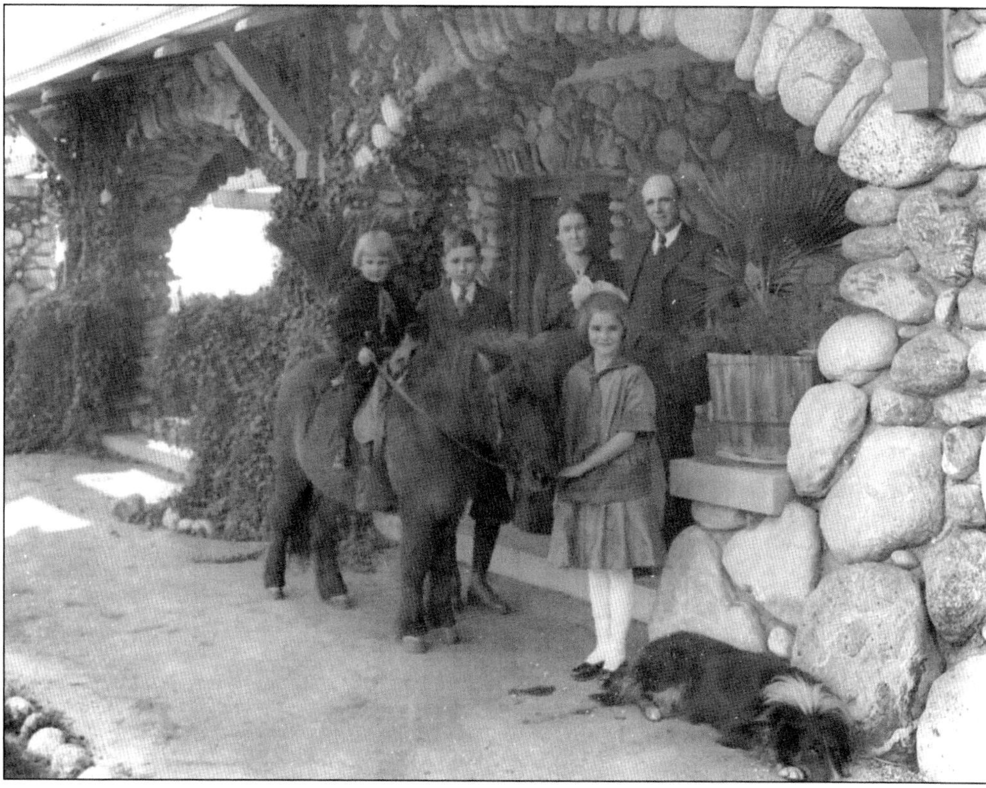

Lee Pitzer Family and House. The influential Pitzer family, seen here in front of their exquisite stone home, settled in Claremont in 1912 after purchasing several hundred acres near Baseline Road and Towne Avenue to grow lemons. The Pitzers found great success as citrus farmers and became highly active members of the community. Lee helped construct the Claremont Manor retirement center, while his wife, Blanche, ran one of the city's first Girl Scout troops.

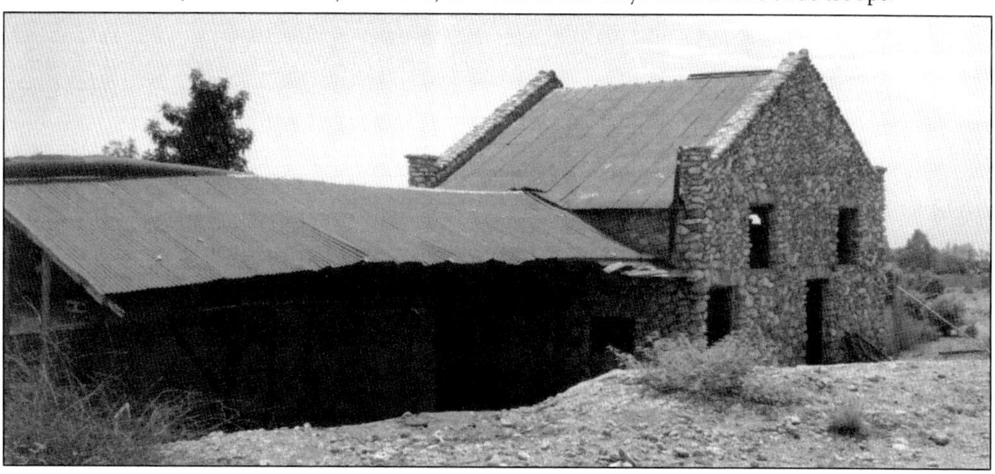

Pitzer Ranch Barn. Pitzer earned the distinction of being the first rancher to grow citrus above Baseline Road, with his farm's rockier soil proving conducive to growing lemons. As news of Pitzer's success spread, land in northern Claremont became highly desirable to citrus growers. Seen here is one of the Pitzer ranch's gable-roofed barns as it looks today, at Baseline Road and Monte Vista Avenue.

Five

Trees and PhDs
The Claremont Colleges

Pomona College quickly gained a reputation as one of the premier liberal arts colleges in the country. With this prestige, however, came the serious problem of overcrowding. By 1920, enrollment was at 750, and the board was emphatically against increasing it any further, despite massive demand.

The solution to this problem was the development of the "group plan," inspired largely by the Oxford-Cambridge system. This plan established the Claremont Colleges, a consortium that included both a graduate school (now the Claremont Graduate University) and "associated colleges," the first of them being Pomona. These undergraduate associated colleges—there would come to be five in total—were independent institutions; however, they all shared some common services and facilities, such as an infirmary and an auditorium. In 2000, after a series of name changes, the Claremont Colleges became the Claremont University Consortium.

The first additional associate college to be built under the group plan was Scripps College for Women. The college was named for its generous benefactor, Ellen Browning Scripps, who wanted to create a school with a focus in the humanities. Just two years after the incorporation of the Claremont Colleges, Scripps's first class entered in the fall of 1927.

For two decades, the consortium's three schools seemed sufficient. However, by the late 1940s, demand increased due to millions of World War II veterans returning home with the GI Bill. Plans were quickly approved for Claremont Men's College (CMC), which was incorporated in 1947 with the aim of educating men interested in careers of public service. CMC became coeducational in 1976 and was renamed Claremont McKenna College shortly thereafter.

The postwar industrial boom in the West soon inspired the 1955 addition of Harvey Mudd College, a liberal arts college with a science and engineering emphasis. In 1963, Pitzer College was incorporated as a women's college to help reach a gender balance within the colleges—in 1962, women were outnumbered by about 700. Later, Pitzer became coeducational, though it retained its specialization in the social sciences. The consortium was completed in 1997 with the establishment of the Keck Graduate Institute of Applied Life Sciences.

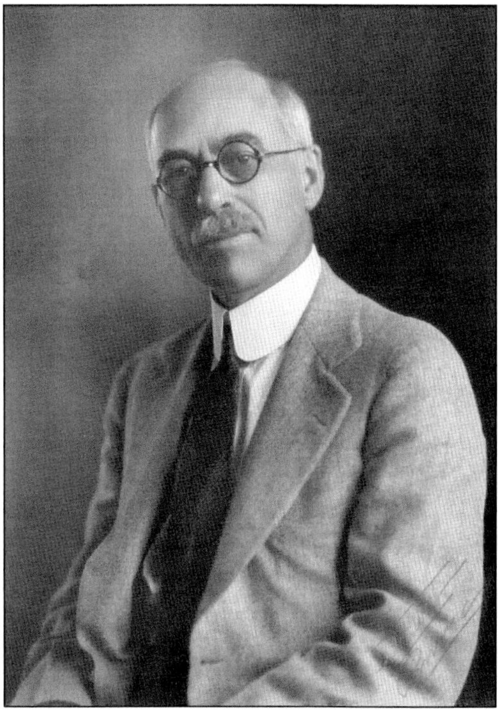

James Arnold Blaisdell. In 1910, former minister James Blaisdell accepted the presidency of Pomona College. Over the course of the next 18 years, Blaisdell would prove to be an exceptional leader, expanding the campus, fundraising admirably, increasing enrollment, and attracting acclaimed professors. Furthermore, Blaisdell can nearly single-handedly be credited with developing the idea of the Claremont Colleges Consortium, of which he served as president for eight years. (Courtesy of Special Collections, Honnold/Mudd Library of the Claremont Colleges.)

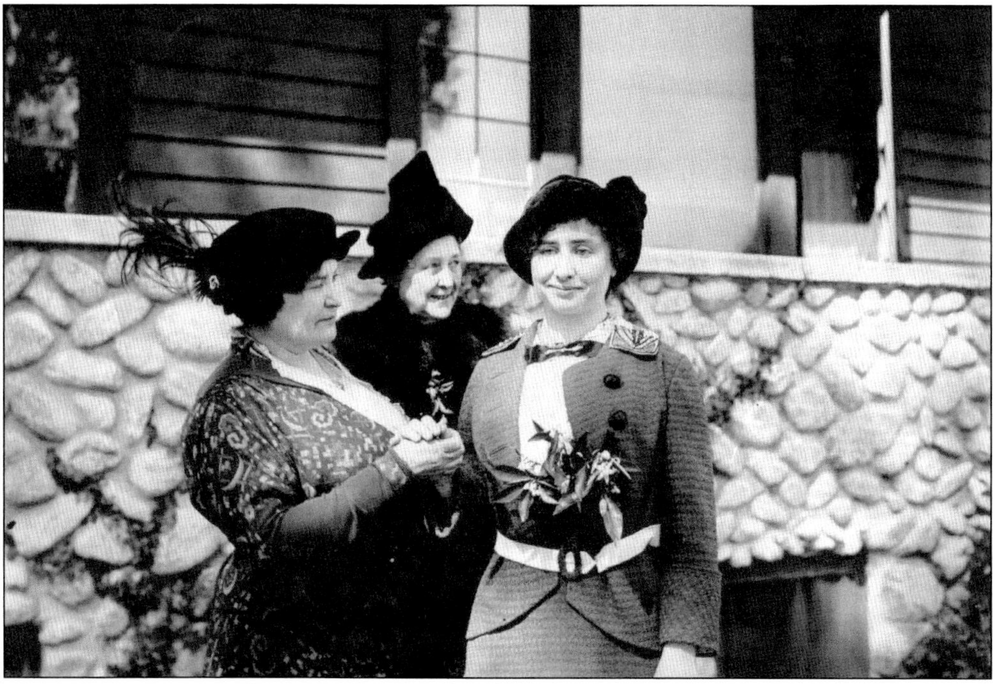

Helen Keller Visits Campus, 1914. Under the presidency of James Blaisdell, many notable people came to speak at Pomona College. Helen Keller (right) visited in 1914. In the same year, Booker T. Washington also came to speak in the college chapel. Blaisdell had carried on this tradition from his predecessor George Gates, who had invited future Nobel Peace Prize recipient Jane Addams and Pres. Theodore Roosevelt to campus.

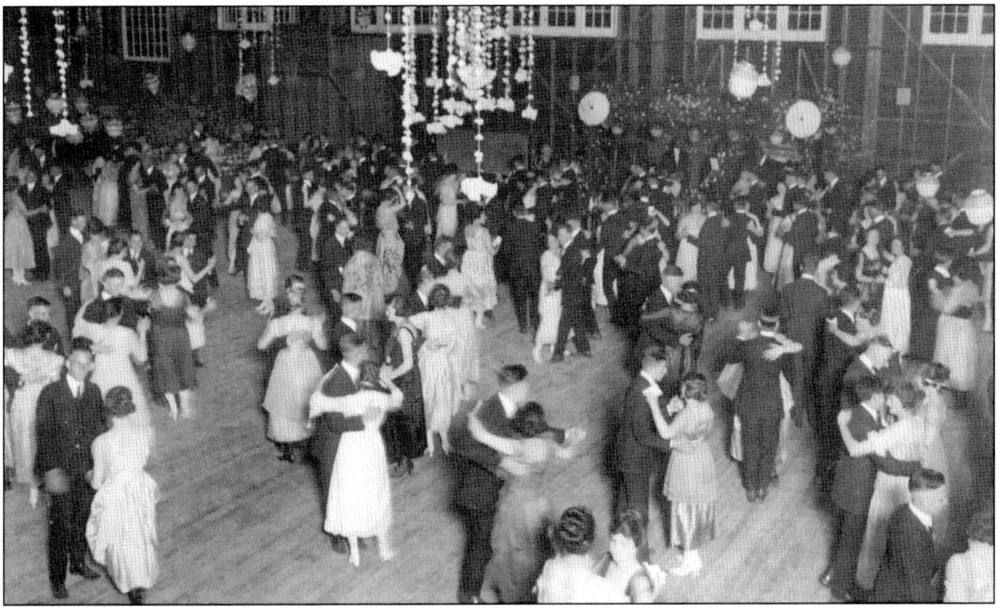

Formal Dance at Pomona, 1923. By the 1920s, Pomona College was moving away from its strict Congregationalist roots. In March 1923, the college hosted this Freshman–Senior Reception in its gym, complete with a jazz orchestra. As a further sign of changes in the student body, four years later, the yearbook reported, "The best bootlegger in the whole neighborhood of Claremont has been caught. The improved behavior of the college men is very noticeable." (Courtesy of Special Collections, Honnold/Mudd Library of the Claremont Colleges.)

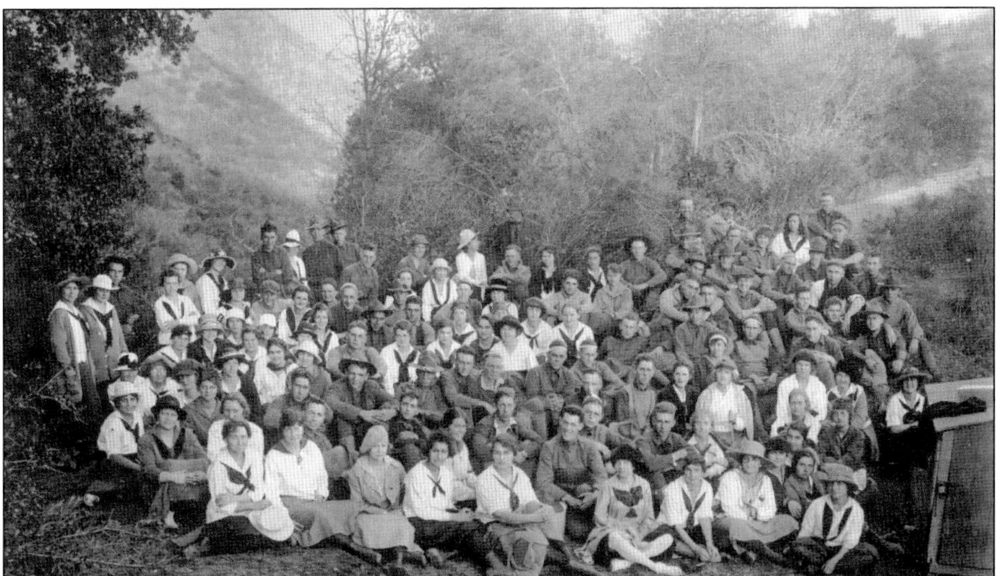

Pomona Students "Clear the P," 1919. Proud Pomona College students pose at the firebox in Palmer Canyon after participating in the "Clearing of the P." This annual activity was one of the school's most cherished traditions. Beginning in 1912, the students would clear a giant "P" on the hillsides of Palmer Canyon before the football game against their biggest rival, Occidental College. The "P" would then be set aflame to burn throughout the game.

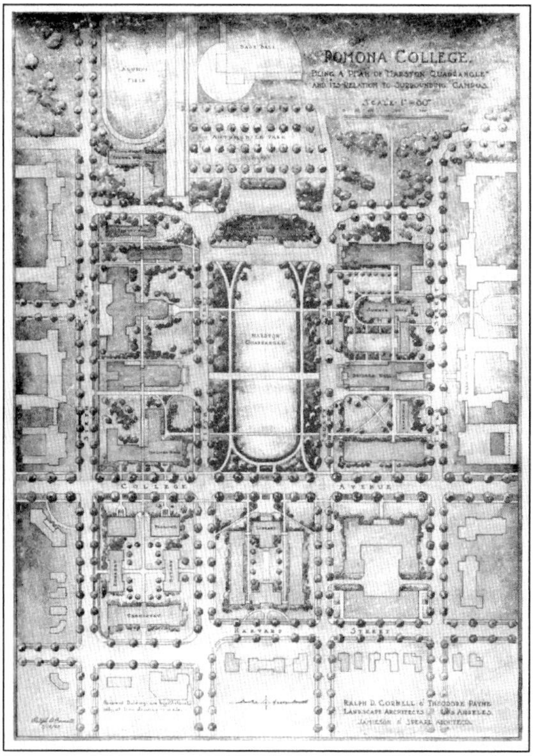

Marston Quadrangle Plan. In a 1908 campus plan designed by architect Myron Hunt, a large quadrangle—an open grassy space with buildings along the perimeter—was a central feature. It was not until 1919, however, that Pomona finally received a donation from founding trustee George Marston to begin construction. To make space for the quad, Sumner Hall, the original college building, had to be moved and rotated, stretching the project out three years. (Courtesy of Special Collections, Honnold/Mudd Library of the Claremont Colleges.)

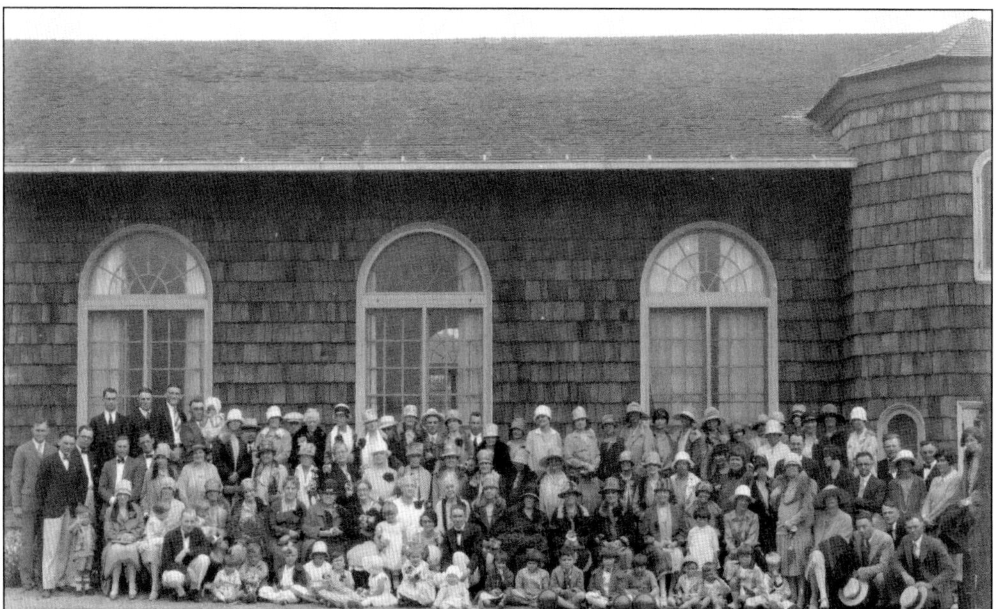

Pomona Faculty, 1917. By 1917, when this faculty picture was taken, Pomona College's reputation was growing across the nation. The downside to this newfound popularity, however, was overcrowding. In 1915, the board of trustees had tried to limit the incoming class's enrollment to 200, but more and more students continued to apply for admission. Soon, college administrators began considering the idea of a "group plan," which eventually led to the Claremont Colleges Consortium.

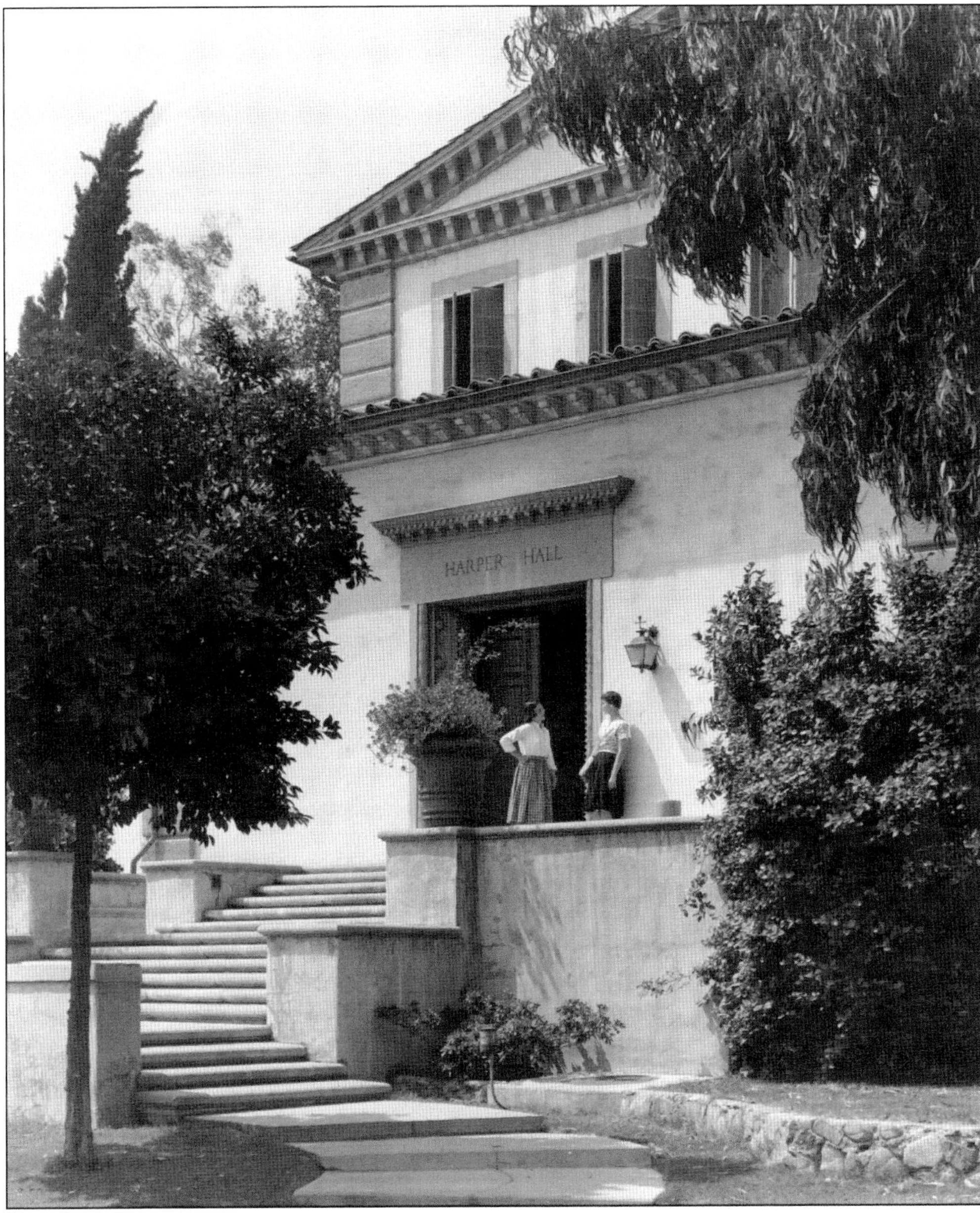

CLAREMONT COLLEGES CONSORTIUM'S HARPER HALL. Pictured here is Harper Hall, once the central administrative building and library of the Claremont Colleges Consortium. The consortium was the fruit of the labor of James Blaisdell, who envisioned "that instead of one great, undifferentiated university, we might have a group of institutions divided into small colleges—somewhat on the Oxford type—around a library and other utilities which they would use in common. In this way I should hope to preserve the inestimable *personal* values of the small college while securing the *facilities* of a great university." Claremont Colleges—the sum of the associated colleges (at the time, only Pomona), a graduate school, and the central institution—was incorporated on October 14, 1925. Blaisdell soon became its president. The consortium has since been renamed the Claremont University Consortium, with Claremont Graduate University operating as a separate institution.

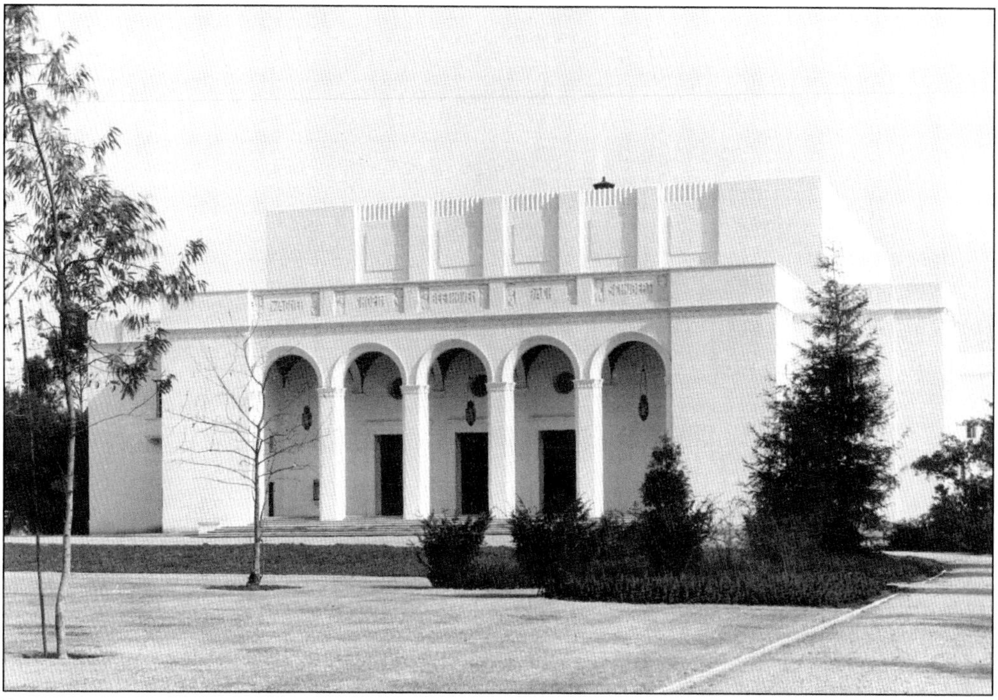

Bridges Auditorium, 1931. Construction on this impressive building was completed in 1931, at the beginning of the Great Depression. "Big Bridges," as it is called, is located on the eastern perimeter of the Marston Quadrangle on Pomona College land; however, it was actually a joint undertaking of the Claremont Colleges. At the time, it was the largest college or university auditorium on the West Coast, with seating for 2,500—the entire population of Claremont. (Courtesy of Special Collections, Honnold/Mudd Library of the Claremont Colleges.)

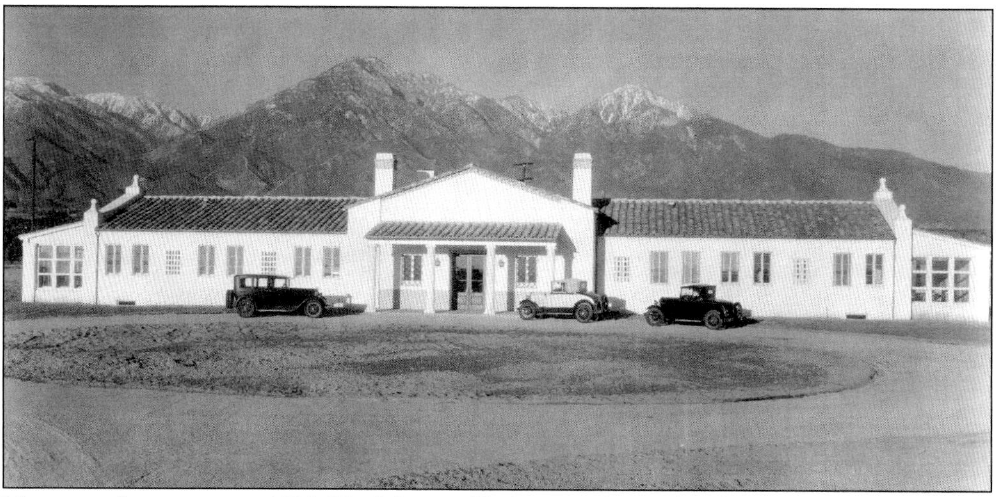

Memorial Infirmary, c. 1931. The Memorial Infirmary, shown shortly after its completion, was another shared venture of the Claremont Colleges, serving consortium students from 1931 to 1975. The one-story stucco building had two wings, one for men and one for women, and was situated north of Foothill Boulevard, purposefully slightly removed from the hustle and bustle of campus. The infirmary has been credited with preventing any major epidemics on campus. (Courtesy of Special Collections, Honnold/Mudd Library of the Claremont Colleges.)

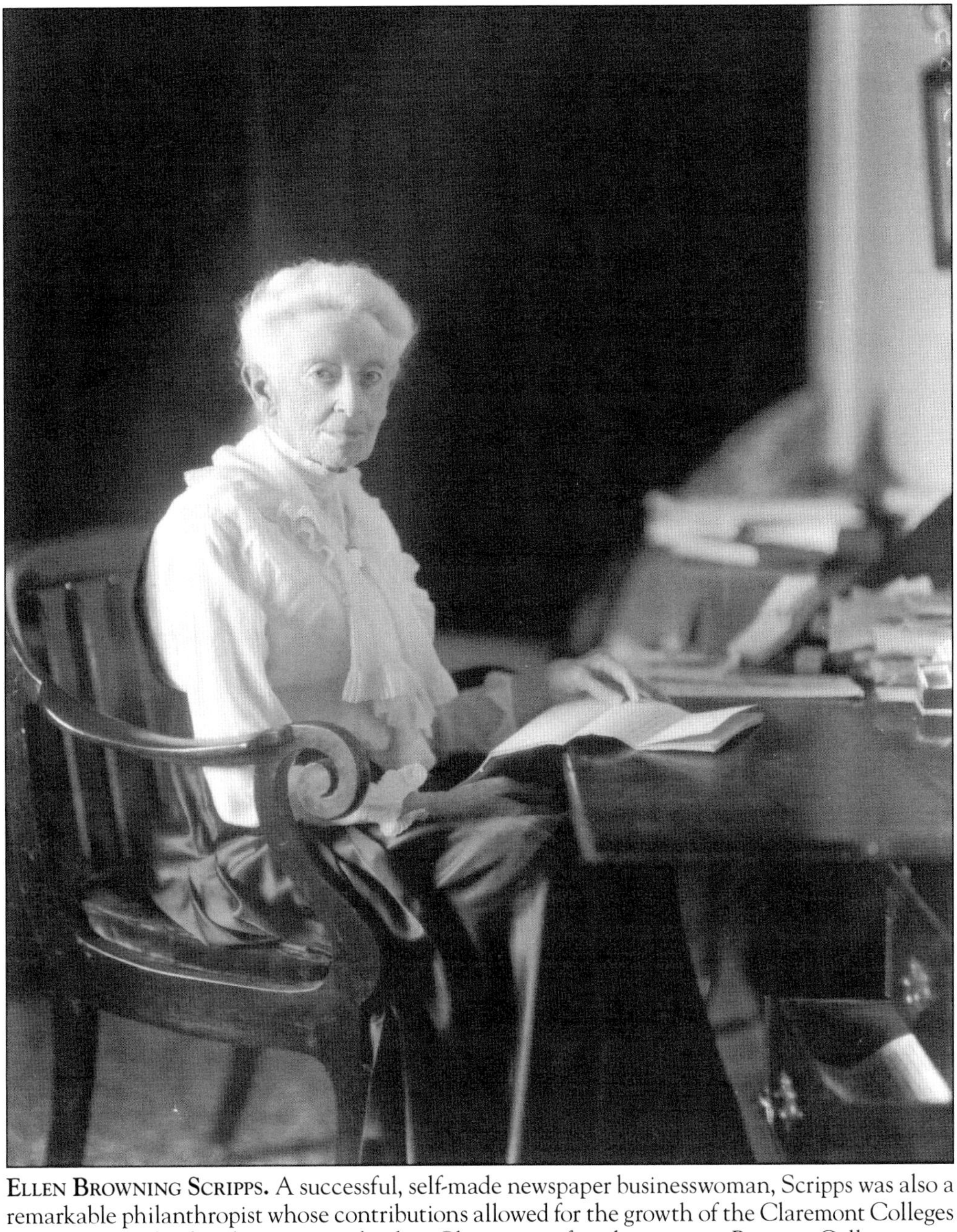

Ellen Browning Scripps. A successful, self-made newspaper businesswoman, Scripps was also a remarkable philanthropist whose contributions allowed for the growth of the Claremont Colleges Consortium. She first became involved in Claremont after donating to Pomona College; soon after, she was convinced by President Blaisdell to help fund the new Oxford-style consortium. From there, Scripps became even more dedicated to the Claremont Colleges, donating not only money, but also time and personal attention. As a former educator and a lifelong supporter of women's rights, at age 90 she set up an endowment for a new women's college. Scripps College, as the school was subsequently named in her honor, was designed to "develop in its students the ability to think clearly and independently, and the ability to live confidently, courageously, and hopefully." In total, Scripps's contributions to the Claremont Colleges amounted to over $2 million. (Courtesy of the Judy Wright collection.)

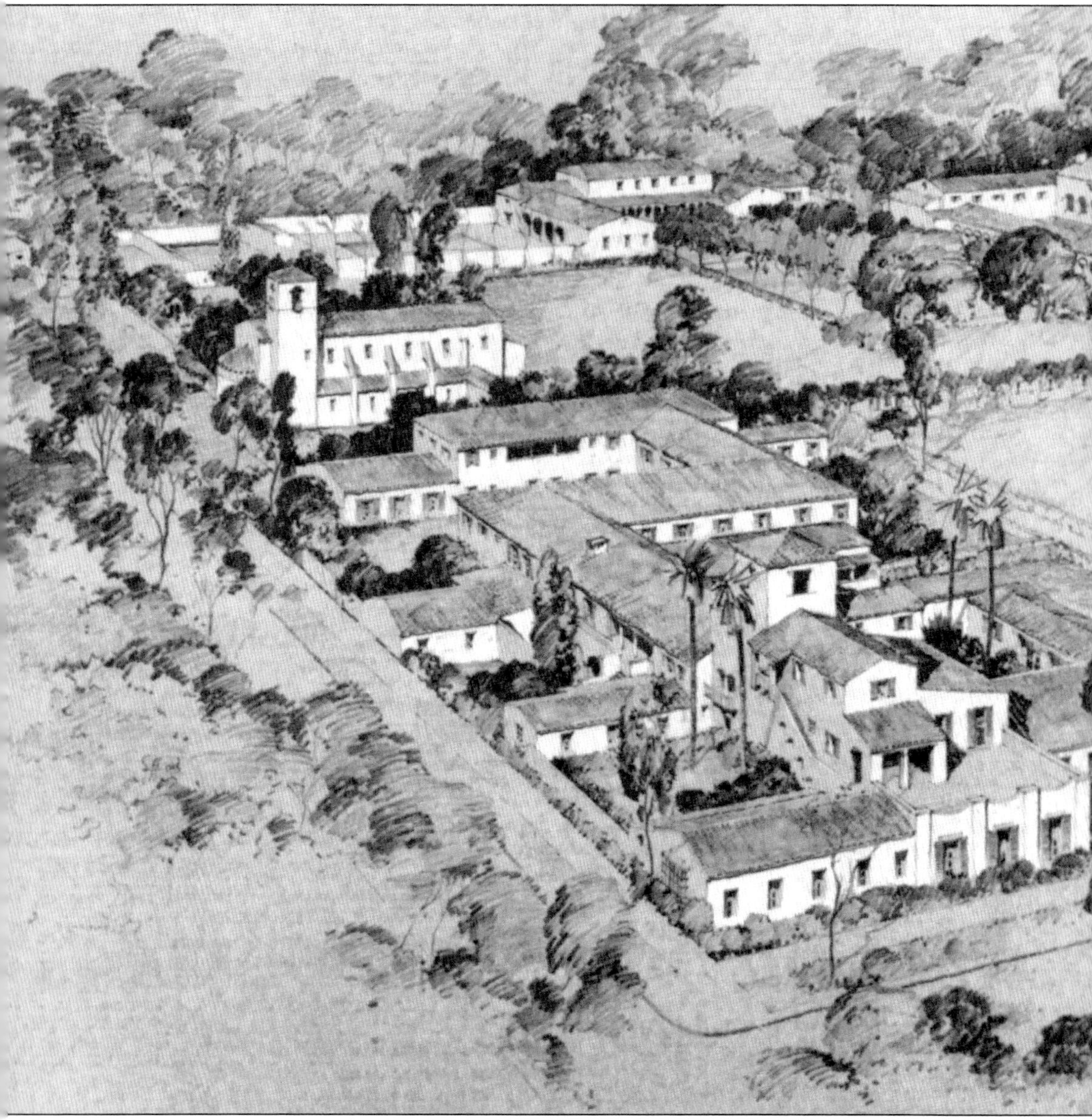

SCRIPPS COLLEGE CAMPUS PLAN. With the Claremont Colleges group plan firmly established, administrators immediately set their minds to the formation of a second college. Enthusiasm for the project was greater than funding, however, and many pinned their hopes on Ellen Browning Scripps, a friend of James Blaisdell who had proved to be a generous benefactor to the consortium already. On September 29, 1925, the fateful letter from Scripps arrived announcing her financial support for the establishment of a Scripps College for Women. No time was wasted establishing

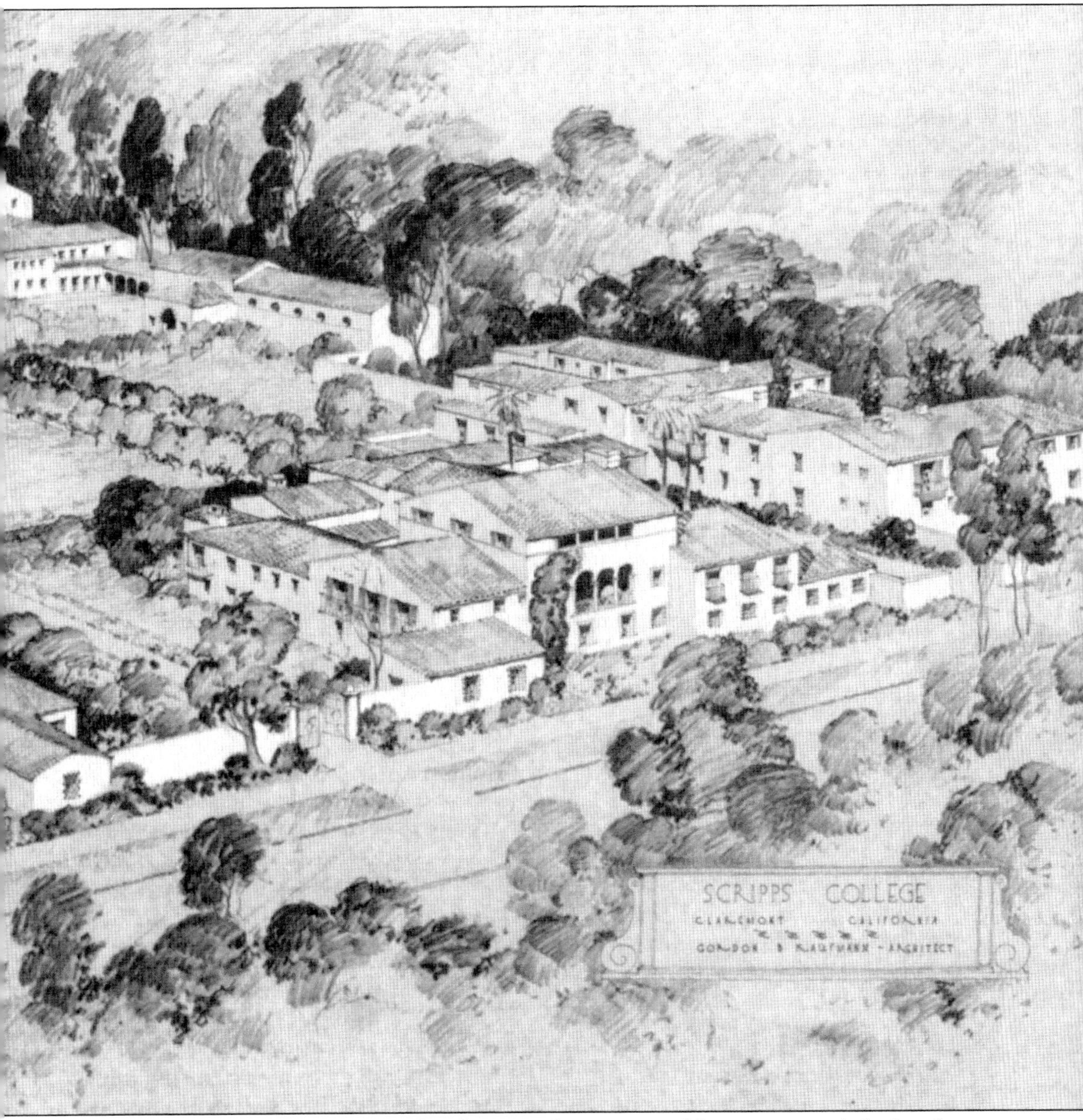

a board of trustees, comprised equally of men and women, and hiring accomplished architect Gordon Kaufmann to design the buildings. The first Scripps College students arrived in the fall of 1927. Within a few years, a beautiful, Mediterranean-style campus abounding with white stucco walls, red tile roofs, and shady courtyards had developed around them. (Courtesy of the Judy Wright collection.)

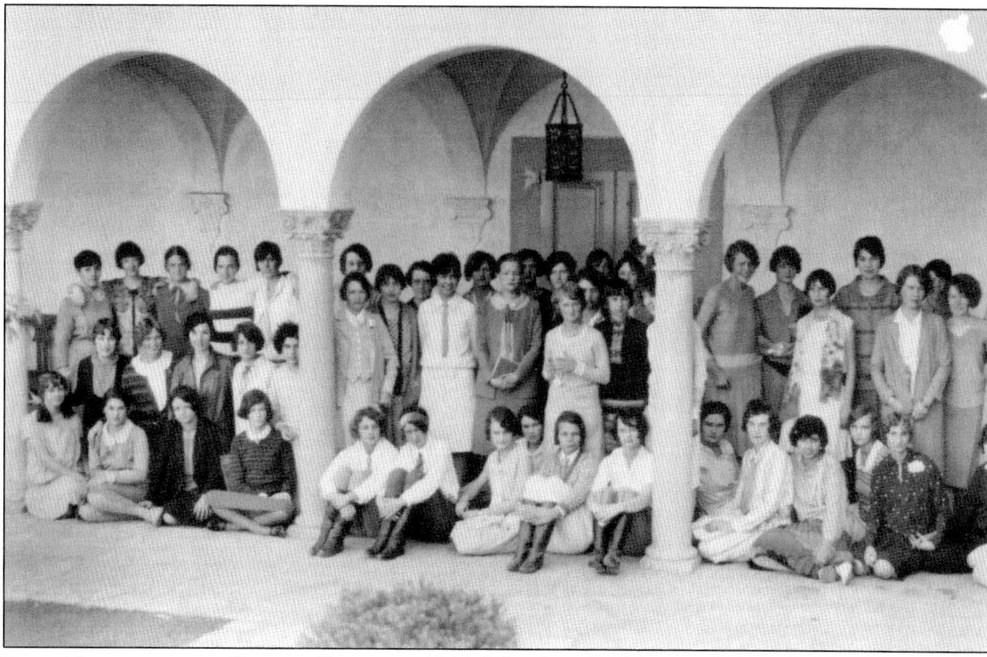

First Graduates of Scripps College, 1931. The first graduating class of Scripps College, the class of 1931, is seen here posing in the courtyard of the Toll Hall dormitory. It was this class that established the famous "Graffiti Wall" by painting on a small section of the wall between Toll and Browning Halls. Each year, graduates of Scripps carry on this tradition, leaving behind an artistic reminder of their time in college. (Courtesy of Ella Strong Denison Library, Scripps College.)

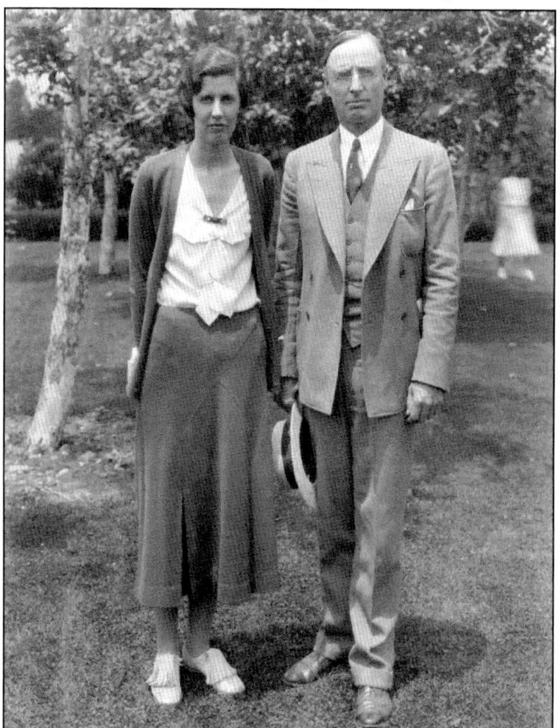

Pres. Ernest Jaqua with Student, c. 1931. After serving as Pomona College's dean of faculty for three years, Jaqua accepted the position of first president of Scripps College. He put much emphasis on attracting and retaining highly skilled faculty. Under his 16 years of leadership, Scripps developed from a tiny, three-room school into a beautiful and lively campus. (Courtesy of Ella Strong Denison Library, Scripps College.)

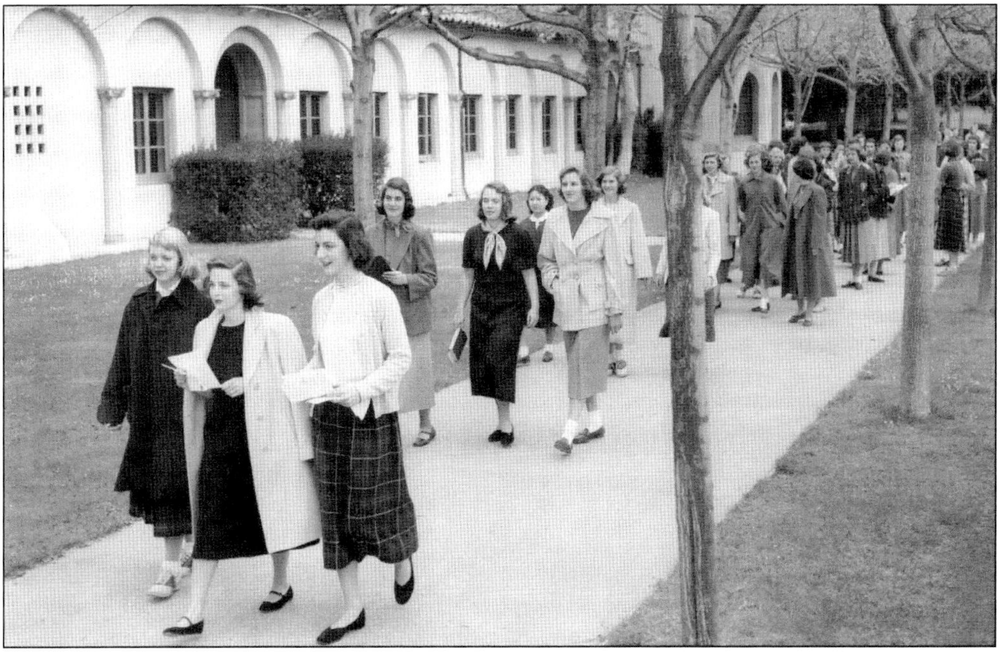

SCRIPPS STUDENTS ON CAMPUS, C. 1959. Scripps students walk in front of Janet Jacks Balch Hall, the school's primary academic facility since its completion in 1929. The grass visible on the right side of the picture was put in thanks to efforts by Scripps students in the mid-1930s. As part of their "Grass Before We Graduate" campaign, they sacrificed their dessert for two years in order to raise sufficient funds to grass the central quadrangle. (Courtesy of Ella Strong Denison Library, Scripps College.)

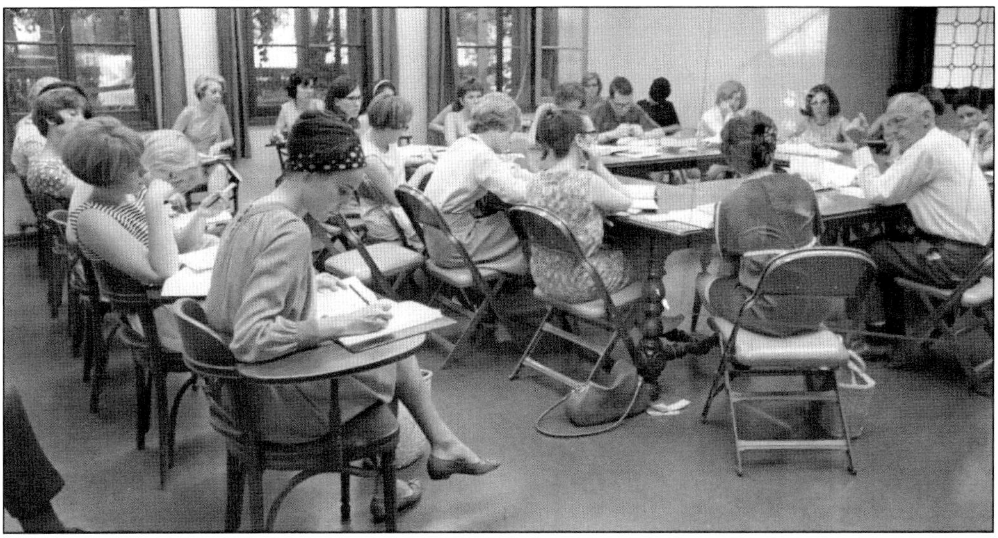

ENGLISH CLASS AT SCRIPPS, C. 1966. In this photograph, Prof. Philip Gray leads a discussion in an English class in Balch Hall. The early curriculum at Scripps was designed to primarily focus on art, psychology, literature, and the social sciences. A Scripps education also involved completion of a two-year class, "The Humanities: History of Occidental Culture," designed to give students a broad yet in-depth perspective on Western culture. (Courtesy of Ella Strong Denison Library, Scripps College.)

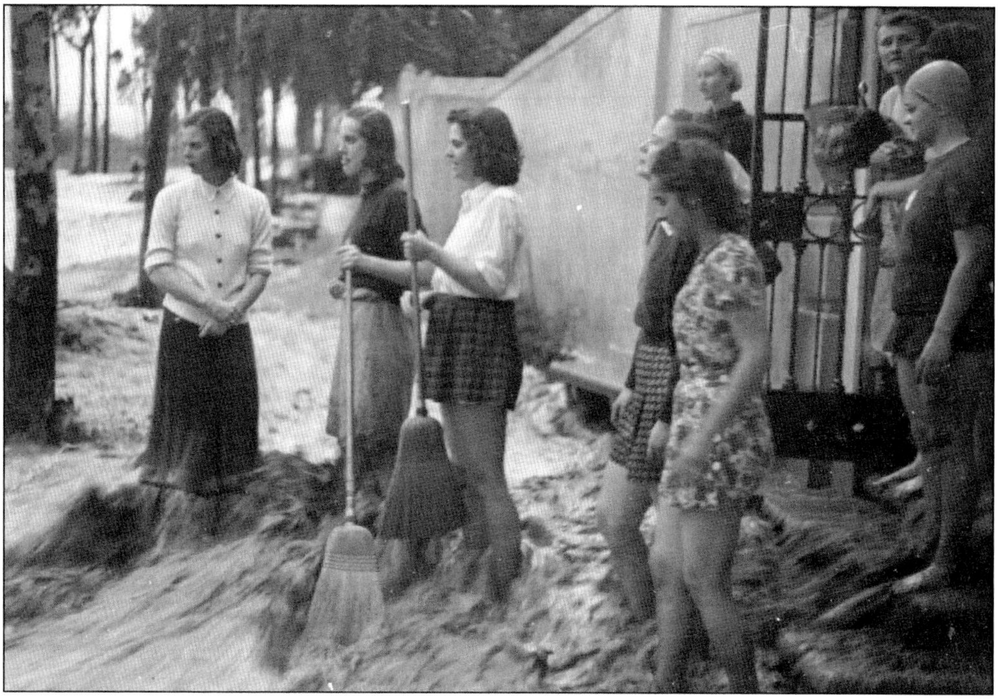

FLOOD WASHES THROUGH CLAREMONT, MARCH 1938. The heaviest prolonged rainstorm in Southern California's history swept through Claremont in March 1938. Water pouring into the valley destroyed the dams and levees in its path, resulting in an estimated $350,000 in damage to the local area. Unfortunately, the college campuses were some of the heaviest-hit areas. Here, Scripps students watch the water rush down the street. (Courtesy of Ella Strong Denison Library, Scripps College.)

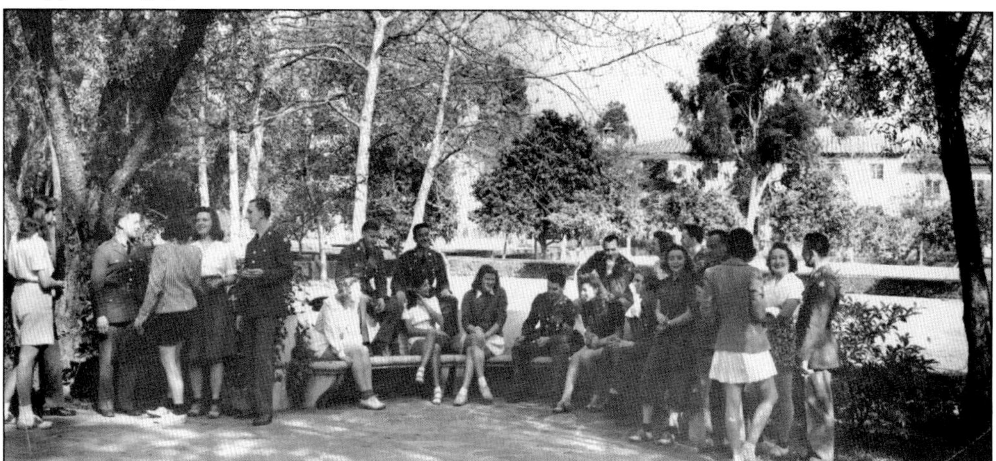

WORLD WAR II AFFECTS THE COLLEGES, 1942. War brought about immense change to college life. In 1940, all Claremont males ages 21 to 35 were required to register for the Selective Service; by the fall of 1943, there were only about 60 male civilian students left on campus. Athletics were discontinued, and, for the first time, a woman was elected president of the associated students. Here, female students socialize with some of the Army men on campus. (Courtesy of Ella Strong Denison Library, Scripps College.)

George Sumner Charles Benson. In the fall of 1946, after nearly two decades of fundraising and organizing, Claremont Men's College (CMC) opened its doors under the leadership of Pres. George Sumner Charles Benson. The college, seen by many as a stabilizing force for the fledgling consortium, attracted many veterans returning home under the GI Bill. A former Army lieutenant colonel himself, Benson sought to train his students to be leaders in business and government. (Courtesy of the Judy Wright collection.)

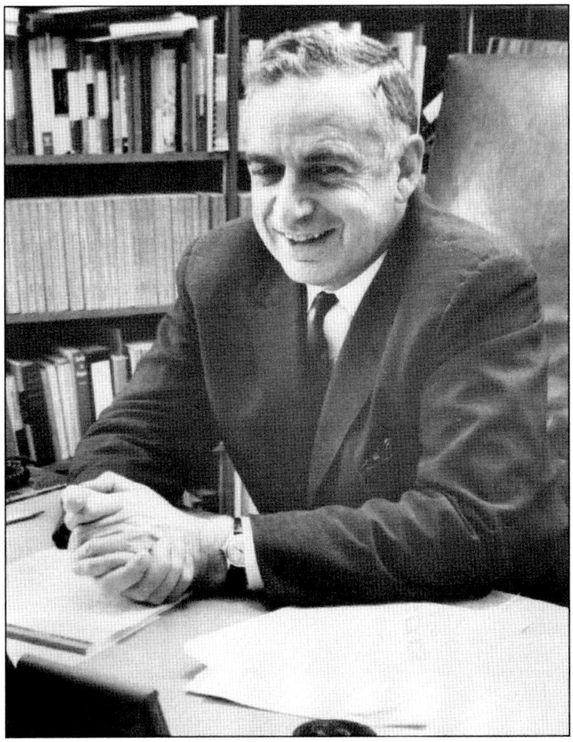

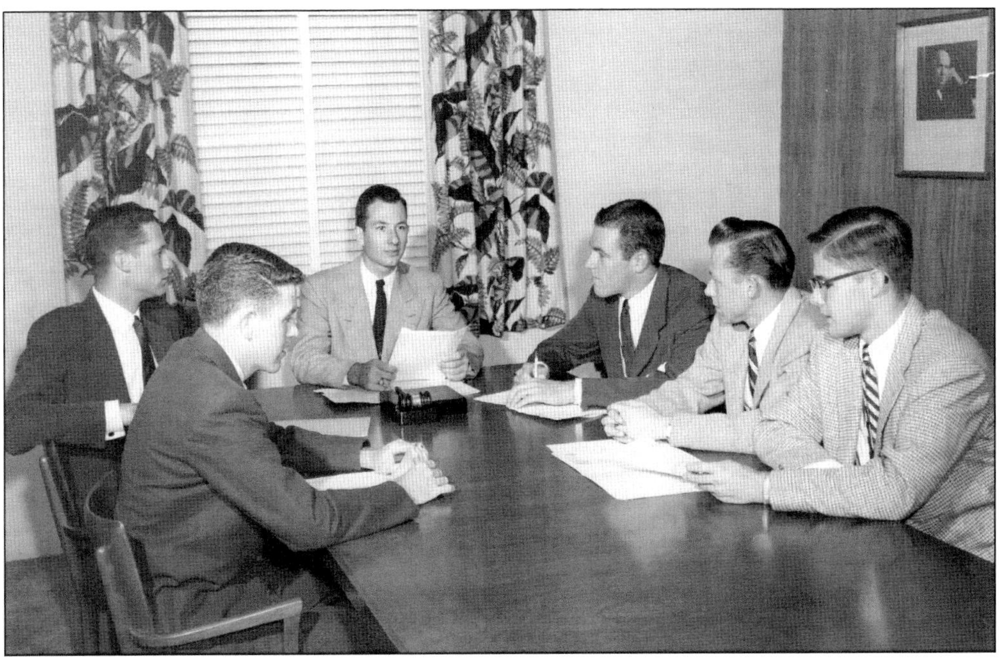

Student Court at CMC, c. 1957. Members of the CMC student government hold court, gaining valuable experience for their lives after college. Since its beginning, CMC aimed to train its students to "help carry on our American free-enterprise way of life," focusing particularly on economics, political science, and administrative theory and practice while still providing a liberal arts education. (Courtesy of Special Collections, Honnold/Mudd Library of the Claremont Colleges.)

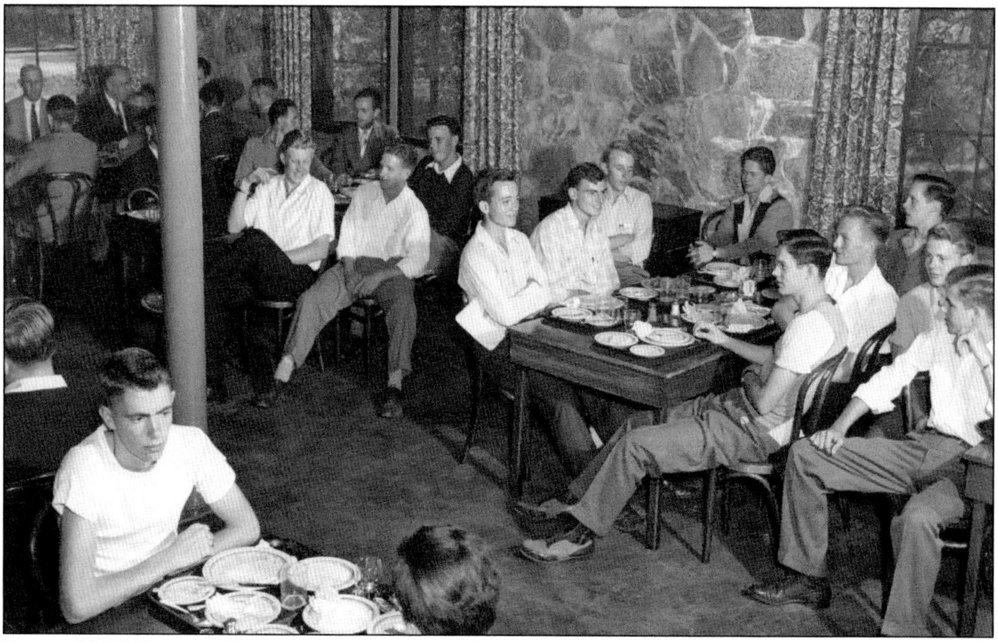

EARLY CMC CAMPUS BUILDINGS, C. 1947. Before CMC had the time to construct a true campus, its first students arrived. The college administrators resorted to using whatever buildings they could to house the 101 men, 15 of whom were already married. The grand former home of Claremont resident Sarah Bixby Smith, also called the Story House, was originally the only permanent CMC building. Above, the first students are seen relaxing in the dining room of the house. Below, former army barracks used during the war were brought in to serve as dorms. Located on the northwest corner of Sixth Street and Mills Avenue, these dorms seemed to symbolize CMC's connection to World War II and no doubt brought back memories for student veterans. (Both, courtesy of Special Collections, Honnold/Mudd Library of the Claremont Colleges; photograph by Robert C. Frampton.)

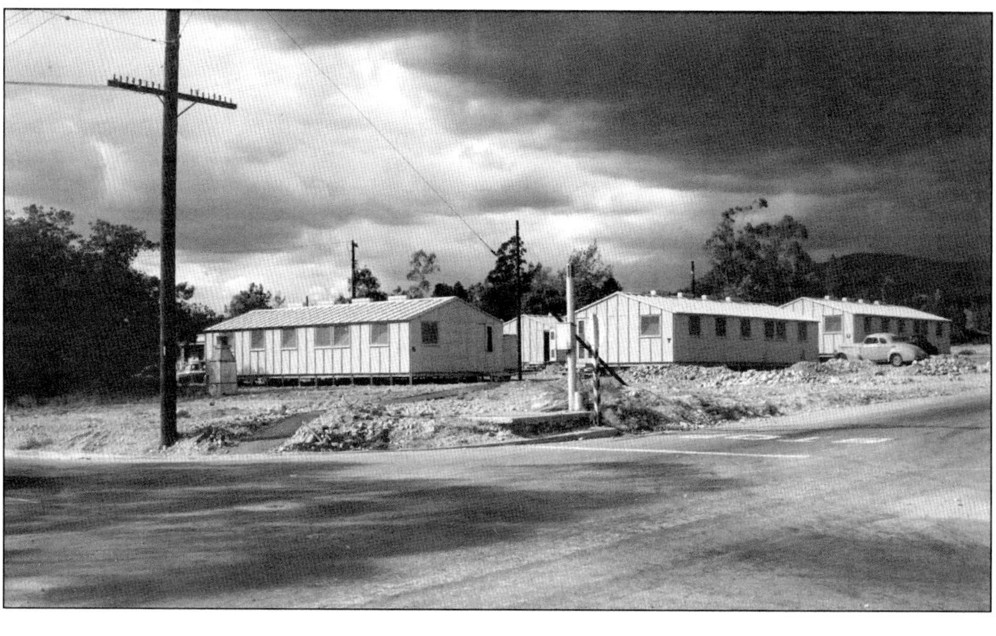

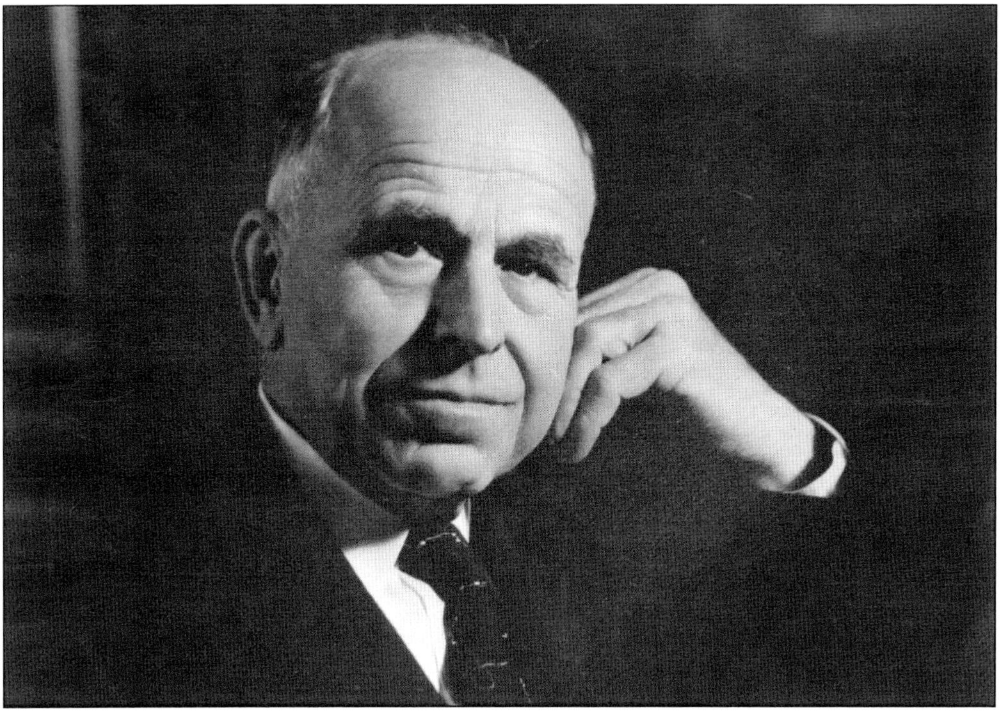

RUSSELL K. PITZER'S CONTRIBUTIONS. A wealthy citrus grower, attorney, and banker, Russell Pitzer, the son of Lee Pitzer, was a major benefactor to the Claremont Colleges. Initially, he offered $500,000 to CMC with the stipulation that the school call itself Pitzer College. The board refused; nonetheless, Pitzer still gave $25,000, which was instrumental in paying for the construction of CMC's first on-campus academic building, Pitzer Hall (below). Unfortunately, the construction of the hall required the razing of a good number of occupied homes, leaving CMC scrambling for funds. To save money, acoustical ceiling tiles were eliminated from the plans—a decision that turned out to be a mistake, as the classrooms became veritable echo chambers until tiles were later installed. Pitzer's quest for a college named in his honor would finally end in 1963 with the founding of the sixth consortium member, Pitzer College. (Above, courtesy of Pitzer College; below, courtesy of Special Collections, Honnold/Mudd Library of the Claremont Colleges.)

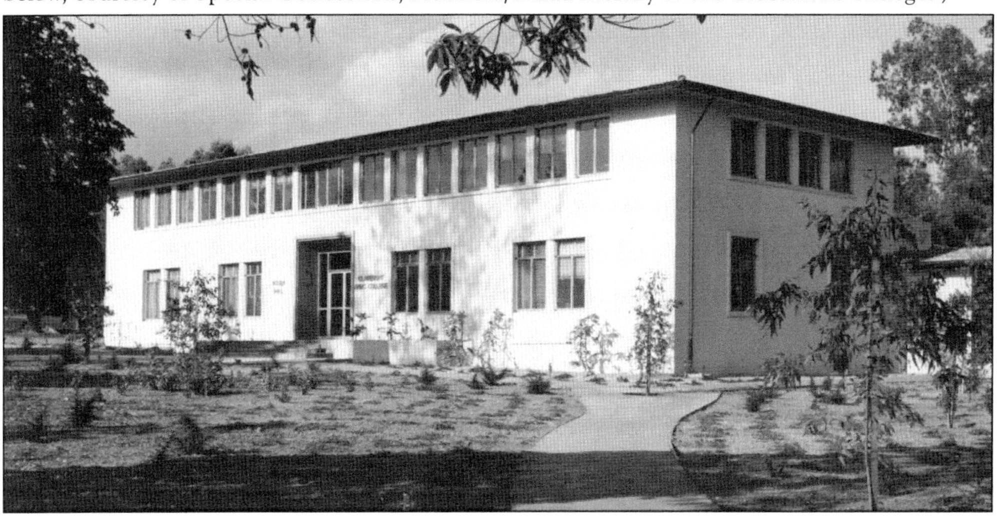

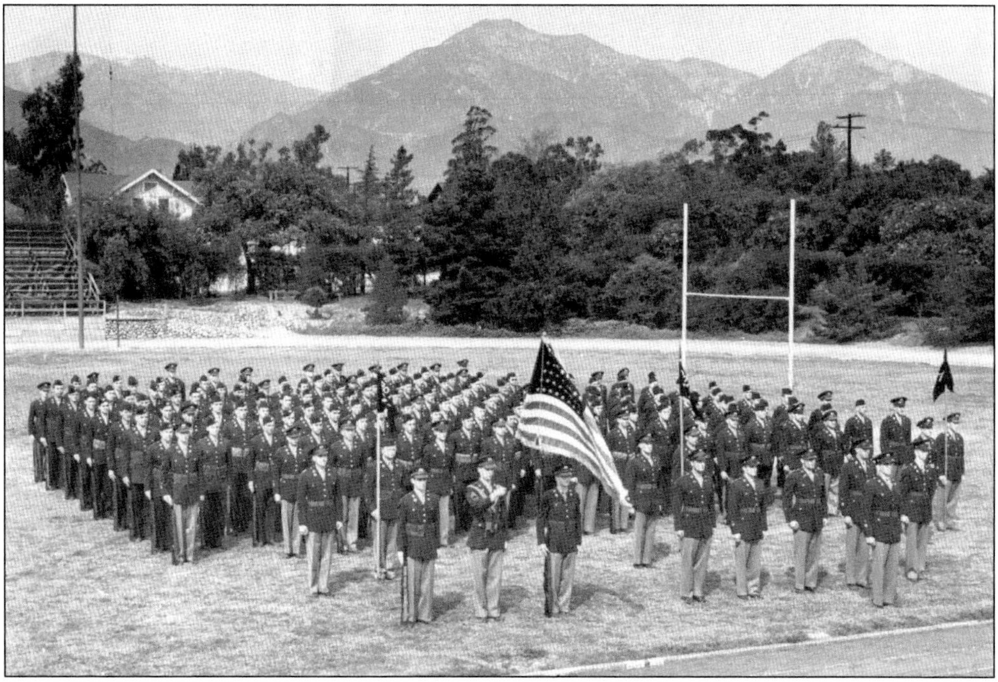

ROTC Drills at CMC, 1950. Here, a Reserve Officers Training Corps (ROTC) unit trains on campus under the leadership of Col. Theodore Bogart. In 1948, a joint Pomona–CMC Unit was established. Despite much anti-ROTC agitation on college campuses in the late 1960s, CMC would firmly maintain its program under the leadership of ardent ROTC supporter George Benson. (Courtesy of Special Collections, Honnold/Mudd Library of the Claremont Colleges.)

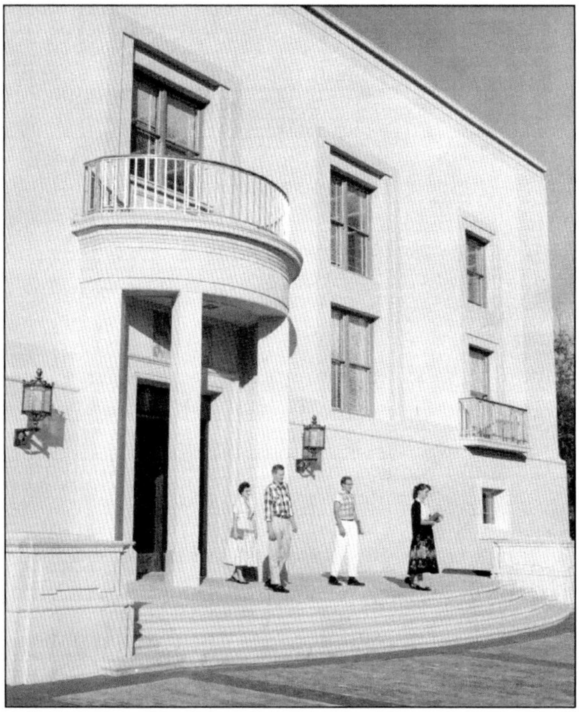

Honnold Library, c. 1952. By 1946, the Claremont Colleges Consortium had three separate libraries, which made research more complicated for students and faculty. Honnold Library, built with a donation from wealthy philanthropists Mr. and Mrs. Willliam Lincoln Honnold, provided a central solution to the problem. The library was designed by architect Gordon Kaufmann, who also designed much of the Scripps campus, and opened in 1952, with 297,000 volumes available to any consortium student.

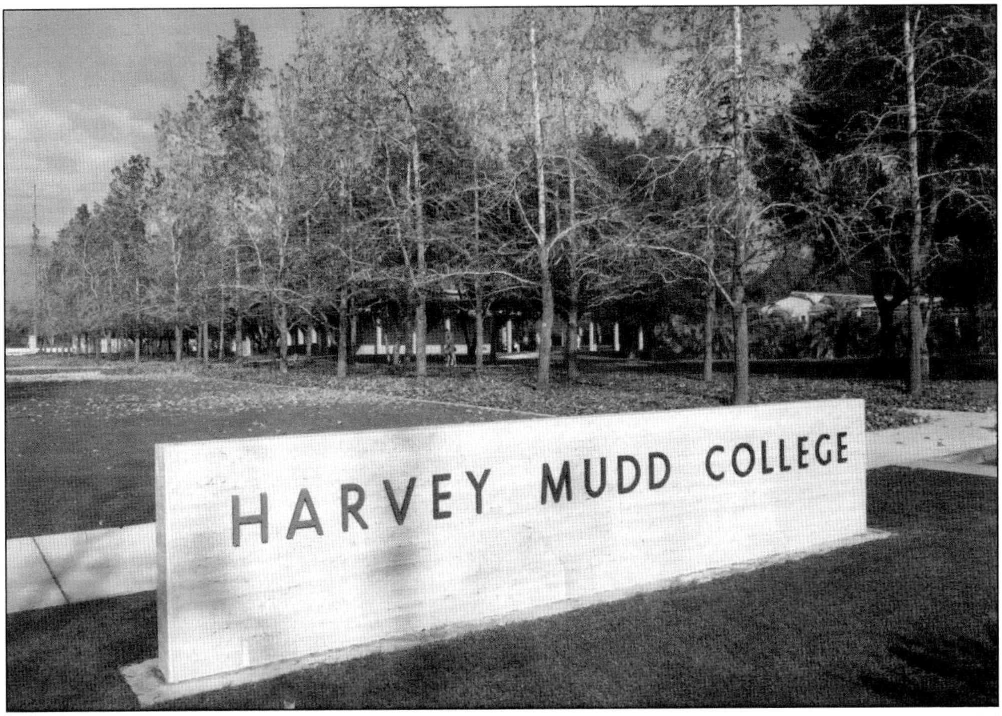

Harvey Mudd College. In the midst of the Cold War–inspired technology boom, Harvey Mudd College opened as the consortium's fourth undergraduate institution, aiming to offer rigorous and scientific technological training alongside a good liberal arts background. Funding for the new school came from Harvey Seeley Mudd, a successful businessman and mining engineer who served as chairman of the board of fellows of the Claremont College (now Claremont Graduate University). Shortly before his death in 1955, Mudd began helping with the planning of the new science-focused college. Two years later, in the fall of 1957, Harvey Mudd College welcomed its first 48 students. The original campus buildings, shown above and below, were designed in a textile block construction style by Edward Durrell Stone. (Both, courtesy of the Judy Wright collection.)

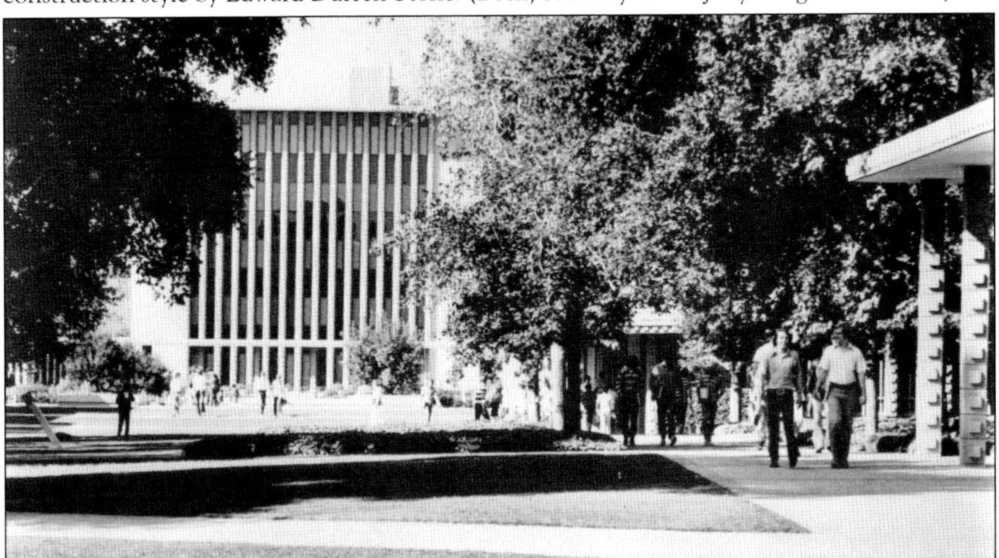

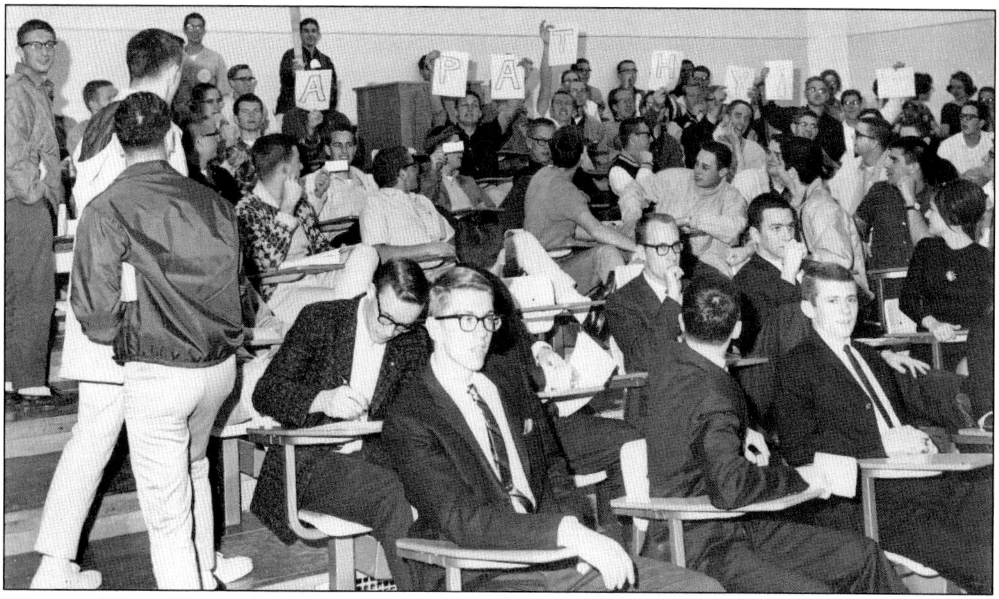

HARVEY MUDD PRANKSTERS, C. 1964. Aside from its academic rigor, Harvey Mudd quickly became known for the pranks its students pulled. Here, students spell out "Apathy" during a lecture; whether it is in reference to the class or world events is unclear. Other pranks were less tame, ranging from "pond dunking" (throwing students and faculty into fountains), to shaving freshmen's heads and flushing them in the toilet, to throwing parties on the roofs. (Courtesy of Special Collections, Honnold/Mudd Library of the Claremont Colleges.)

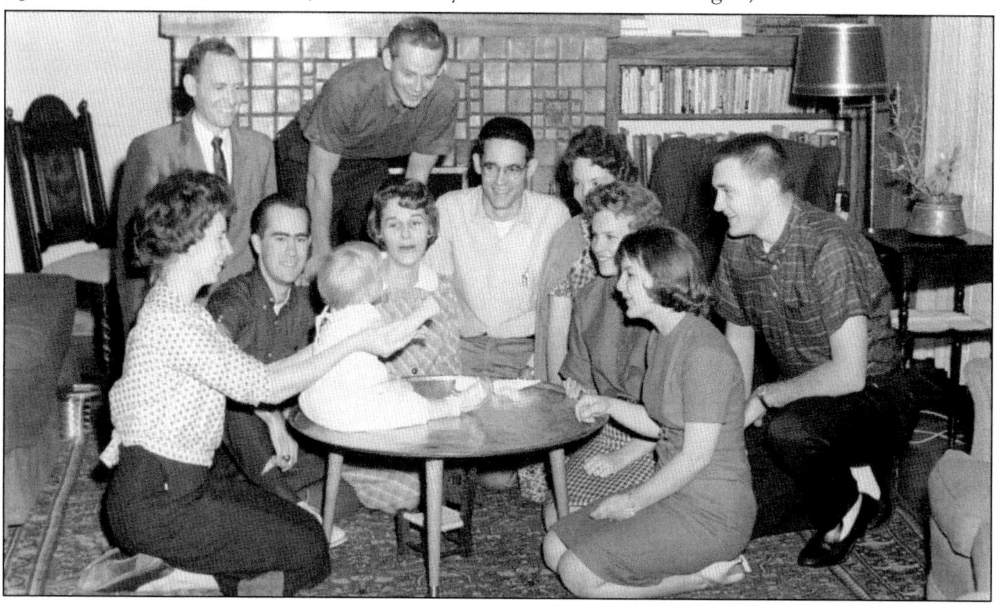

MARRIED COUPLES CLUB AT HARVEY MUDD, 1961. Harvey Mudd College's Married Couples Club, which functioned in the 1960s, was indicative of the times. With the baby boom in full swing, many young men looked to the booming aerospace engineering industry as a means of supporting their families. Harvey Mudd, which specialized in mathematics and the sciences, attracted a good number of married students interested in joining the lucrative field. (Courtesy of Special Collections, Honnold/Mudd Library of the Claremont Colleges.)

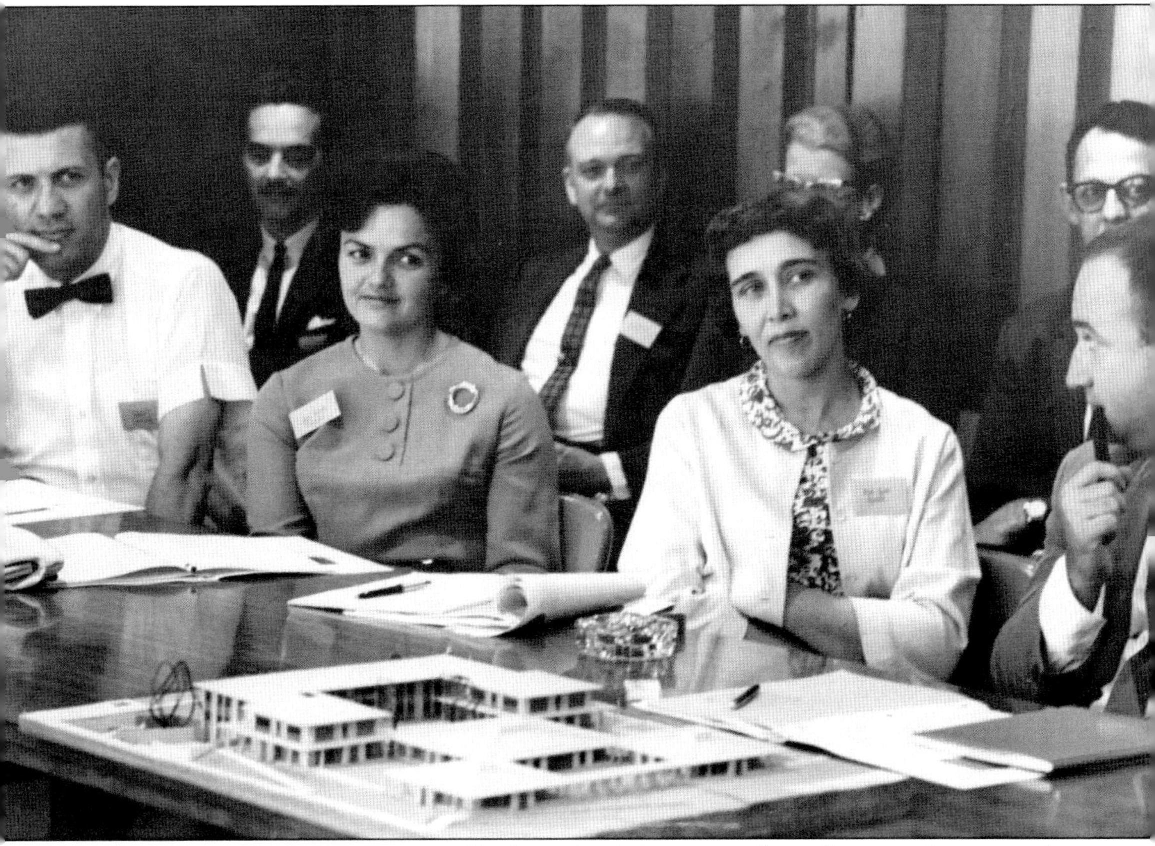

Pitzer College Faculty, June 1964. By the early 1960s, increased enrollment at Pomona and CMC resulted in a disproportionate amount of men at the Claremont Colleges. In response to this, Pitzer College, named in honor of major benefactor Russell K. Pitzer, opened in the fall of 1964 as the consortium's second women's college. The school's mascot, an orange tree, was also chosen in honor of Pitzer, whose family made its money in the booming Southern Californian citrus industry. Pitzer College put special emphasis on the social and behavior sciences, offering degrees in anthropology, psychology, and sociology, in addition to economics and political science majors offered through CMC. Here, some of the early faculty members hold a meeting shortly before the first students arrived that fall. An architectural model of the future campus is shown on the table. (Courtesy of Special Collections, Honnold/Mudd Library of the Claremont Colleges.)

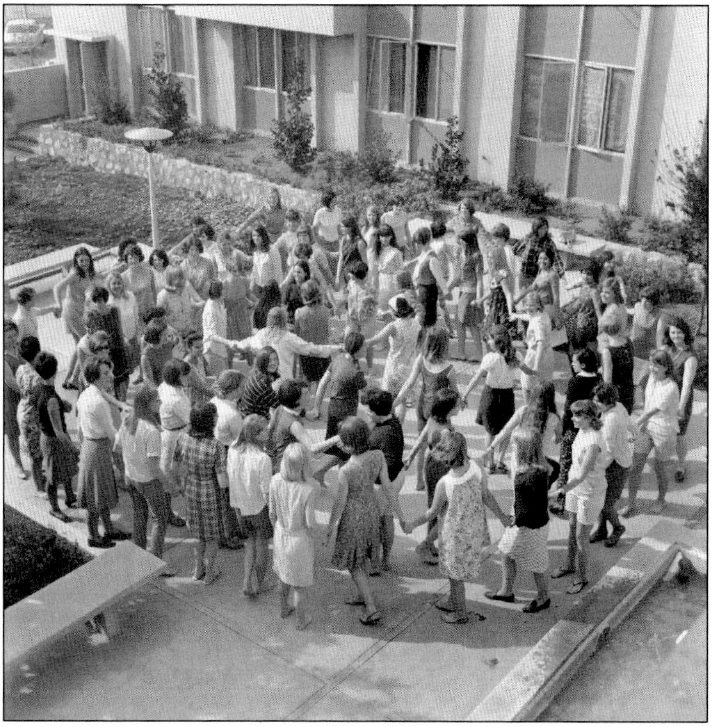

Pitzer's First Students, c. 1964. In Pitzer's first year, 153 women enrolled as undergraduates; that spring, three of them would graduate. This photograph shows some of the school's first students gathered for a celebration in the courtyard of Sanborn Hall, the first dormitory. Six years after its founding, Pitzer would become coeducational, accepting 80 men in the fall of 1980. (Courtesy of Special Collections, Honnold/Mudd Library of the Claremont Colleges.)

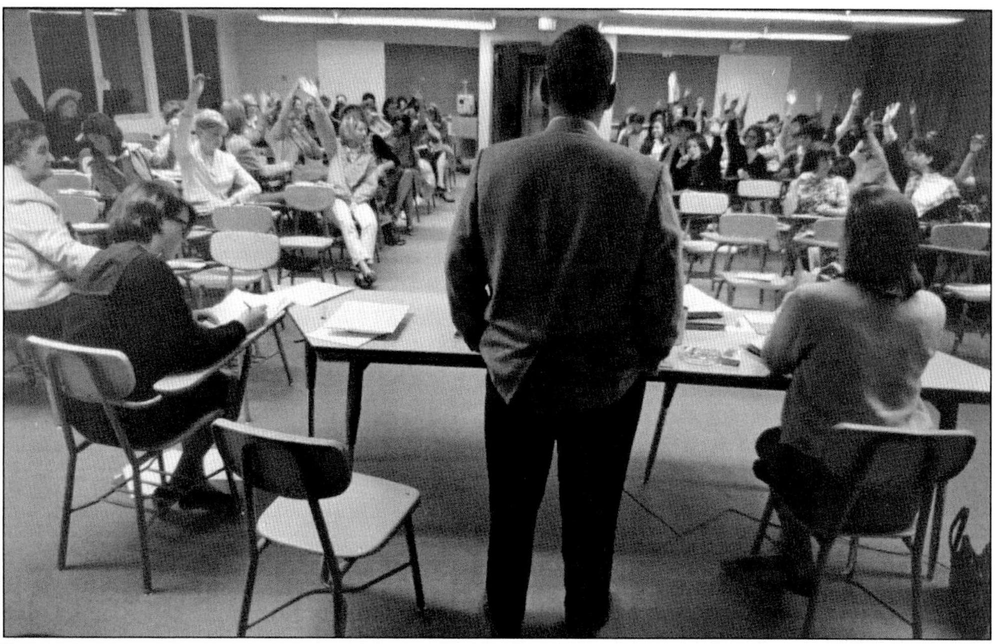

Pitzer's First Town Hall Meeting, c. 1964. Students would come to have a larger role at Pitzer than at many other schools. The original faculty decided to wait until the students arrived on campus before discussing in detail the nature of the college. In the fall, a series of town hall meetings were run in order to solicit input from the students regarding the college's future direction. Shown standing is moderator and professor of classics Steve Glass. (Courtesy of Special Collections, Honnold/Mudd Library of the Claremont Colleges.)

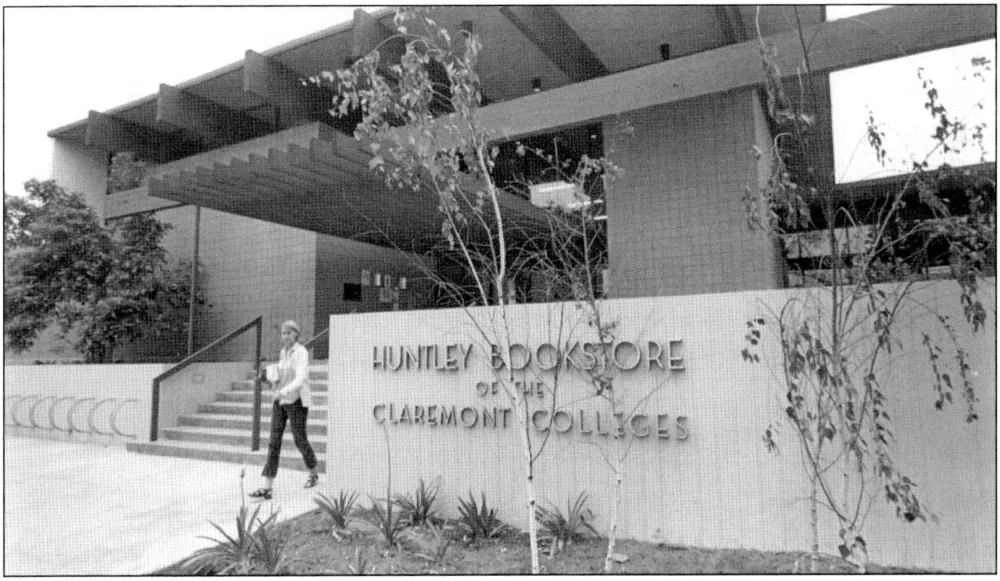

HUNTLEY BOOKSTORE, 1969. There was much celebration in November 1969 when the A. Quincy Jones–designed Huntley Bookstore opened its doors. For years, the colleges had been in need of a bookstore, but funding such a group enterprise had proved difficult. Fortunately, with a generous donation from the Earl W. Huntley Foundation, the Claremont University Center, as the consortium was then called, was able to build its bookstore, which served all six consortium schools. (Courtesy of Special Collections, Honnold/Mudd Library of the Claremont Colleges.)

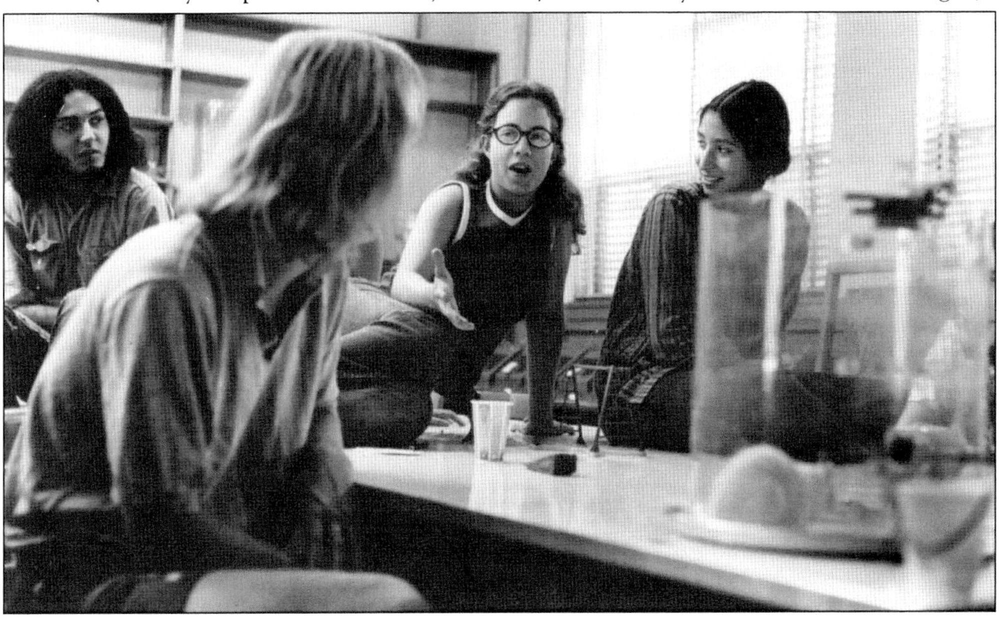

W.M. KECK SCIENCE FOUNDATION, 1972. In 1964, at the height of the Cold War technology boom, three of the Claremont Colleges came together to form a joint science program larger than any one of the colleges could individually provide. The W.M. Keck Science Department, as it is now called, clearly highlighted the advantages of a consortium, serving students from Scripps, Claremont McKenna, and Pitzer College. (Courtesy of Special Collections, Honnold/Mudd Library of the Claremont Colleges.)

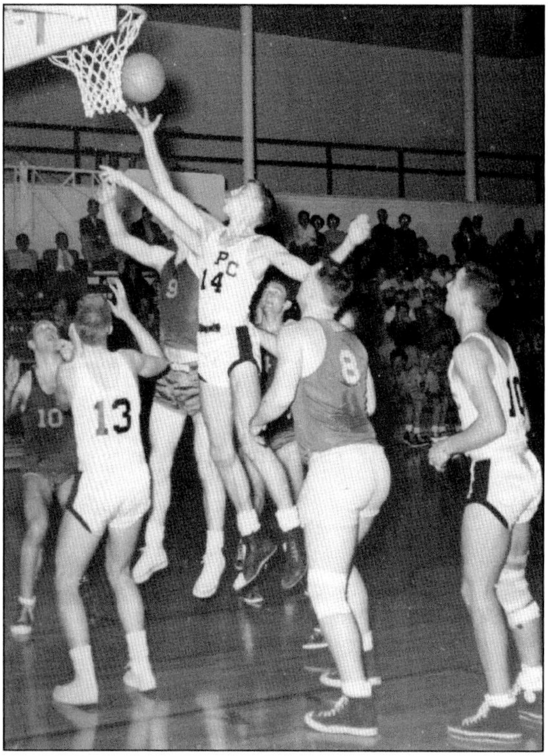

CMS Basketball, c. 1980–1985. The consortium's first multi-school athletic team, the Pomona-Claremont Sagehens, formed in 1946 with the union of Pomona and CMC. The two schools competed together successfully for 12 years until their split in 1958. CMC quickly joined with Harvey Mudd and, later, Scripps. Since 1976, the Claremont-Mudd-Scripps (CMS) Stags and Athenas have competed as one team. Here, the CMS men's basketball team plays in the gym. (Courtesy of Special Collections, Honnold/Mudd Library of the Claremont Colleges.)

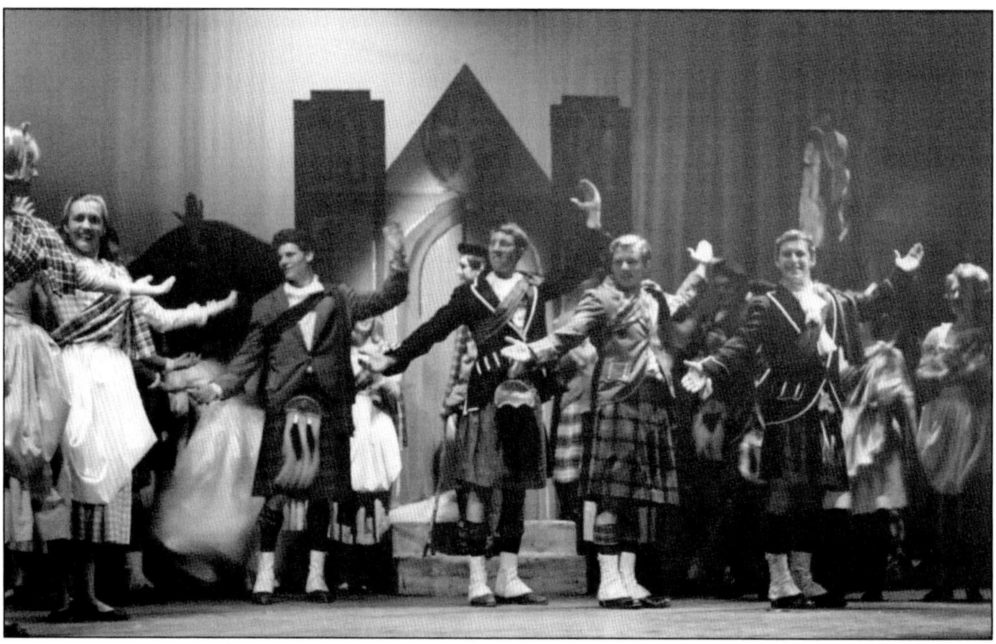

Brigadoon, 1965. The Claremont Colleges also frequently came together for recreation, and theater was especially popular. In this photograph, drama students from a number of the schools perform together in Scripps College's *Brigadoon*, a musical set in a mystical Scottish village. Recreation opportunities such as this provided students with a much broader social experience. (Courtesy of Ella Strong Denison Library, Scripps College.)

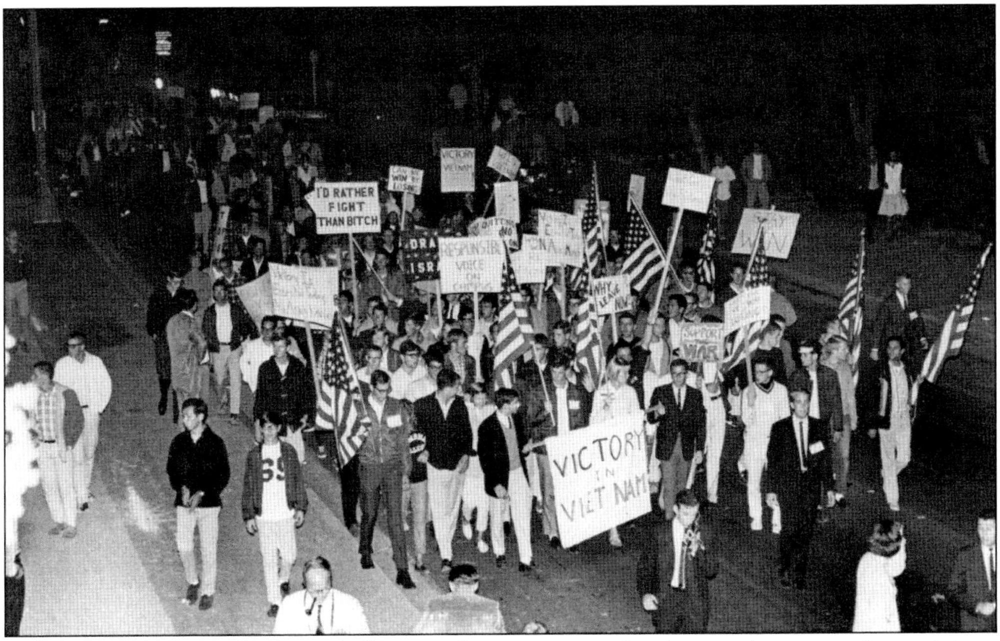

STUDENT PROTESTS. Claremont Colleges students came together frequently to voice their opinions on various issues. Though the topics changed, the regularity of protests did not. In the 1960s, demonstrations both in favor and in opposition to US involvement in Vietnam attracted students and townspeople alike. Above, a nighttime pro-involvement student march, in the 1963–1964 school year, passes by the Harvey Mudd campus. Over a decade later, a new topic concerning students was funding for the Black and Chicano Studies Center. On May 6, 1975, students staged a sit-in at the Pendleton Business Building in support of continued funding for the center's pre-freshman program, which helped minority students entering college adjust to the new environment. (Both, courtesy of Special Collections, Honnold/Mudd Library of the Claremont Colleges.)

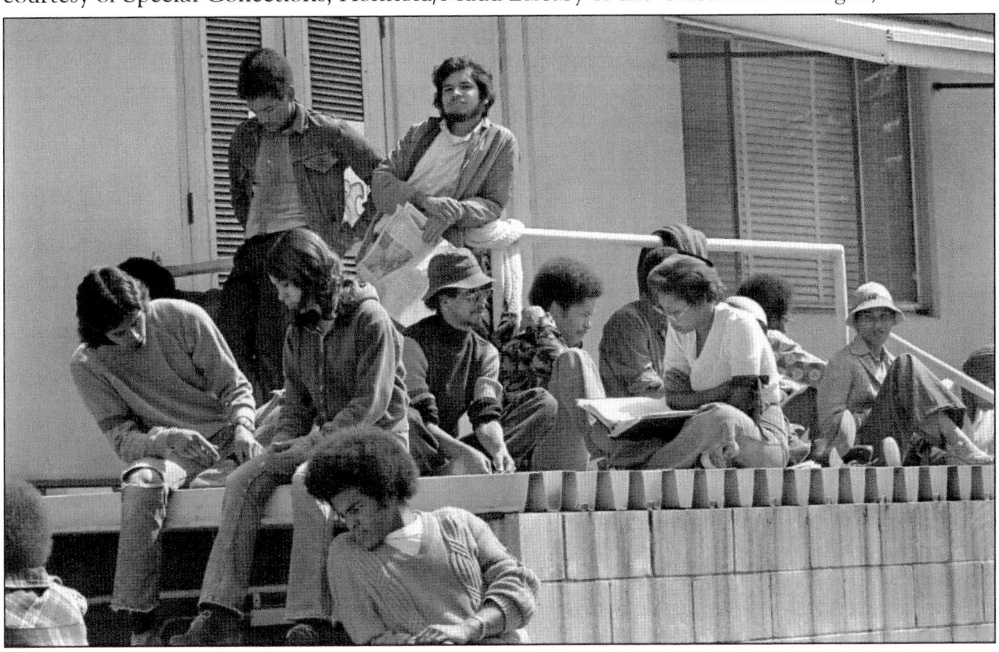

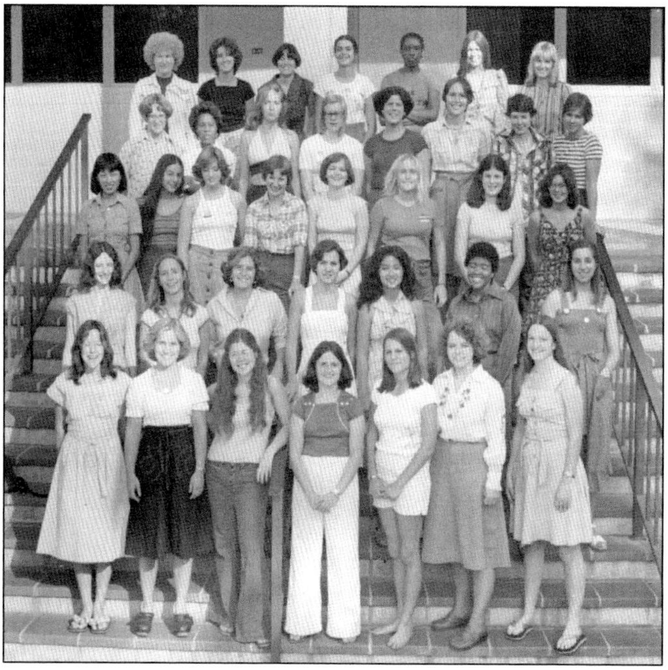

CMC BECOMES COEDUCATIONAL, SEPTEMBER 1976. Claremont Men's College first accepted women in the fall of 1976, following the national trend of many traditionally all-male schools, like Yale, Princeton, Williams, and Amherst, going coeducational. It was the last all-male college west of the Mississippi to do so. Here, 30 of the first women to enroll at CMC stand together outside a campus building. (Courtesy of Special Collections, Honnold/Mudd Library of the Claremont Colleges.)

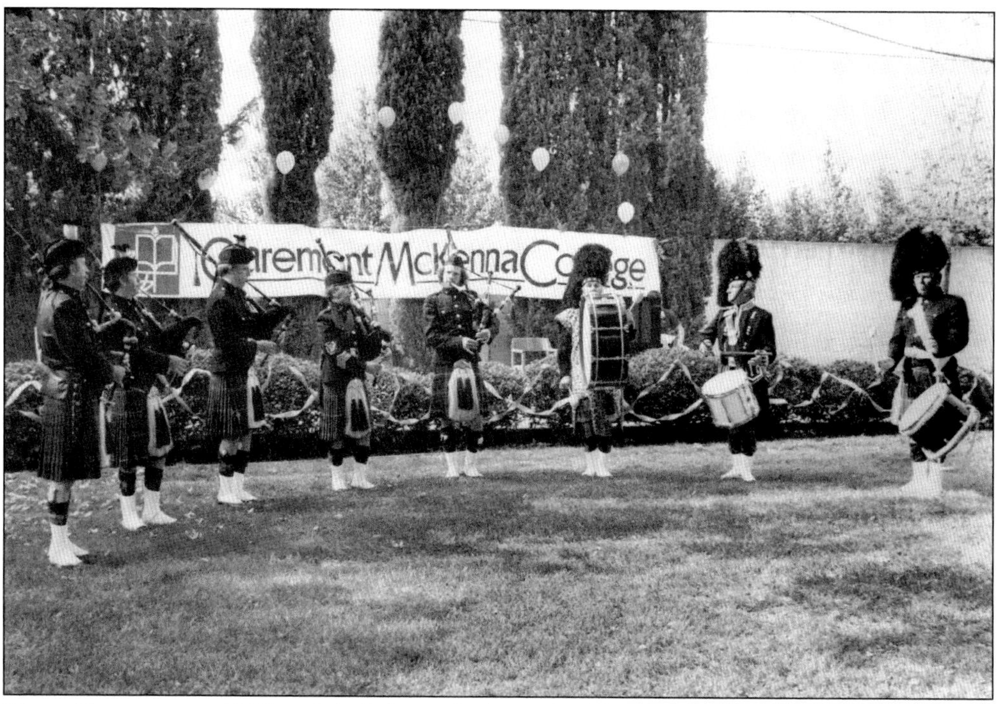

NAME CHANGE FOR CMC, 1981. A Scottish-themed celebration was held in 1981 to celebrate Claremont Men's College's official name change to Claremont McKenna College, five years after the school became coeducational. "McKenna" was selected in honor of trustee Donald C. McKenna for his immense contributions to the founding of CMC. The guest of honor at the celebration, McKenna would later wryly remark that he was "thankful that my father's surname began with an 'M.'" (Courtesy of Special Collections, Honnold/Mudd Library of the Claremont Colleges.)

Six

War and Beyond
The Boom

By the 1940s, Claremont was well accustomed to booms. It had been birthed from the railroad boom, nearly killed by the land boom, and was now in the midst of a prosperous citrus boom. However, none of these had prepared it for the massive, Cold War–inspired industrial engineering boom of the coming decades. The population of Southern California was sent skyrocketing, and, as newcomers arrived, they flocked to quiet, safe Claremont. Soon, the town was well on its way to becoming a bustling suburb.

The completion of new freeways brought in huge waves of new residents, many of whom commuted to larger cities to work. By 1970, when the boom began to subside, Claremont's population had increased nearly 800 percent in just three decades. Housing tracts were constructed practically overnight as Claremont expanded northwards. Numerous schools and parks, such as the once controversial Memorial Park, opened to meet the needs of the growing population.

In this new, suburban Claremont, the citrus industry—long one of the town's two main industries, along with the colleges—struggled to survive. The groves were increasingly vandalized as they became surrounded by housing developments, and growers soon found they made a larger profit selling their land to developers than using it to grow oranges. The packinghouses along the Santa Fe Railroad tracks began to close, and, by the 1970s, the industry was on its last legs.

Aside from the declining citrus industry, however, Claremont's transformation was a remarkably smooth one, due in part to the clever foresight of its residents. Just prior to the boom, in 1944, the Claremont Chamber of Commerce had established the Post-War Planning Committee. Comprised of about 50 to 70 residents, the committee dedicated itself to issues such as the development of parks and schools and the maintenance of city trees and streets. It also dealt with zoning, and proposed new commercial areas and housing tracts were discussed in depth before being approved. With thoughtful planning, Claremont was able to maintain its small-town appeal while still expanding into a modern suburb.

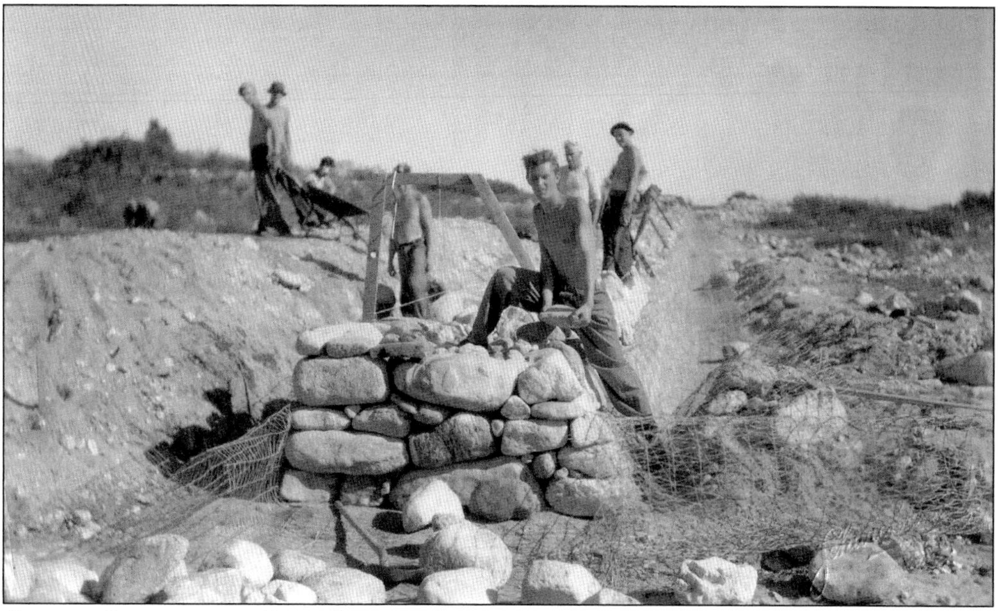

Civilian Conservation Corps Camp, c. 1934. CCC Camp F239 operated in the foothills above the Claremont, providing work to young men who labored daily to help construct dams, levees, walls, and roads at the base of the San Gabriel Mountains. Meanwhile, in town, Pomona College employees took reduced salaries, while many other residents, like millions of Americans, lost their jobs entirely. (Courtesy of the Judy Wright collection.)

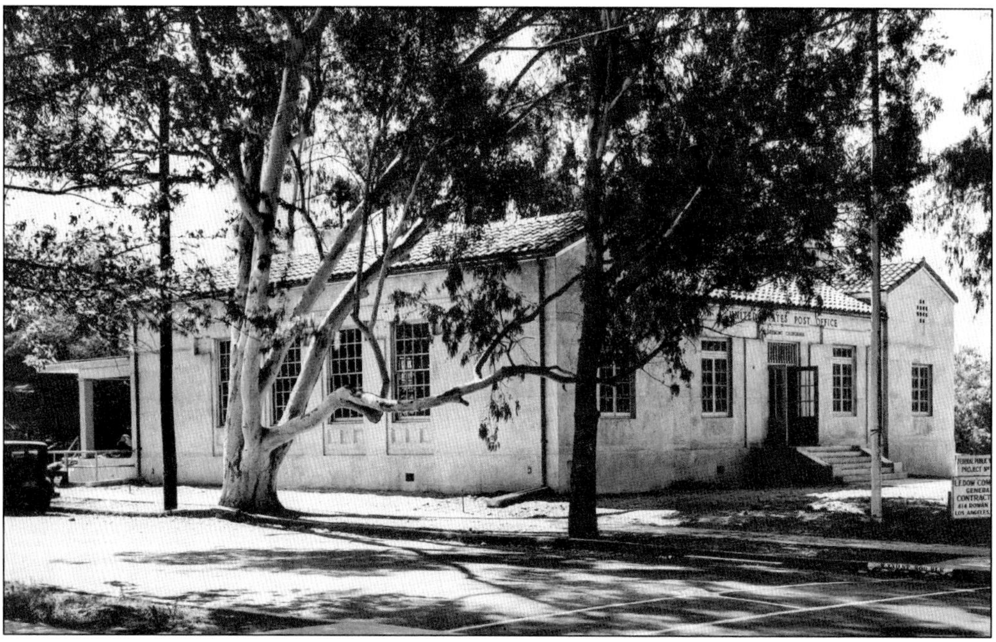

Claremont Post Office, 1936. Claremont's Spanish Colonial Revival post office was completed in 1936 as a Works Progress Administration project. Its construction provided jobs to unemployed men in the area and finally gave a stable home to the Claremont Post Office, which had originally been housed in various general stores. In 1980, local artist Milford Zornes painted the colorful mural depicting life in 1930s Claremont that now adorns the walls.

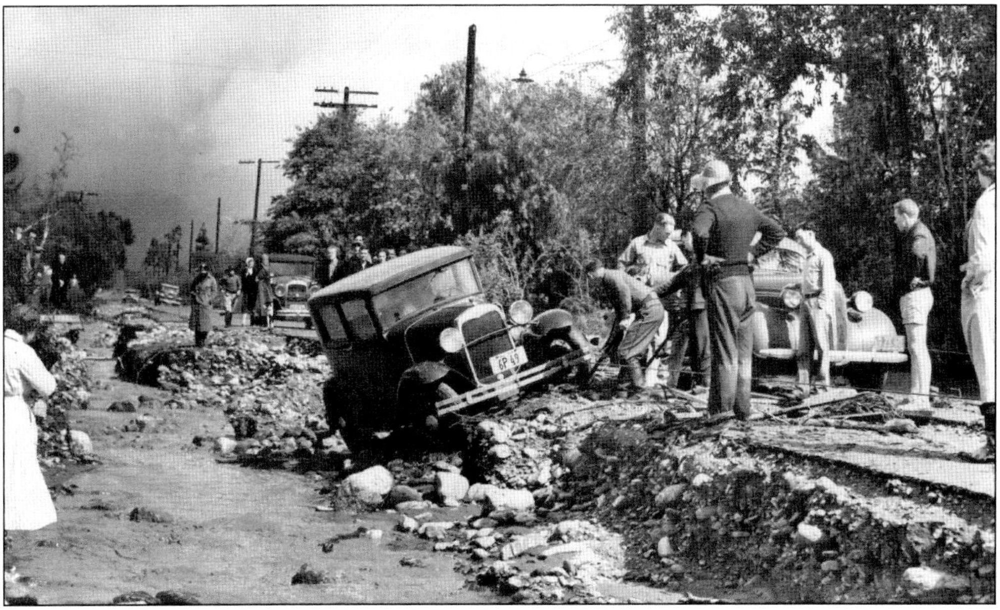

The Great 1938 Flood, March 2, 1938. The flood of 1938, which washed through Claremont on March 2 and 3, came as a result of the heaviest prolonged rainstorm in the region's recorded history. The Los Angeles Basin faced 9.18 inches of rain, and water rushing down from San Antonio Canyon crumbled the check dams and levees designed to protect the town. Many buildings were damaged, streets were entirely destroyed, and a few residents lost their lives in the terrible natural disaster. However, the disaster also highlighted the community spirit found in Claremont: 400 residents volunteered for days to create sandbag barriers and clear debris, while others helped organize the clothing and food donations that poured into the chamber of commerce for victims of the flood. (Both, courtesy of the Judy Wright collection.)

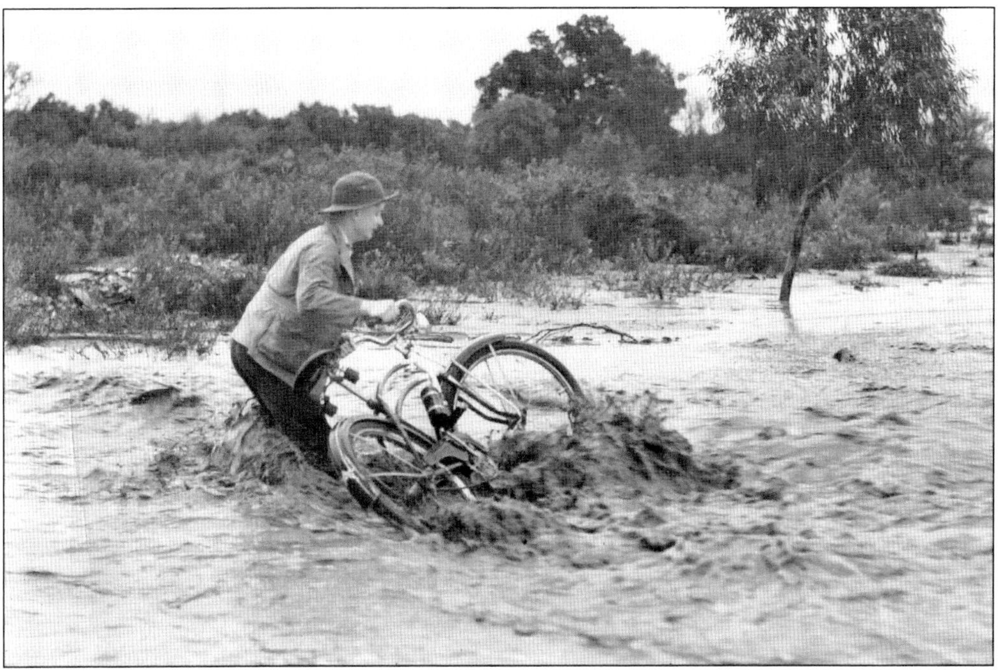

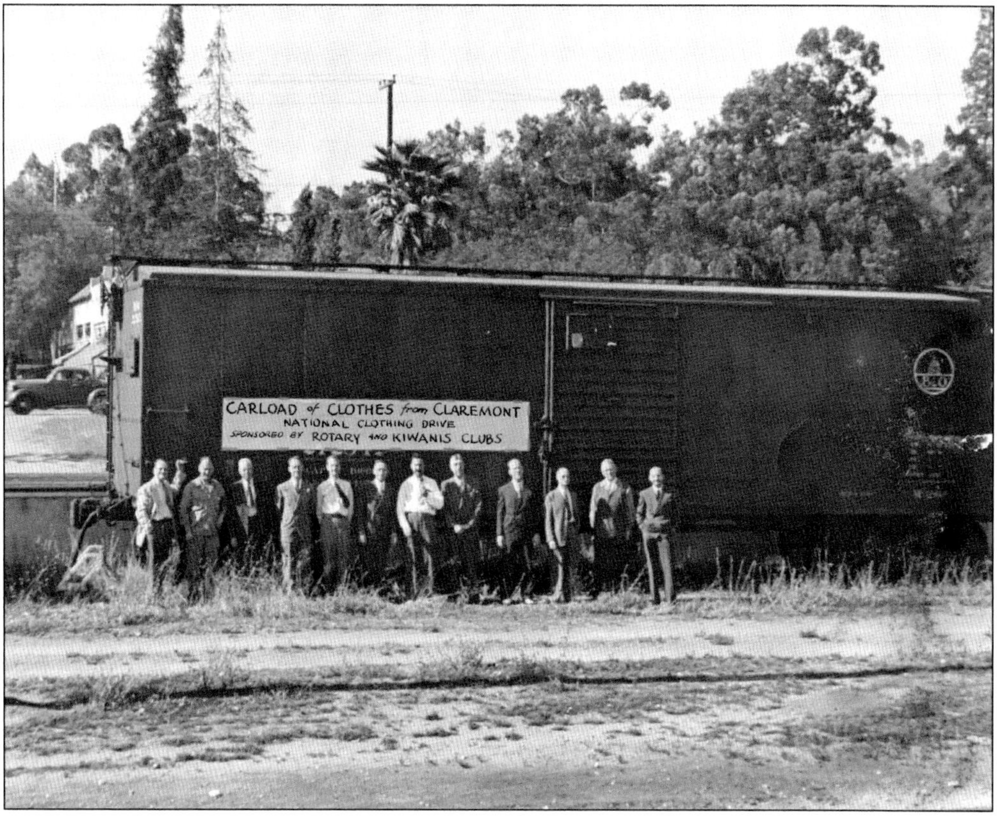

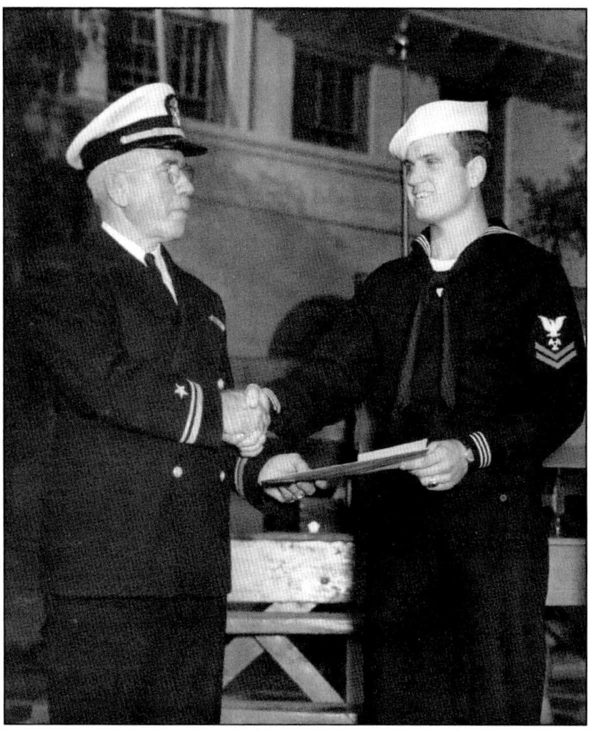

World War II and Claremont. When the United States entered World War II in 1941, Claremont, like cities all across the nation, focused its attention on contributing to the war effort. Many, like Kenneth H. Chidlaw (left, in October 1942), joined the armed forces. Chidlaw had graduated from Claremont High School less than two years earlier. Meanwhile, those left on the home front did their part by buying war bonds, planting Victory Gardens, and collecting over five tons of clothing for the United National Clothing collection. The clothing drive seen above was organized by the local Kiwanis and Rotary Clubs, which worked together to fill a freight car with clothing for European war victims. (Above, courtesy of the Judy Wright collection; photograph by Robert C. Frampton.)

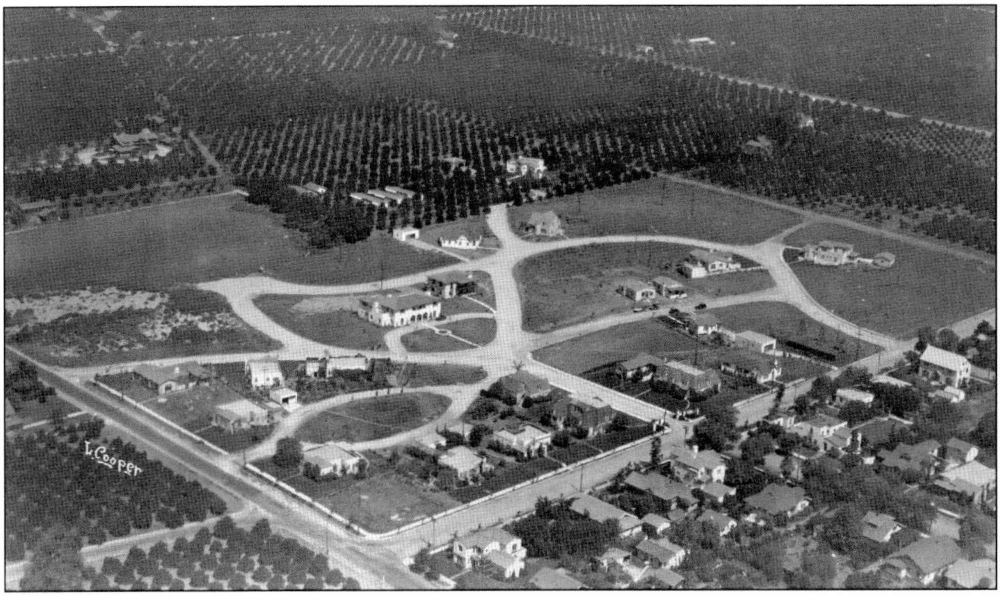

PILGRIM PLACE. In 1914, James Blaisdell founded the Claremont Missionary Home, later known as Pilgrim Place, to bring "some vivid association with the cosmopolitan world" to the tiny Claremont. It was intended to be a home for the children of missionaries and a temporary hostel for missionaries on furlough. In 1924, Pilgrim Place moved to its present location off Berkeley Avenue between Harrison Avenue and Eighth Street, which was originally swampland. The aerial photograph above shows it in 1930. Soon, it became internationally known as a place for missionary furloughs and a residential community for retired Christian workers, attracting people from all over the world. Pilgrim Place has grown to become a community of 150 homes, with winding lanes and landscaped gardens. It still continues to host its Pilgrim Place Festival around Thanksgiving each year, a tradition that began in 1948.

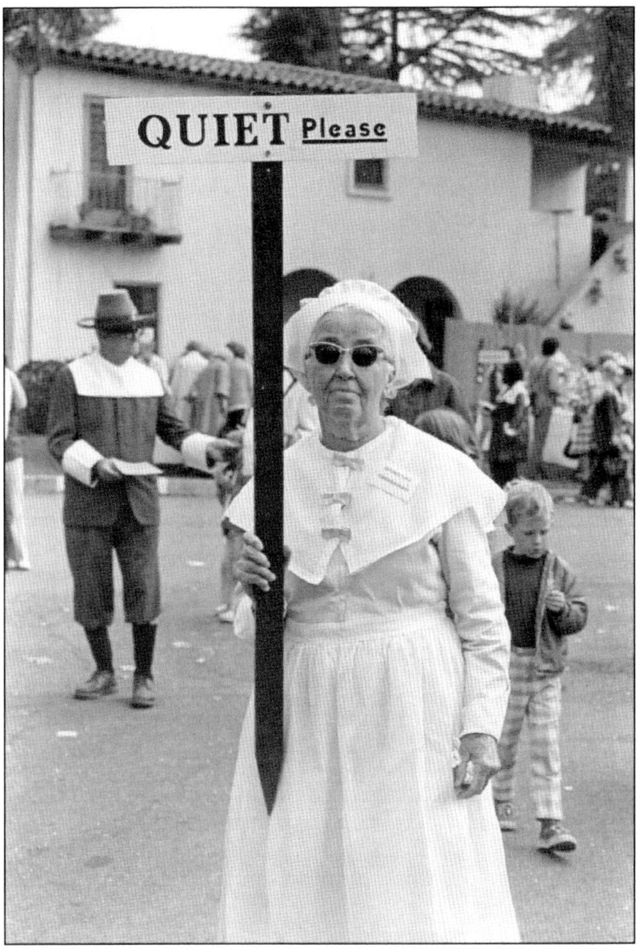

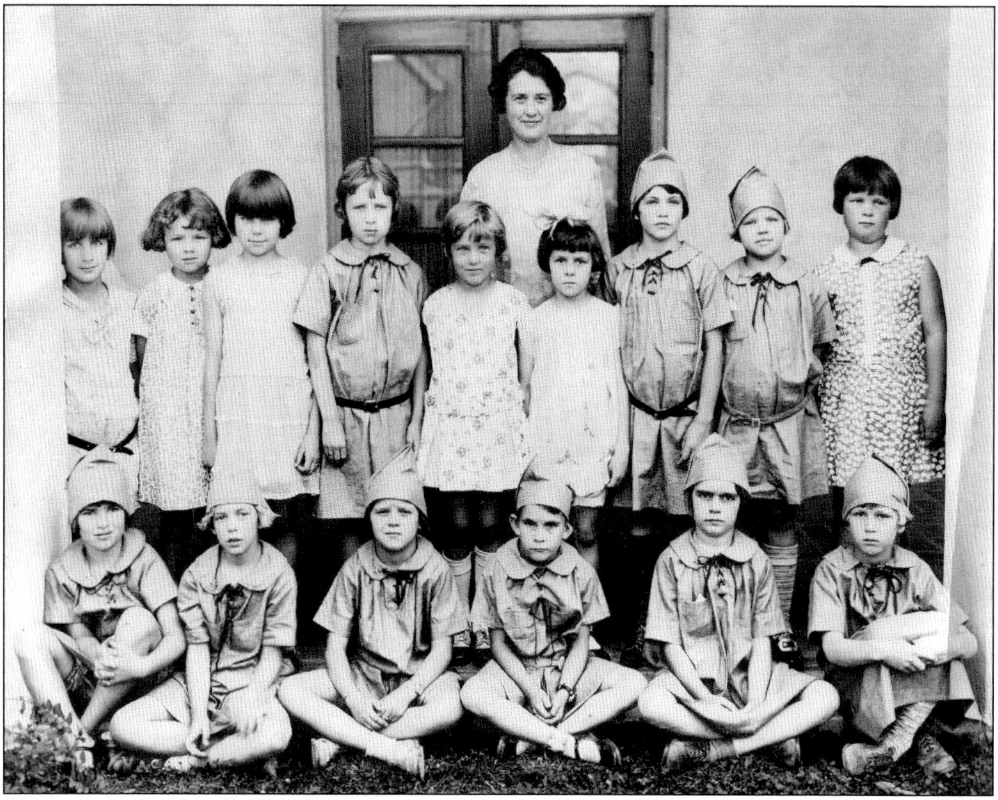

CLAREMONT BROWNIE TROOP, C. 1930. Pictured here are the girls of Claremont's first Brownie troop in the 1930s, in front of the Claremont United Church of Christ. Blanche Pitzer, the wife of successful citrus grower Lee Pitzer, was one of the early troop leaders. The Pitzers would soon purchase land in the foothills and build a Girl Scout cabin, La Casita, for future generations of Scouts to enjoy.

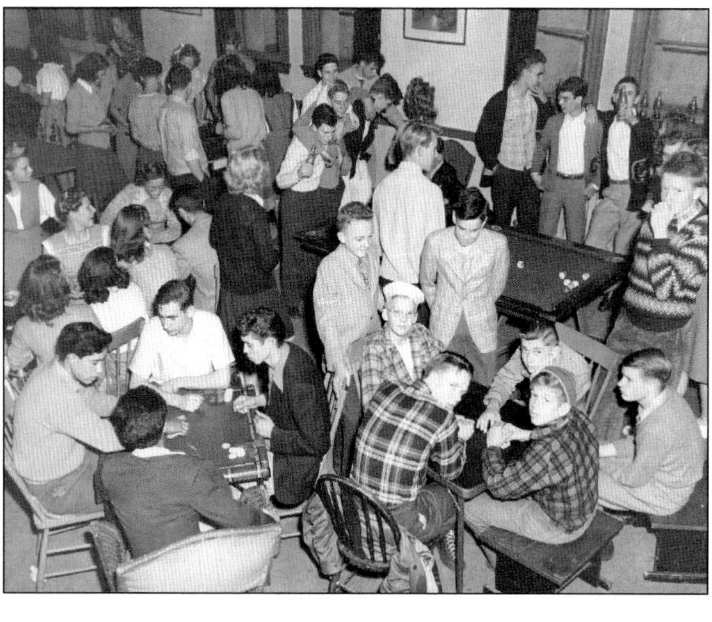

CLAREMONT YOUTH CENTER, DECEMBER 7, 1945. Claremont's teenagers finally had a place to gather when the youth center reopened in 1945. Students from the high school would gather here to play pool, poker, and card games or simply to socialize. The boy in the far right corner wears an original Claremont High School varsity letter sweater, a precursor to today's leather varsity letter jackets. (Photograph by Robert C. Frampton.)

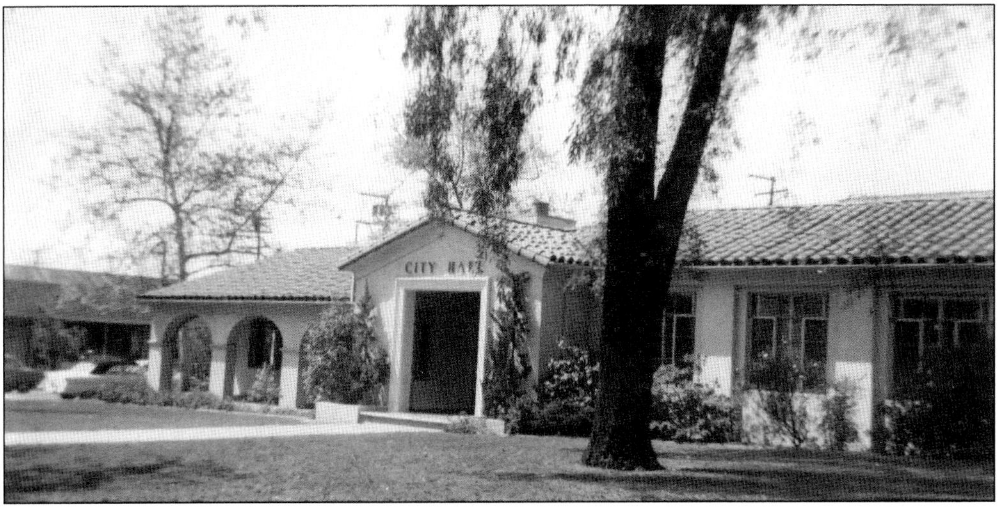

CLAREMONT CITY HALL, 1957. Now one of Claremont village's landmarks, city hall was once split into three separate buildings. The first building, now the western portion of city hall, was constructed in 1925 as a dual firehouse and city council chamber. In the following decades, two more buildings were added to house additional offices and the chamber of commerce. A remodeling in 1948 transformed the three city hall buildings into one. (Photograph by Robert C. Frampton.)

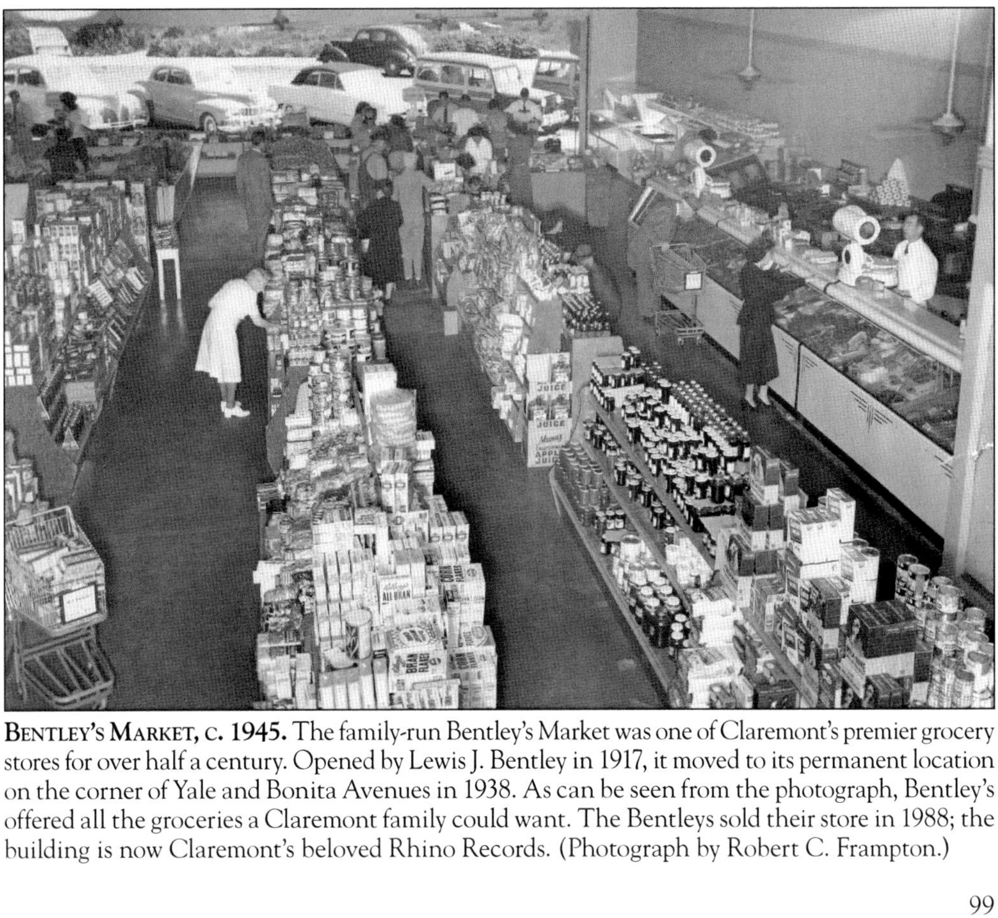

BENTLEY'S MARKET, C. 1945. The family-run Bentley's Market was one of Claremont's premier grocery stores for over half a century. Opened by Lewis J. Bentley in 1917, it moved to its permanent location on the corner of Yale and Bonita Avenues in 1938. As can be seen from the photograph, Bentley's offered all the groceries a Claremont family could want. The Bentleys sold their store in 1988; the building is now Claremont's beloved Rhino Records. (Photograph by Robert C. Frampton.)

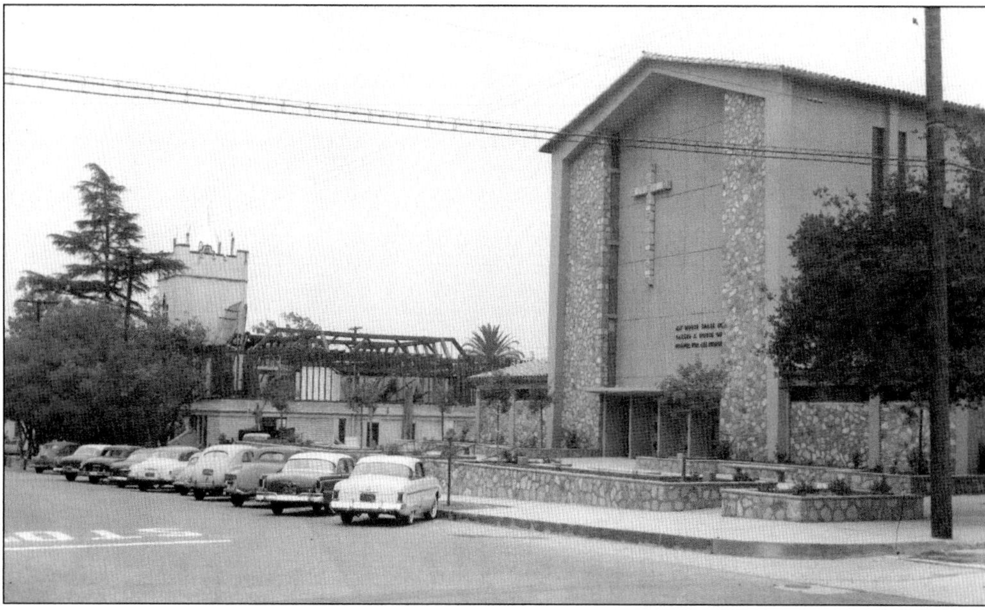

UNITED CHURCH OF CHRIST CONGREGATIONAL CHURCH, C. 1955. Since 1906, the United Church of Christ Congregational Church, on the corner of Harrison and Harvard Avenues, had served as the center of Claremont religious life. By 1955, however, a new, more modern sanctuary was needed to accommodate the growing congregation. This photograph shows the new church with its beautiful stone masonry in the foreground while the old church undergoes demolition in the background. (Photograph by Robert C. Frampton.)

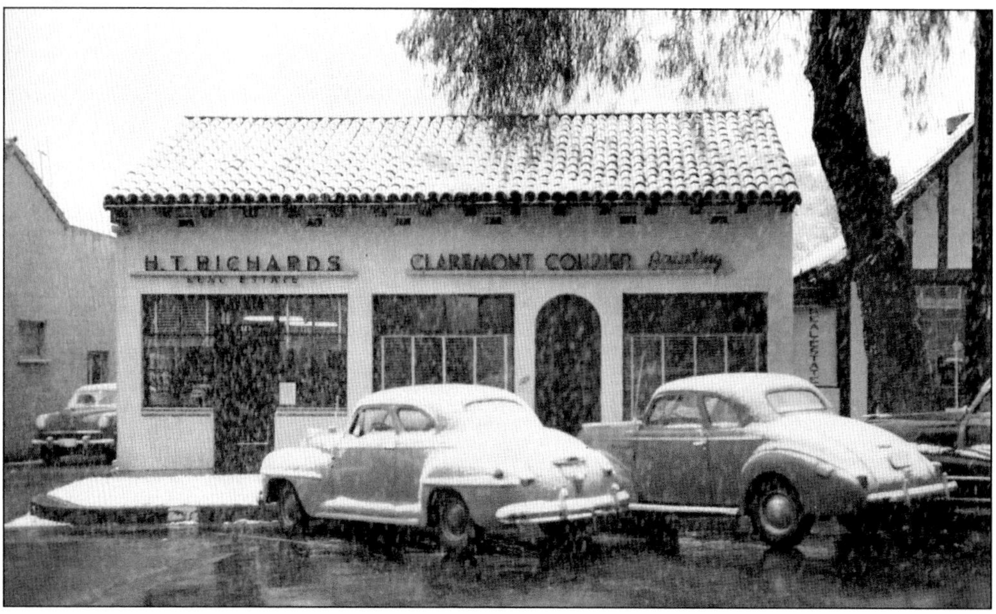

SNOWFALL IN CLAREMONT, JANUARY 1949. Pomona Valley's Mediterranean climate means that snow is rare. January 1949 saw Claremont's first snowstorm in 17 years, with a total of three inches blanketing the city and providing much fun for the younger residents. The offices of Claremont's newspaper, the *Claremont Courier*, are shown here in the flurry. (Courtesy of Milford Zornes; photograph by Robert C. Frampton.)

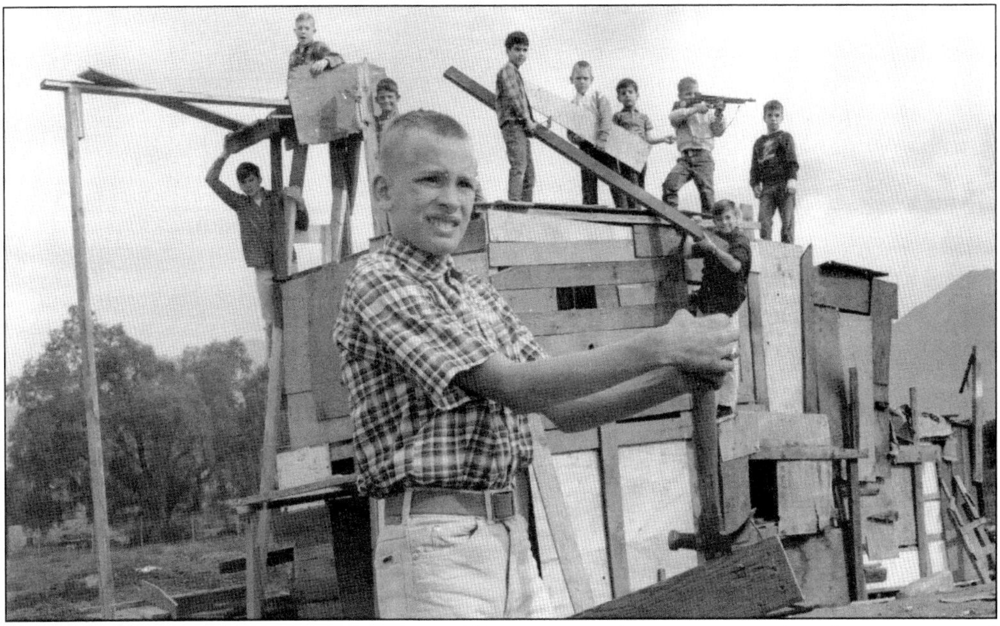

MEMORIAL PARK, 1965. Here, some young Claremont residents pose in a fort they constructed in Memorial Park. The park came into existence in 1946, after much controversy. The first bond measure, which planned for a swimming pool within the park, failed. The second, sans pool, was successful and provided Claremont with its first large park. Memorial Park was dedicated in honor of the men and women who fought in World Wars I and II.

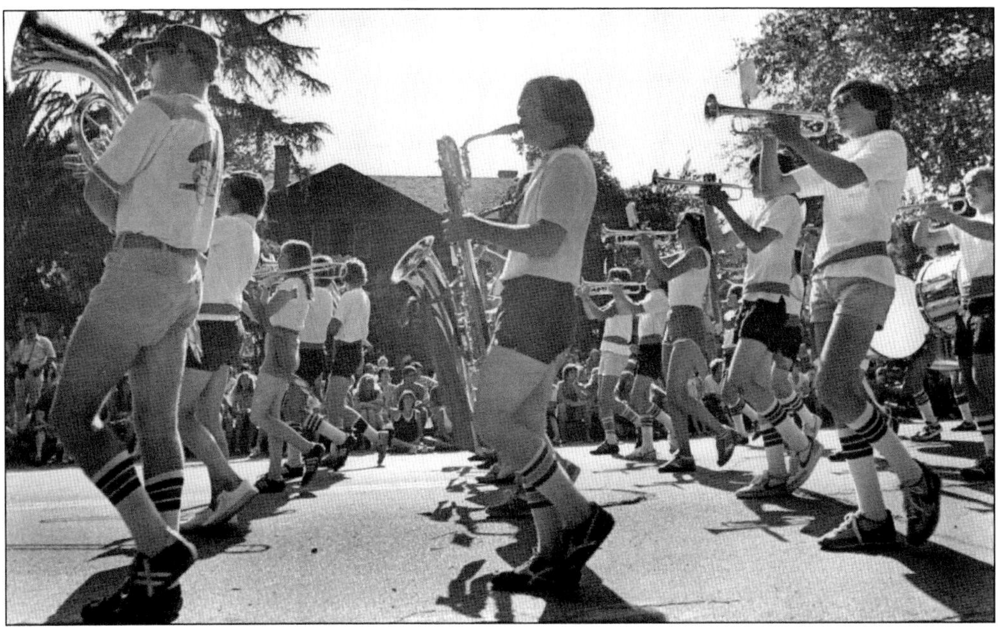

FOURTH OF JULY PARADE, C. 1980. Independence Day has long been a special holiday in Claremont. Picnics, games, and food booths were popular throughout the early 1900s. Once Memorial Park opened, it quickly became the new hub for festivities, hosting a pie-eating contest, a picnic supper, and folk dancing. The tradition of an afternoon parade through the village featuring floats, decorated vehicles, and bicycles began in 1955 and continues to this day.

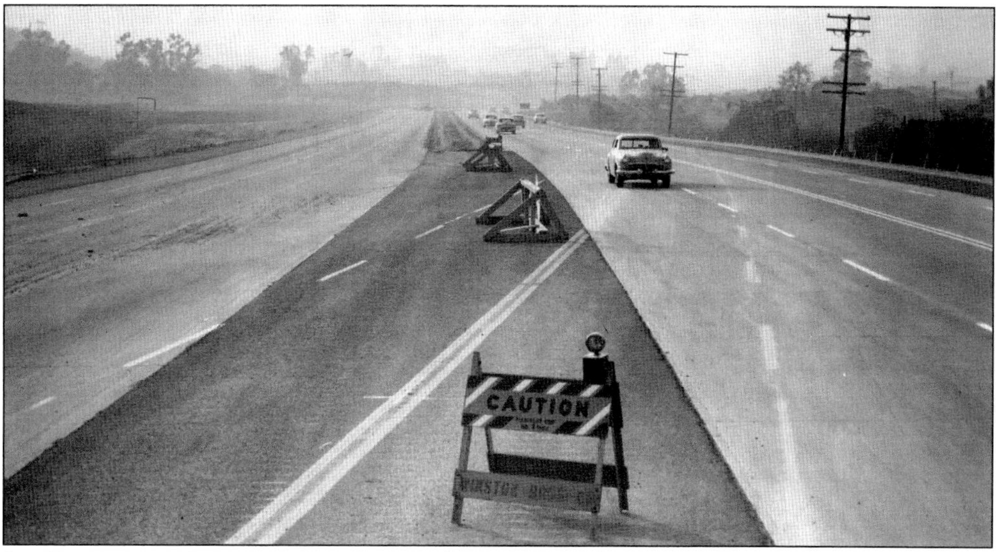

San Bernardino Freeway, c. 1954. By mid-century, Southern California was one of the nation's most rapidly developing regions, and many freeways were built to accommodate this growth. The first freeway through the Pomona Valley was the four-lane Ramona Freeway, which opened in 1954. It was soon renamed the San Bernardino Freeway and, later, Interstate 10. Running from Los Angeles to the San Bernardino County line, it helped bring thousands of new residents to Claremont. (Courtesy of the Judy Wright collection.)

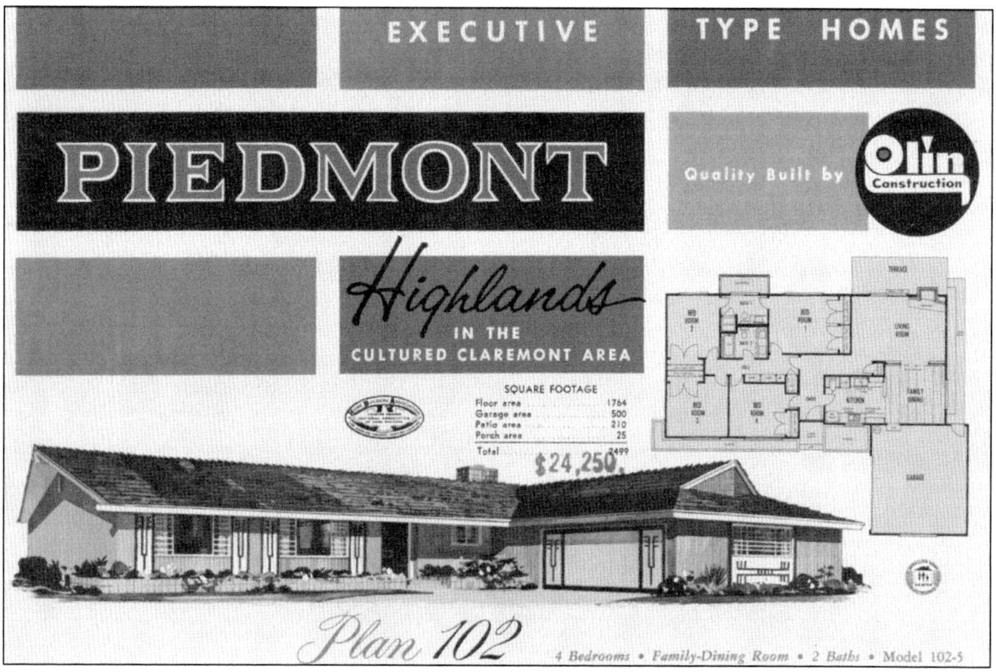

Piedmont Highlands Development Brochure. Freeways allowed new Californians to live away from the commotion of the city and make their homes in suburbs like Claremont. Particularly in the northern portion of the town, sprawling housing tracts came to replace citrus groves. This developer's brochure features a typical suburban home. The changing face of Claremont led to some conflict between "Old Claremont" and the "North of Foothillers."

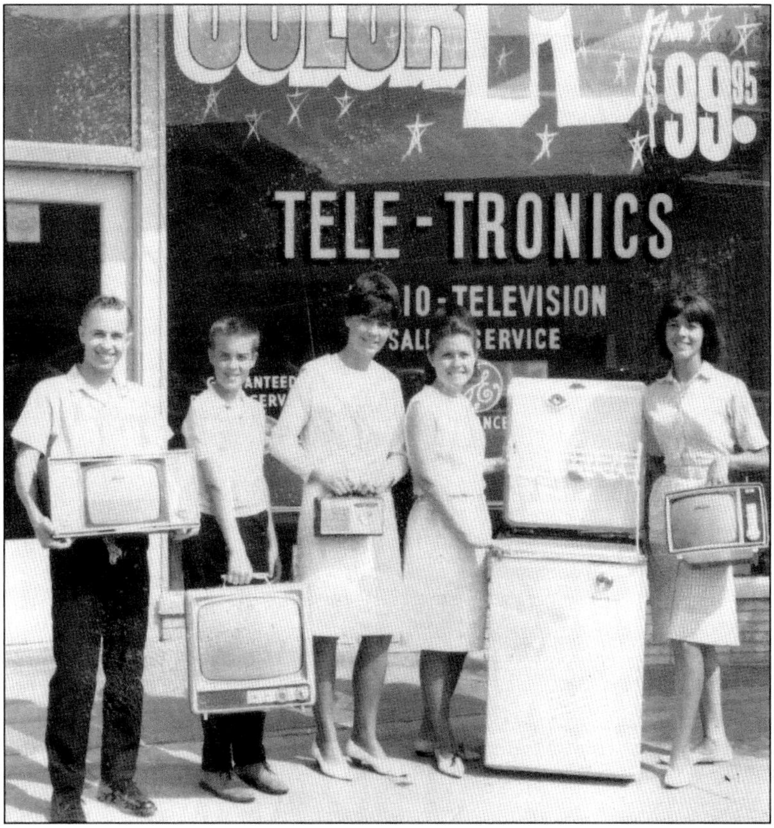

TELE-TRONICS TV AND REPAIR SHOP, C. 1960. The technological advances of the 20th century changed life in Claremont. Tele-tronics TV and Repair Shop, located on Yale Avenue in the village, provided the latest equipment to residents for many years before going out of business. Here, some happy shoppers pose outside the store with their recently purchased radios and televisions.

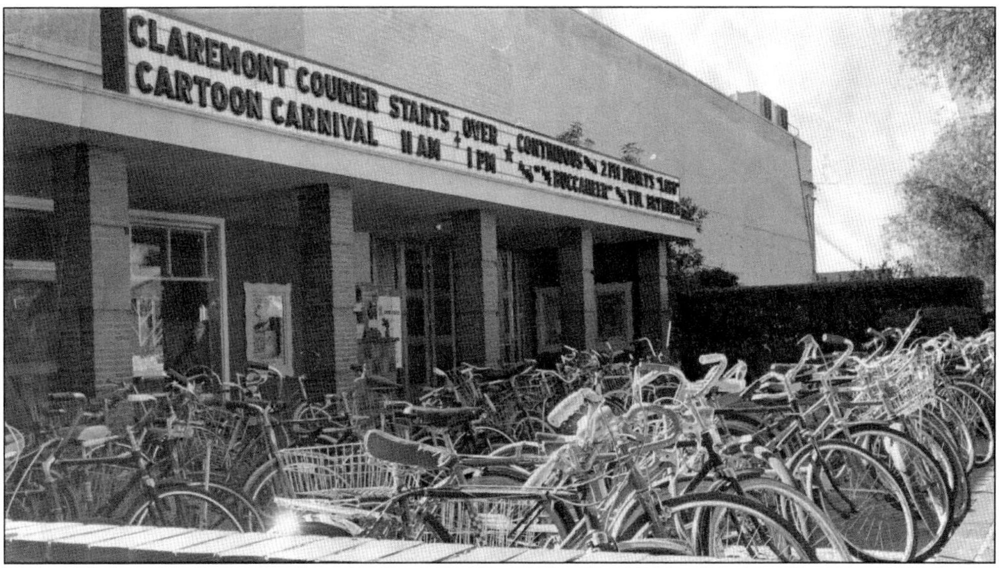

VILLAGE THEATRE, 1962. From its opening night on January 19, 1940, until its closing nearly four decades later, the Village Theatre provided entertainment to Claremont residents, who previously had to travel to other towns to see the latest movies. The theater's convenient location on the corner of Harvard and Bonita Avenues meant Claremont youth and college students could easily bike there in the afternoons.

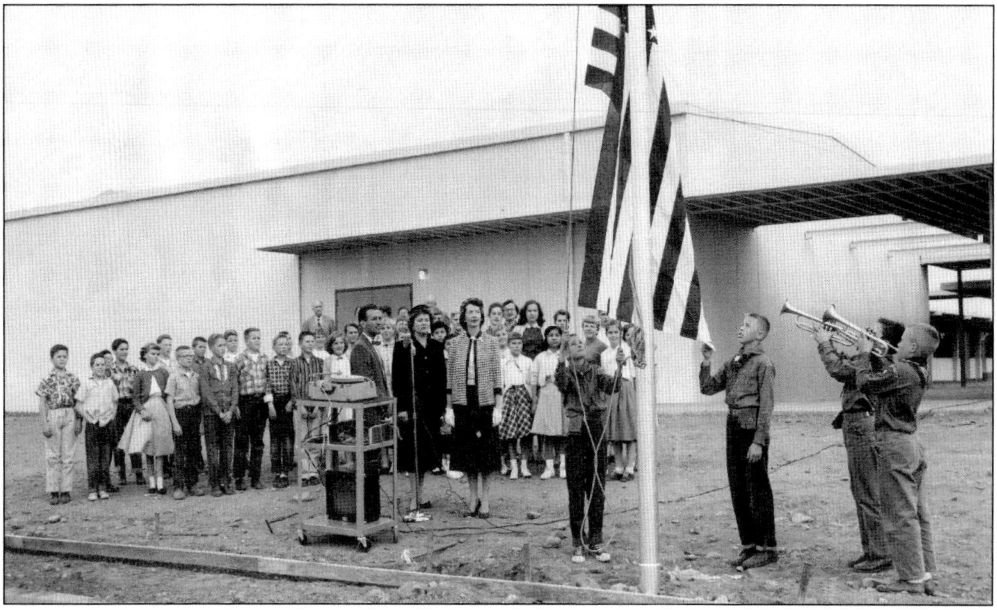

CONDIT ELEMENTARY SCHOOL, JANUARY 1958. As Claremont's population exploded, so too did the number of students enrolled in the school district. From 1950 to 1970, Claremont opened six new elementary schools, two new junior high schools (one of which, La Puerta, closed in the 1970s), and a new, larger Claremont High School. Here, a ceremony is held prior to the opening of Condit Elementary School, named for beloved Claremont educator Eleanor Daly Condit. (Photograph by Robert C. Frampton.)

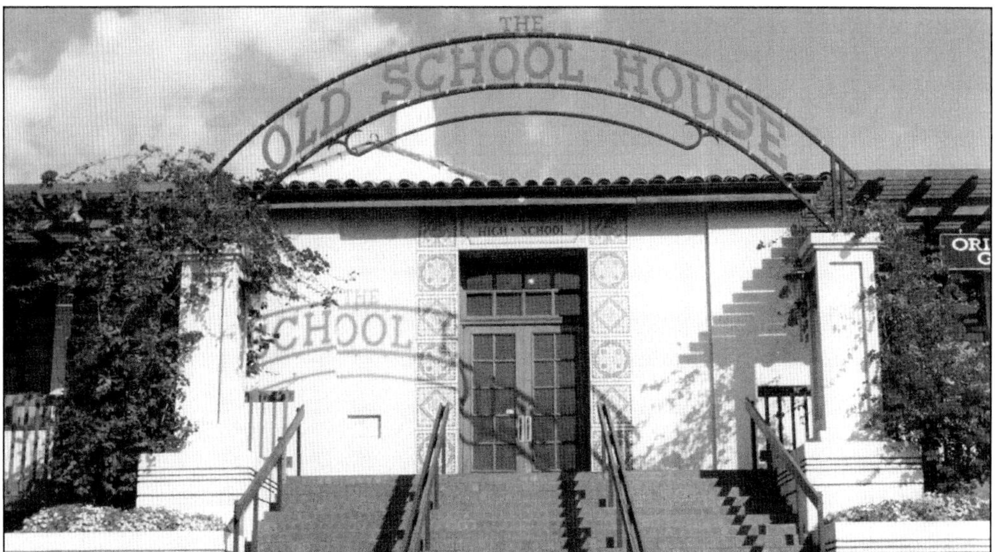

GRISWOLD'S OLD SCHOOL HOUSE. With the opening of the new Claremont High School campus on Indian Hill, the beautiful old school building was left for commercial purposes. For decades, it functioned as Griswold's Old School House, a shopping center, with Griswold's Smorgasbord and Inn nearby. Its location along Route 66, once seen as an inconvenience (pedestrian tunnels had to be built under Foothill Boulevard to allow students to cross safely), now helped bring in many customers.

FRANK WHEELER, "GRANDFATHER OF FOOTHILL BOULEVARD." Wheeler, a real estate developer and English native who came to Claremont in 1893, was one of the city's greatest civic leaders. As vice president of the Foothill Boulevard Association, he was an outspoken proponent of Foothill Boulevard becoming a state highway. Wheeler saw his work come to fruition in 1931 when Claremont's portion of Route 66 was opened, transforming the town into a thriving suburb. (Courtesy of the Judy Wright collection.)

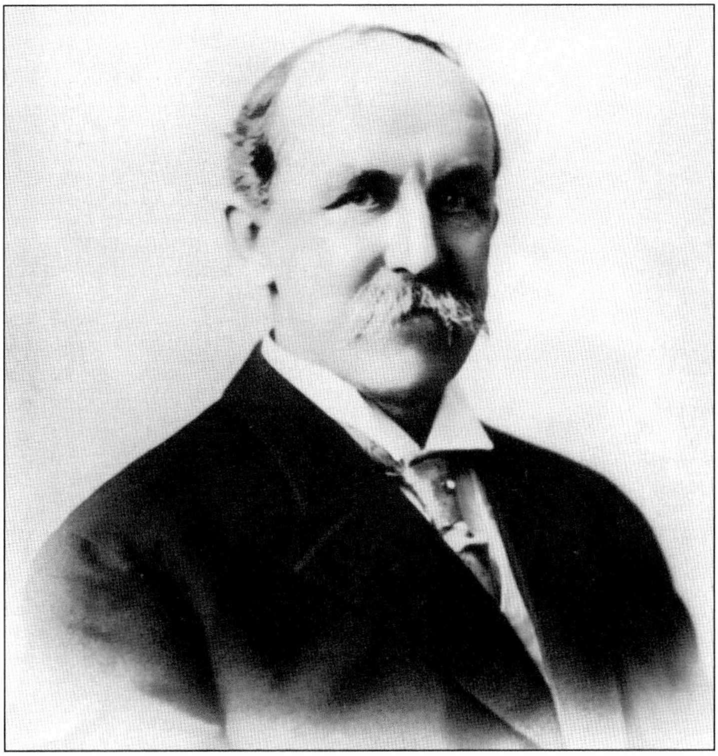

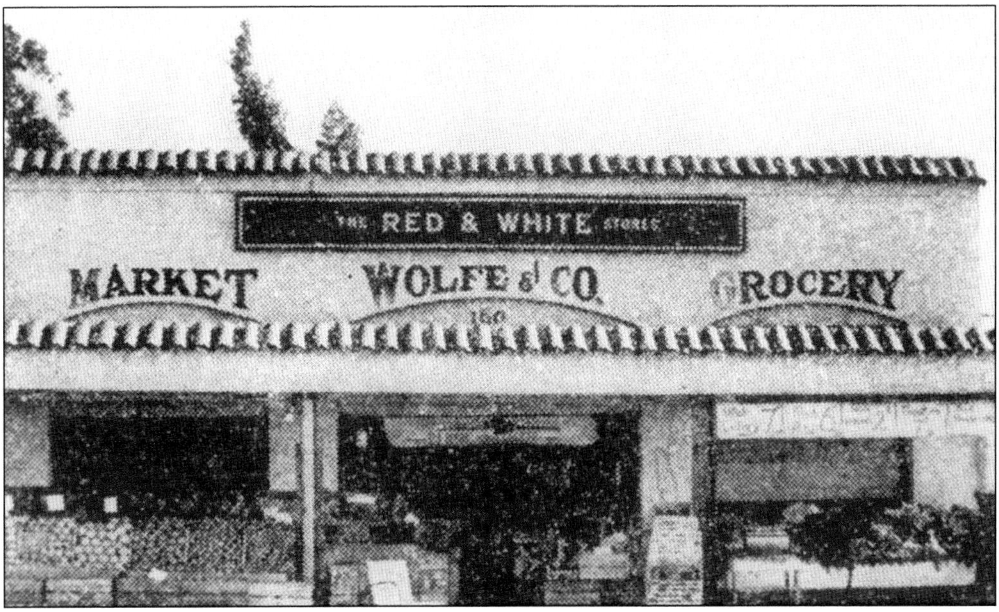

WOLFE'S MARKET. This Claremont commercial landmark was opened by John Wolfe in 1917 as a gas station. At the time, it was the only station between San Bernardino and Pasadena. In 1933, Wolfe's moved to its present location on Route 66 and became a food market under the leadership of John's son Claude. Interestingly, while at Claremont High School, Claude and his friends were called the "Wolfepack," and a wolf later became the school's mascot. (Courtesy of the Judy Wright collection.)

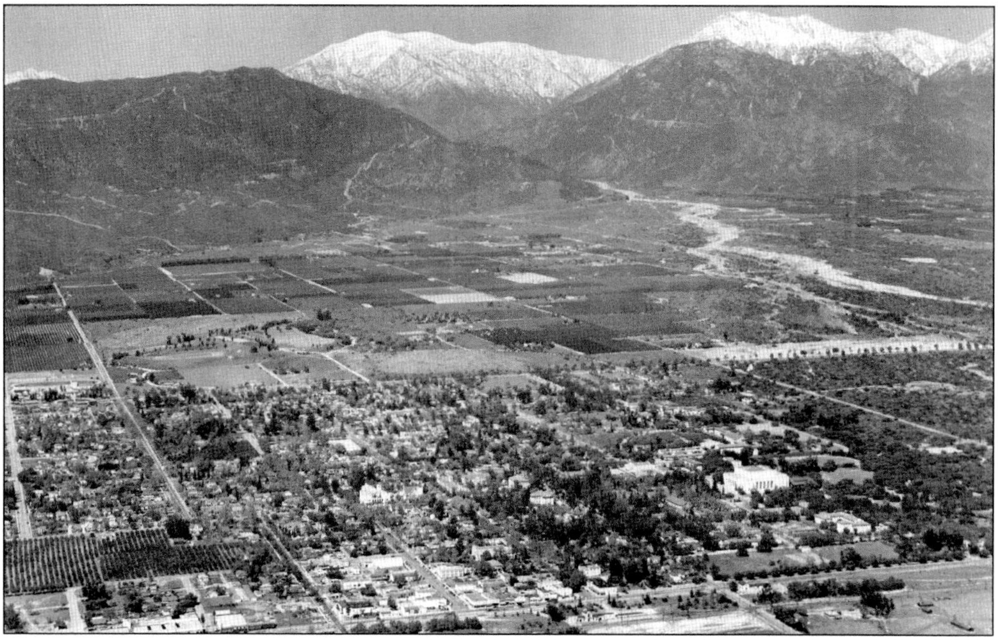

Development of Claremont, 1946 and 1973. These two aerial photographs of Claremont highlight the city's impressive growth over almost three decades. In 1946, Claremont was just emerging from the devastating Great Depression and World War II. By the time the photograph below was taken, its population had increased by over 20,000 people, nine new schools had been built, three new colleges had been founded, the massive San Antonio Dam had been constructed, and housing developments had replaced the old citrus groves north of Foothill Boulevard. No longer a sleepy little college town, Claremont was now a bustling suburb. Despite this, however, it still maintained much of its small-town charm. The village remained a popular commercial center, family businesses continued to thrive, new parks and community centers encouraged neighbors to get to know one another, and traditions like the Fourth of July celebration proved timeless. (Both, photograph by Robert C. Frampton.)

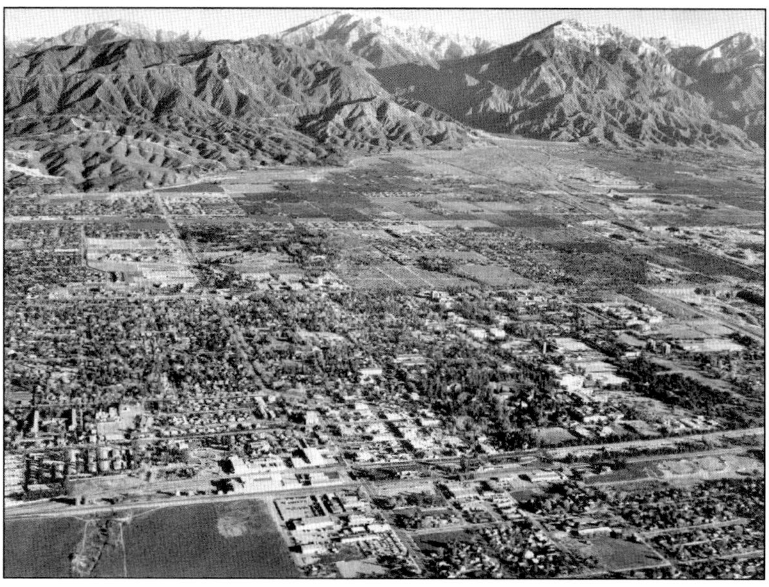

Seven

Art and Architecture

An Artists' Enclave

By the early 1900s, Claremont's residential district was composed of a variety of architectural styles: Victorian, Neoclassical Revival, Mission Revival, Craftsman, American Four Square, and more. Russian Village, a neighborhood south of the village, contained 13 unique houses and bungalows built from salvaged material. Grand stone citrus homes, including the notable Pitzer-Peairs House, now in the National Register of Historic Places, dotted the northern part of town. Despite being located in the western wilderness, Claremont was an architecturally sophisticated town.

The combination of the beauty of the area and the resources of the colleges was ideal. By the 1940s, Claremont was the center of a growing studio art movement that emphasized the use of natural materials. Pomona and Scripps Colleges both continued to expand their art programs, adding highly influential artists to their faculty. Across the campuses, public art works, including murals by Ramon Martinez and José Clemente Orozco, offered inspiration to budding student artists. Experienced artists also flocked to Claremont, and the town quickly became known as an art mecca.

Padua Hills Theatre, built in 1930 in the hills overlooking Claremont, further encouraged this. From 1937 to 1974, the theater served as home to the Mexican Players, who performed hundreds of shows in their native language and drew audiences from around the region. Furthermore, each summer, the Padua Hills Art Fiesta brought 30 or so local artists together for a celebration of "Art in Action," with the artists creating their work in front of delighted visitors. For years, Padua Hills thrived as an artists' colony, and the presence of such a community was of immeasurable cultural value to Claremont.

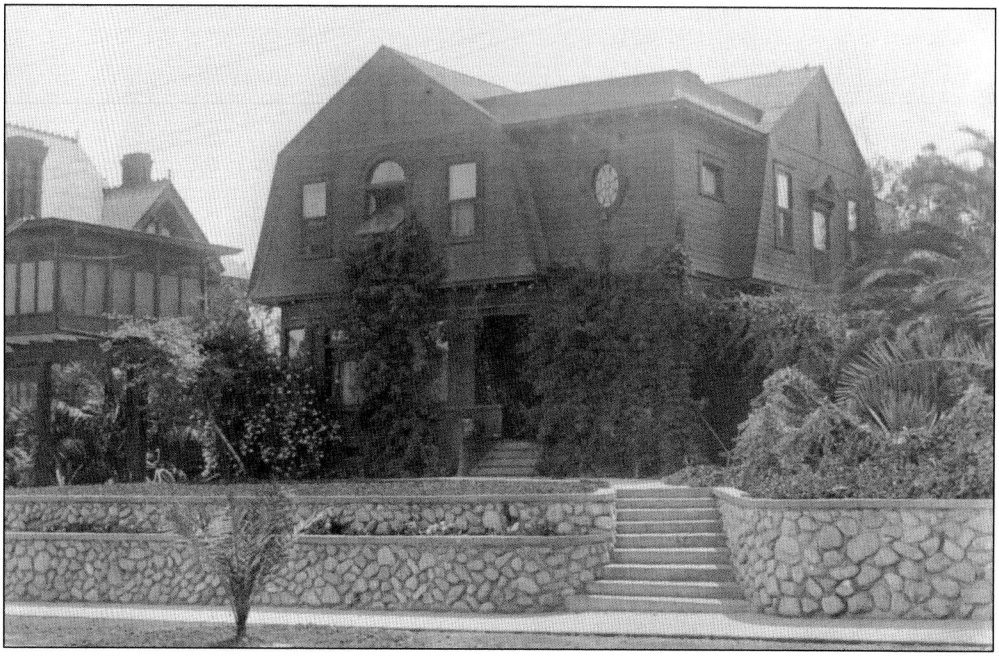

VICTORIAN HOMES. Many of Claremont's early homes were built in the Victorian style. Popular from the mid-1800s to around 1900, Victorian homes differed in scale and ornamentation but featured the same verticality of structure. Mass production of building ornaments, including columns, pediments, and decorative friezes, allowed homeowners to easily customize their homes to fit their personal tastes. The Cook House (above) was built about 1896. It mixes a variety of styles, including Queen Anne Victorian and Dutch Colonial Revival. Below is the Gillette family home, which was located on the corner of Yale Avenue and Fourth Street but has since been demolished. (Both, courtesy of the Judy Wright collection.)

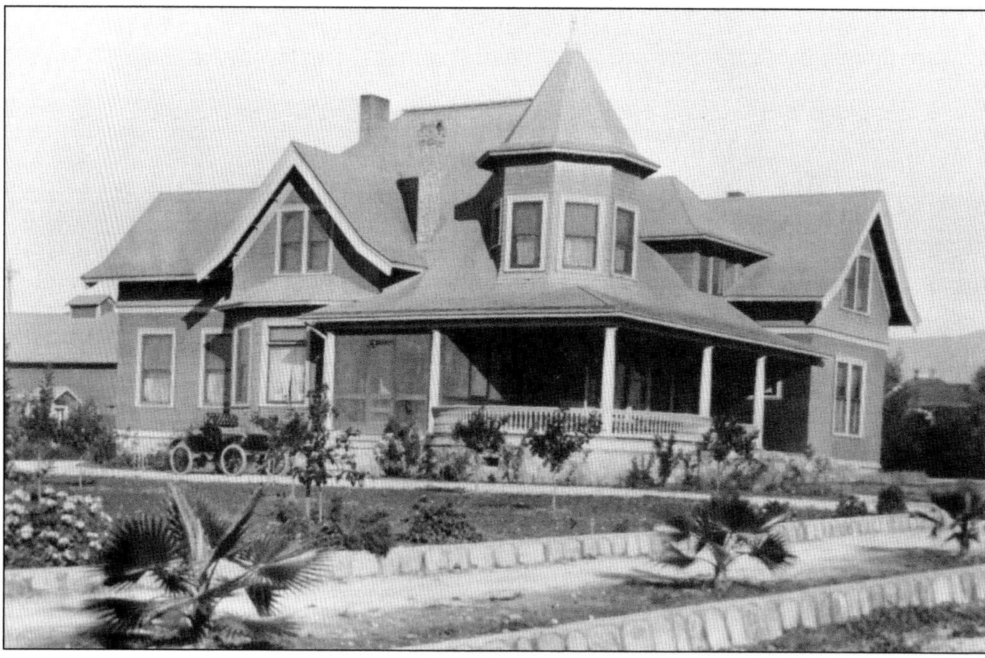

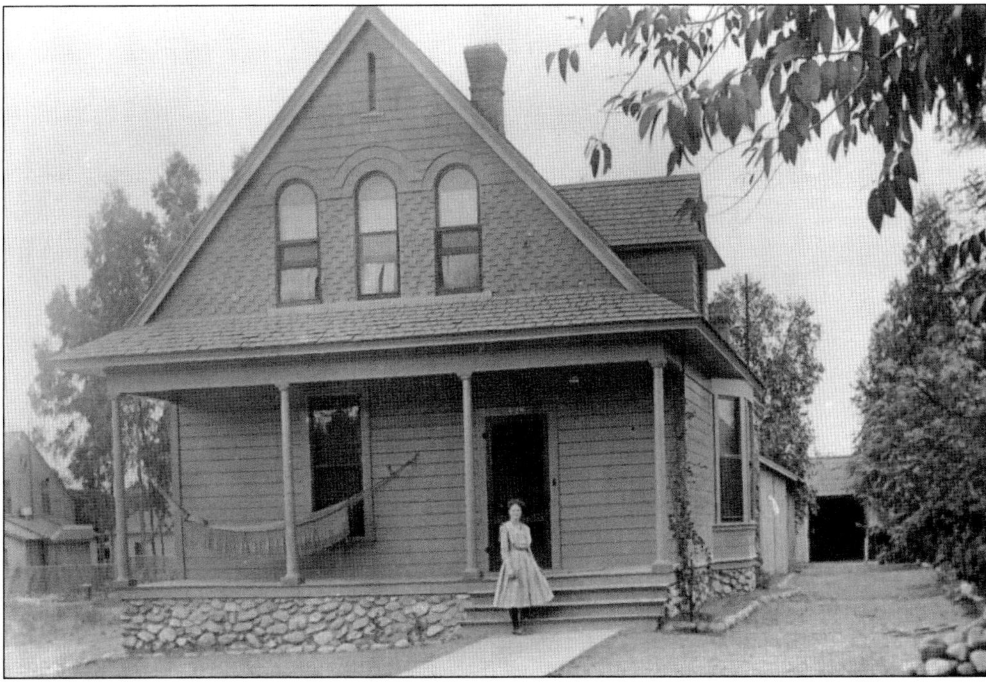

MISS LEE HOUSE. This modest home holds the distinction of being one of Claremont's oldest standing homes. The house, which combines Victorian and Craftsman styles, was originally built about 1890 on what is now Bonita Avenue but was later moved to its present site at 355 West Seventh Street. Here, original owner Miss Lee stands in front of her home at its Bonita Avenue location. (Courtesy of Special Collections, Honnold/Mudd Library of the Claremont Colleges.)

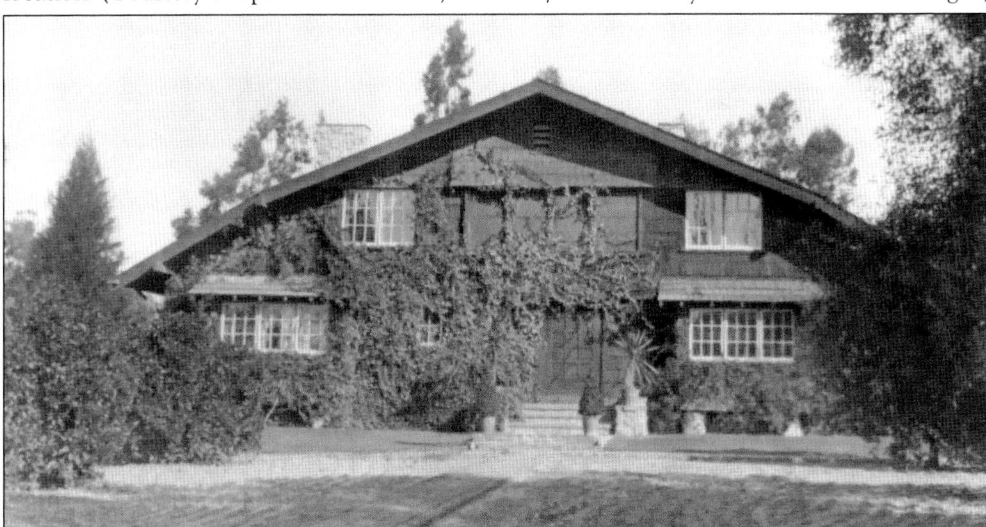

DARLING HOUSE. The Craftsman style called for a return to simplicity, rejecting ostentatious designs. These "democratic" houses were designed to utilize simple, unadorned surfaces and natural materials, often taking designs from pattern books. E.E. List, George Coulson, and Greene & Greene were exceptional Craftsman architects who helped to design many homes in Claremont. This beautiful Craftsman bungalow was designed by Greene & Greene in 1903. (Courtesy of the Judy Wright collection.)

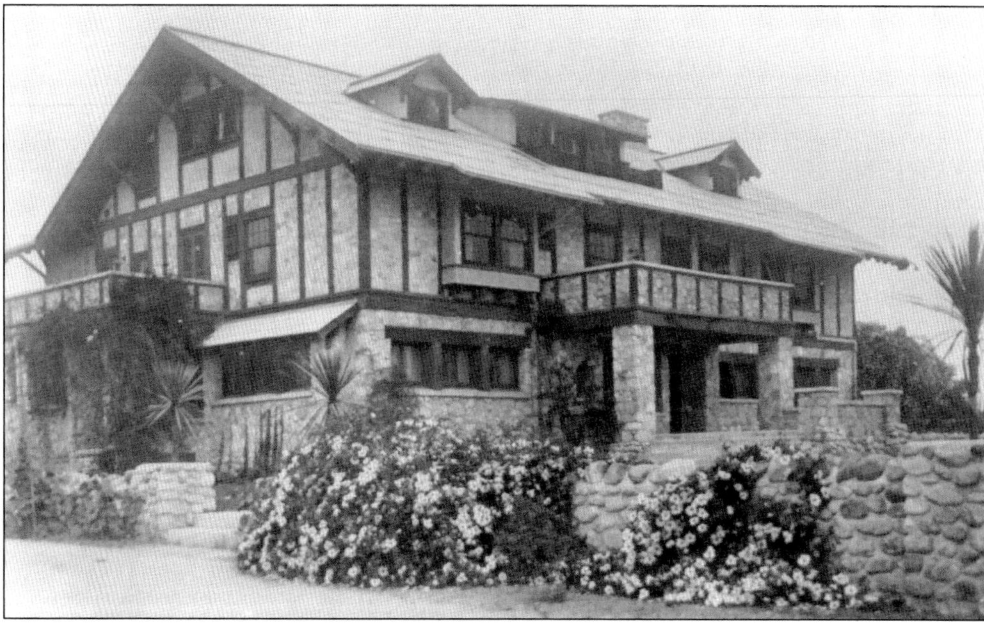

Stone Houses. From the 1900s to the 1930s, stone architecture was hugely popular in Claremont, as the city's location on top of an alluvial fan provided an abundance of natural rock, known as "Claremont potatoes." Sarah Bixby Smith's grand stone home (above) was one of the finest residences in the city when it was built in 1910. At three stories tall, it was perfect for hosting lavish parties and even briefly served as a dormitory for Claremont Men's College. Sadly, it was later destroyed by fire. Below, a more modest example of stone architecture is seen in this dormitory for citrus workers on the Johnson Brothers Ranch in northern Claremont. (Both, courtesy of Special Collections, Honnold/Mudd Library of the Claremont Colleges.)

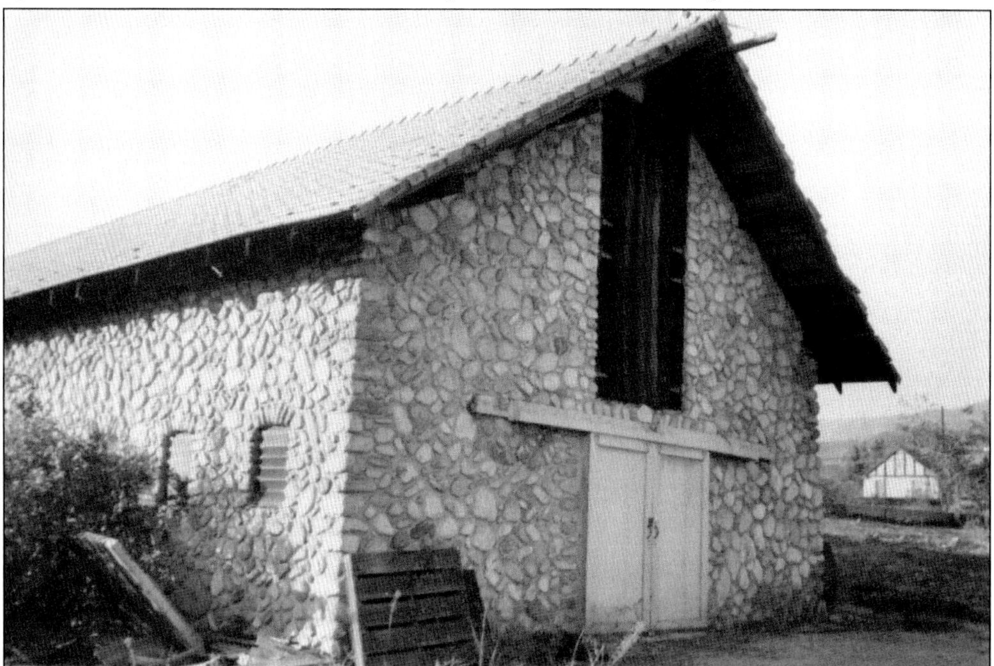

ROBERT ORR. Pomona architect Robert Orr was hired by the Pitzer family in 1911 to design a house for their large citrus ranch. The resulting Pitzer-Peairs House has been described as "one of the finest stone house in Southern California." Orr also designed several other well-known local buildings, including the Pilgrim Congregational Church in Pomona and the original Claremont High School. (Courtesy of the Judy Wright collection.)

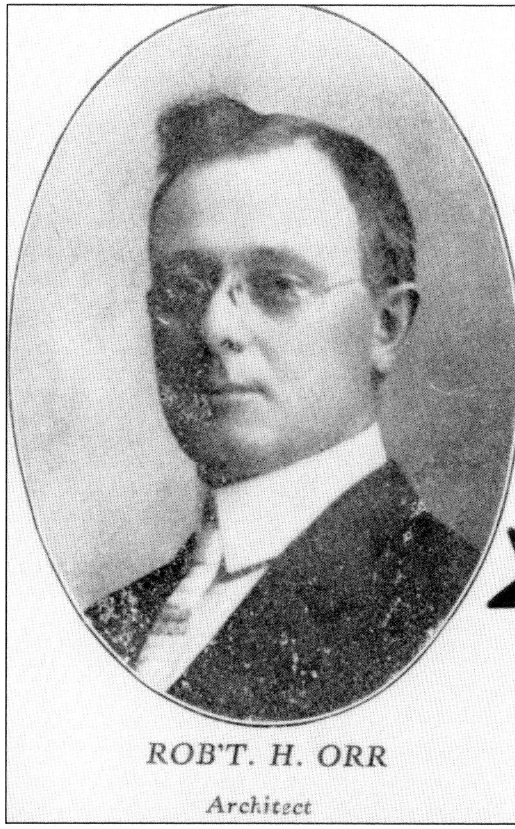

STONE CURBS. Stonework was not limited to homes, it was also utilized on the city's street curbs. Nicknamed "elephant toes," these stone curbs were standard in Claremont until about 1930. Stones were arranged in rows, and the gaps were filled with concrete mortar, creating a beautiful streetscape for the city that is still present today. (Courtesy of the Judy Wright collection.)

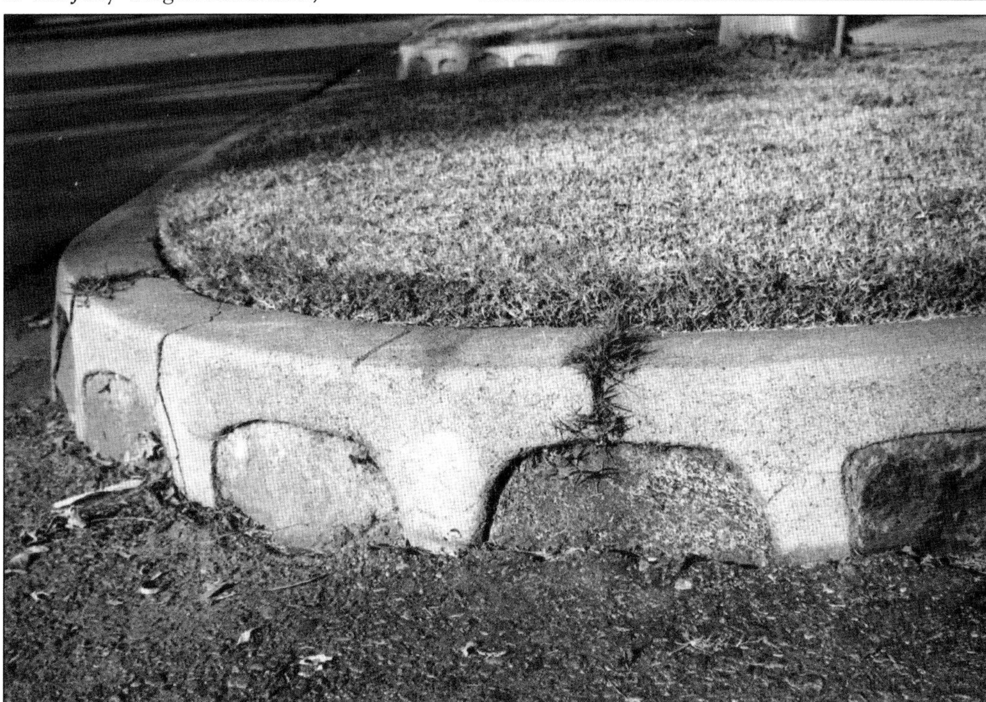

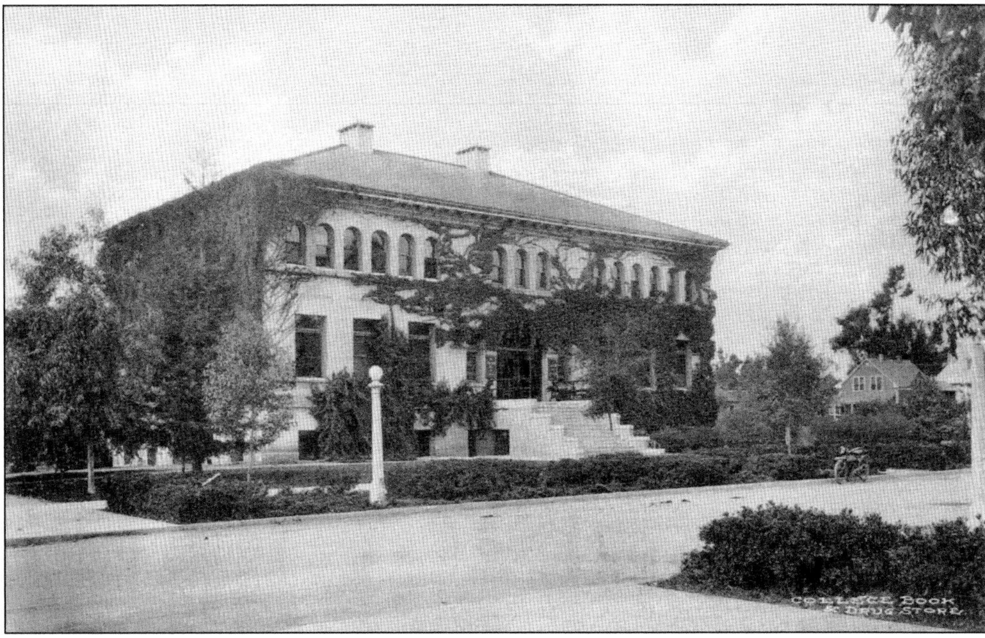

PEARSONS HALL, C. 1898. Classical Revival architecture appeared in Claremont in the early 1900s, paying homage to a more ancient, grander style. Pearsons Hall, designed by C.H. Brown and built in 1898 with money donated by D.K. Pearsons, served as a science hall for Pomona College. The symmetrically designed building with a balanced facade is a great example of the Classical Revival motif.

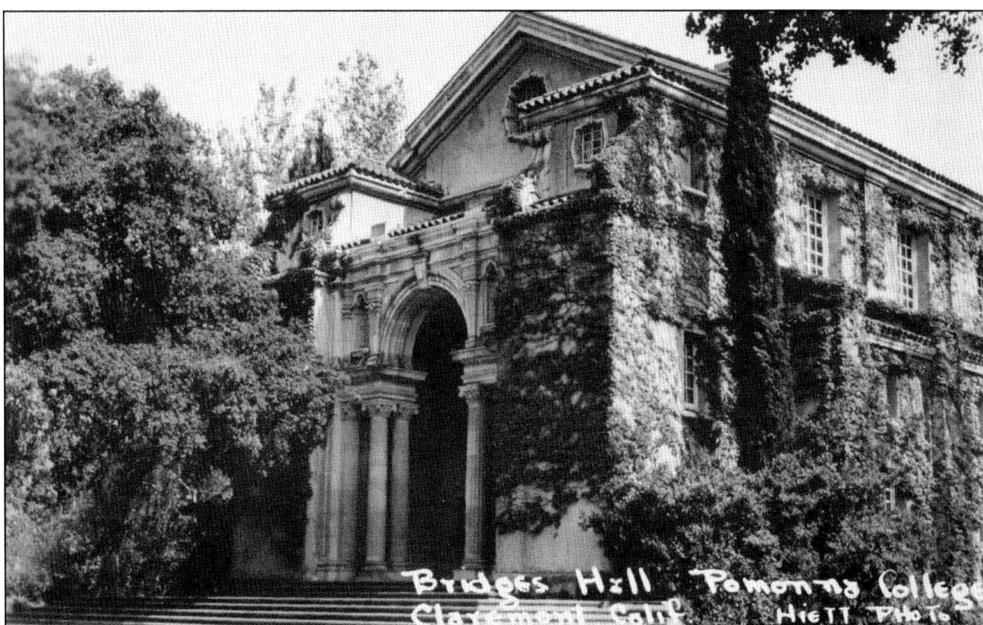

BRIDGES HALL OF MUSIC. "Little Bridges," as Bridges Hall of Music is affectionately called, was built in 1915 with a generous donation from the parents of late Pomona College student Mabel Shaw Bridges. Renowned architect Myron Hunt designed the Romanesque building, which is known for its wonderful acoustics and its stunning Classical Revival architecture.

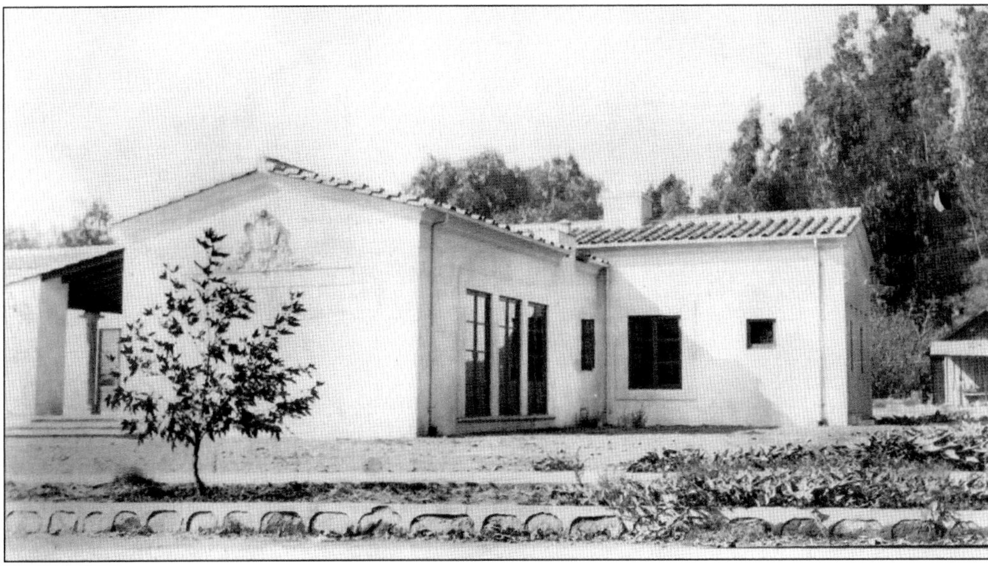

Spanish Colonial Revival Houses. Spanish Revival architecture became popular in the West after the Pan American-California Exposition was held in San Diego in 1915, showcasing renowned architect Bertram Grosvenor Goodhue and Mexican Baroque architecture. Some of the characteristics of Spanish Revival homes include low-pitch red-tiled roofs, plastered exterior and interim walls, carved or cast ornamentation, balconies, and window grilles. Though initially met with some hostility, Spanish influence had a profound effect on Claremont, with buildings like the 1927 Santa Fe depot showcasing beautiful architecture as well as the Spanish heritage of California. The 1928 library at Harvard Avenue and Second Street (above, now demolished) and the Warner House at Pilgrim Place (below) are two great examples of Mediterranean influence in Claremont. (Both, courtesy of the Judy Wright collection.)

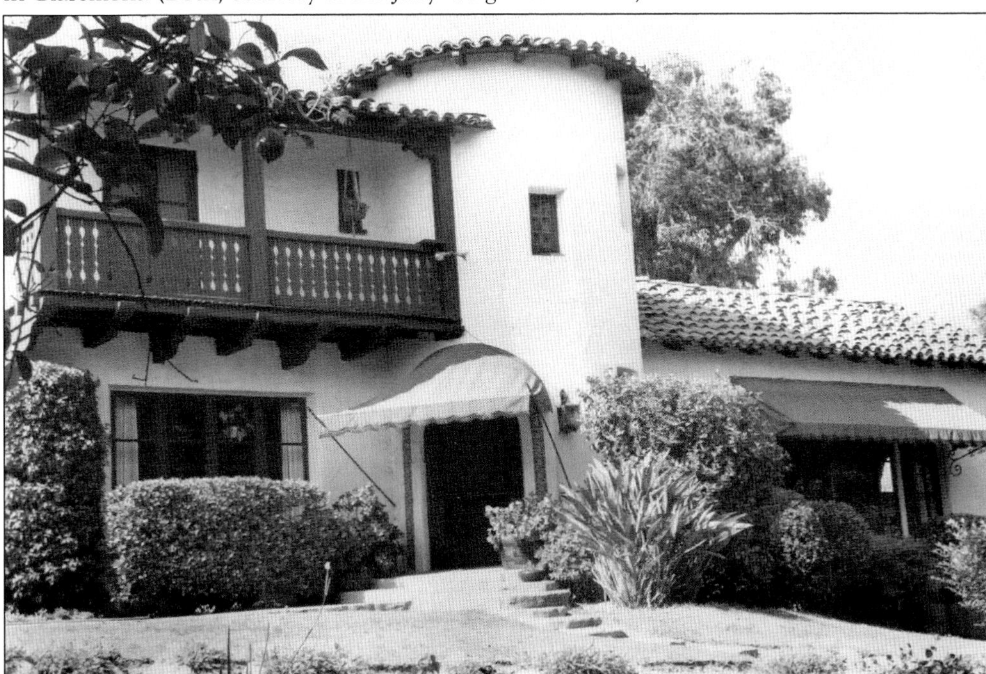

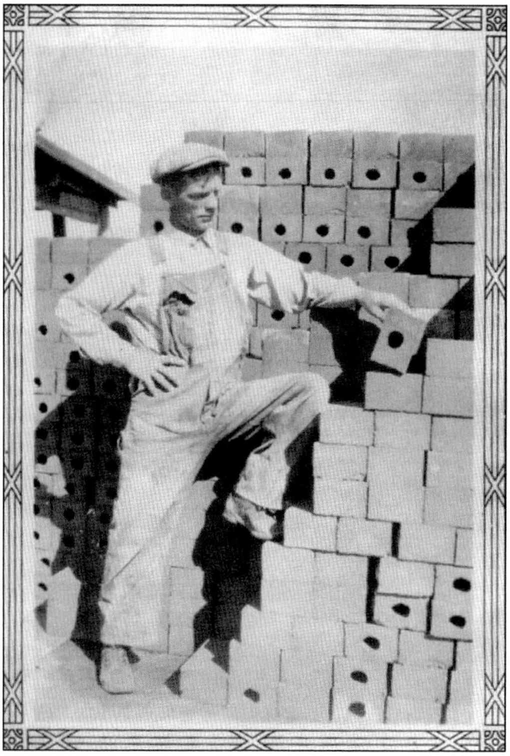

Kostany Stys and Russian Village. A unique individual in Claremont's history, Polish immigrant Kostany Stys helped design and build many of Claremont's famous rock houses in the Russian Village area. Stys immigrated to Claremont in 1921 with his wife, Antonina, buying land on the eastern side of Mills Avenue and building many houses there, despite having no formal training in engineering or architecture. As much of his building was done during the Great Depression, the resourceful Stys used recycled or salvaged material. Stones came from cleared citrus orchards, slab segments of concrete were taken from damaged streets, scrap sheet metal was used to design gates, and recycled tile and wood were bought from razed or damaged buildings. This was not only economically practical, but it also gave Russian Village its distinctive folk architecture. (Both, courtesy of the Judy Wright collection.)

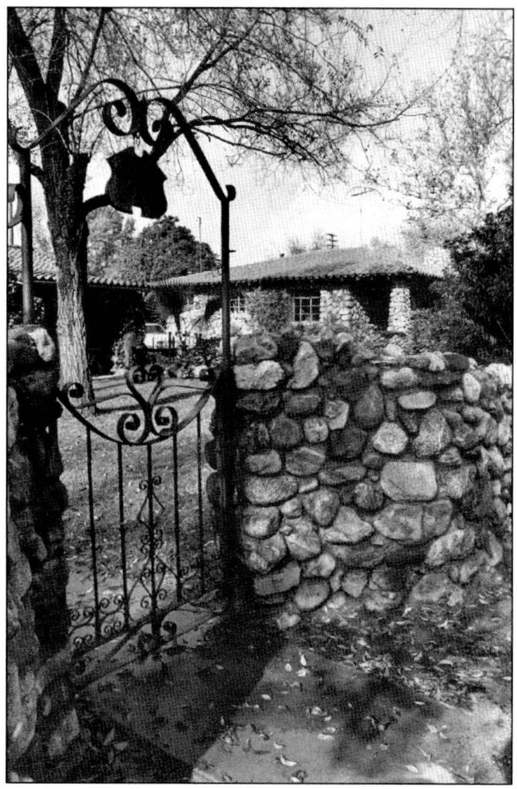

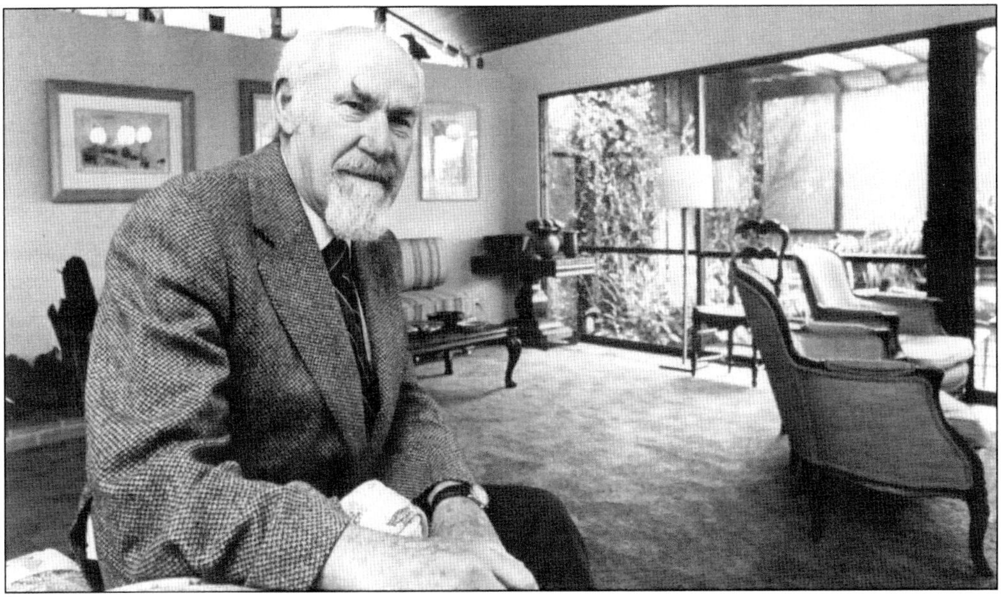

Theodore Criley Jr. and Fred McDowell. Two of Claremont's most famous architects, Criley and McDowell were among the leaders of the architectural movement known as California Modernism. Criley earned his degree from the Massachusetts Institute of Technology, later opening a private practice and working as a lecturer at Scripps College and the University of Southern California. In 1957, McDowell, a young architect and former understudy of Richard Neutra, joined Criley's practice, cementing together two great architectural minds. The Criley-McDowell partnership is best known for its work on the Claremont Colleges' campuses, including master plans for the dormitory and classroom buildings at Pitzer College, halls at Scripps College, and buildings at the Claremont Graduate School and University Center. The two prolific architects worked and designed together until Criley's death in 1987.

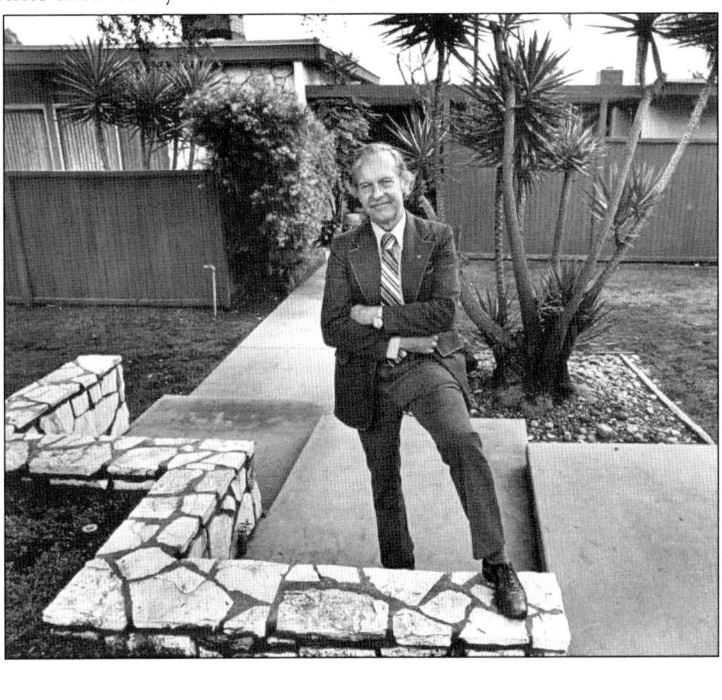

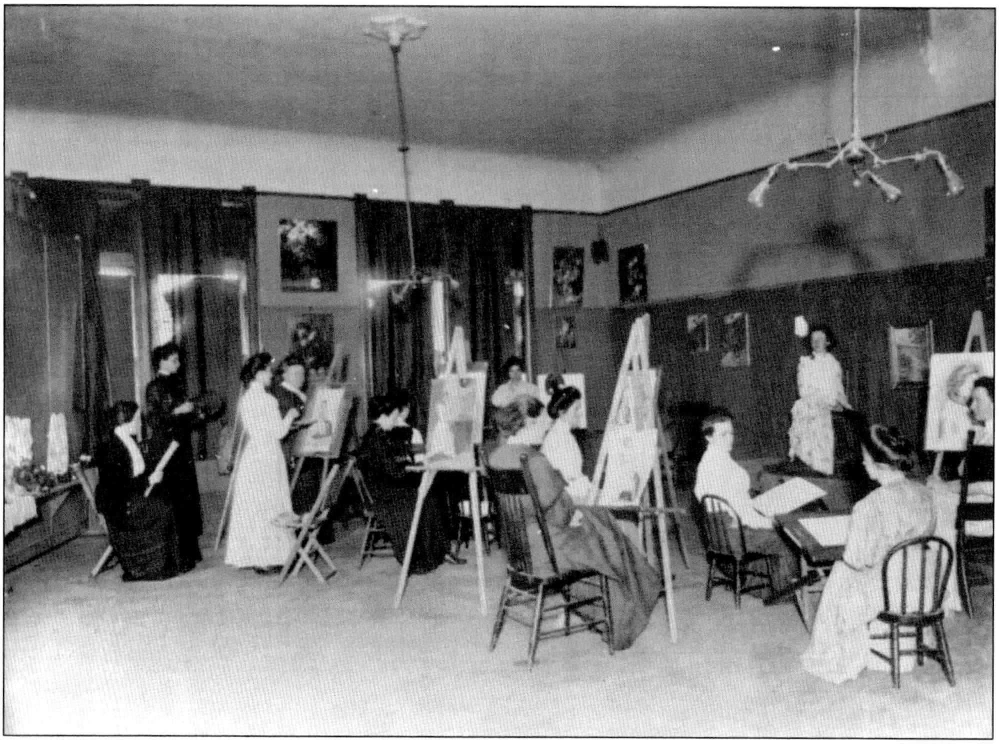

POMONA COLLEGE ART CLASS, C. 1900. The arts quickly became an important part of the culture at the Claremont Colleges, with art classes like this one held in the earliest days of Pomona College. Later, the founding of the Fine Arts Foundation of Scripps College, in 1935, helped develop greater opportunities for the study of fine art by providing an art studio, equipment, and scholarships. The foundation also sponsors monthly exhibits and lectures. (Courtesy of the Judy Wright collection.)

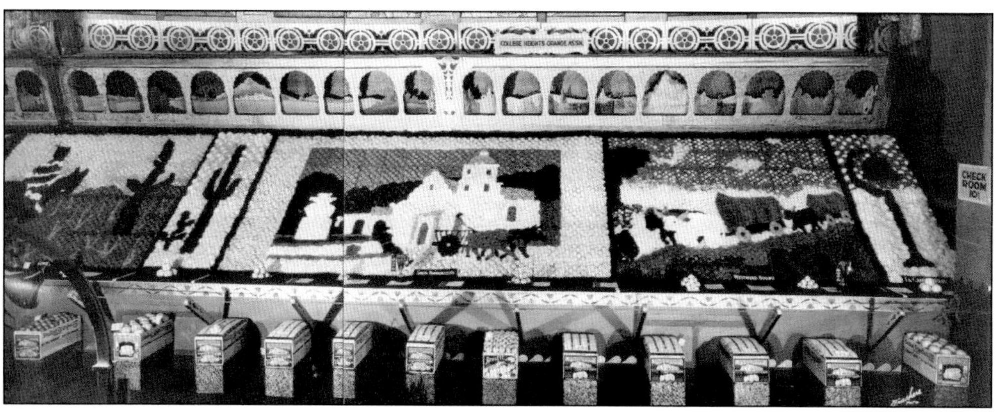

LOS ANGELES COUNTY FAIR ARTWORK. Claremont was regularly represented in the fine arts and home arts competition at the Los Angeles County Fair, allowing many of the city's talented artists to show off their creations. Even companies, like the College Heights Orange and Lemon Association, created pieces for the fair, as seen here. This winning display illustrates early California history, and all the designs are made from many individual oranges and lemons. (Courtesy of the Judy Wright collection.)

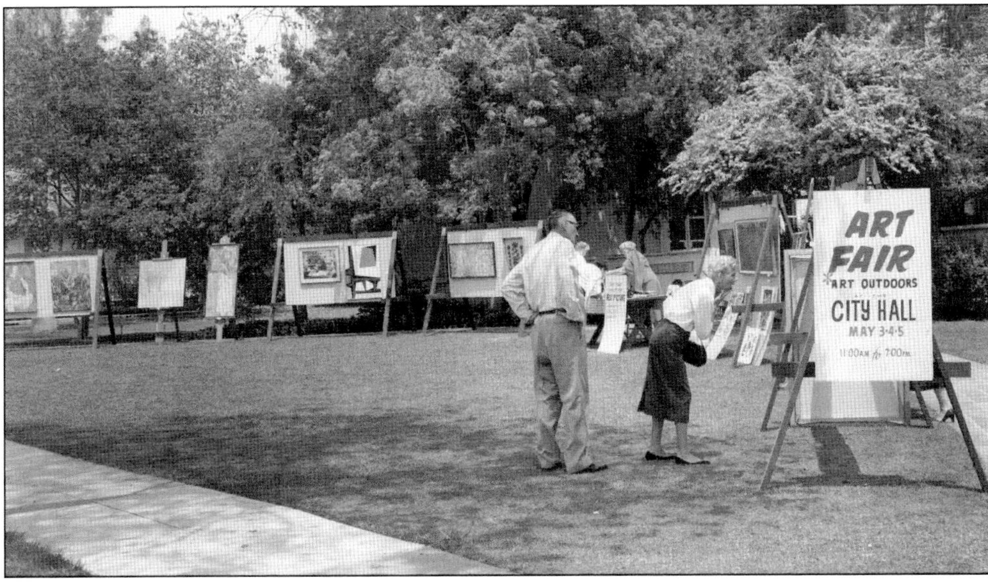

CLAREMONT ARTS FAIR, C. 1958. A true art mecca from the 1930s through the 1950s, Claremont was home to a number of annual art shows beginning in the 1950s. The Lively Arts in Claremont show was an annual indoor and outdoor exhibition held over the summer at Scripps College, showcasing the work of students, faculty, and local artists. Downtown Claremont's annual Claremont Arts Fair, meanwhile, featured up-and-coming artists. With its first annual show in 1958, the fair helped grant exposure to some of Claremont's great artists, including Paul Darrow, Milford Zornes, Harrison McIntosh, Karl Benjamin, Phil Dike, and many more. Drawing crowds of thousands, the art fair exposed Claremont's artistic scene to people from all over Southern California. These photographs show local artwork on display at the first annual Arts Fair. Below, jurors Sueo Serisawa and Thomas Leavitt choose the best pieces. (Both, photograph by Robert C. Frampton.)

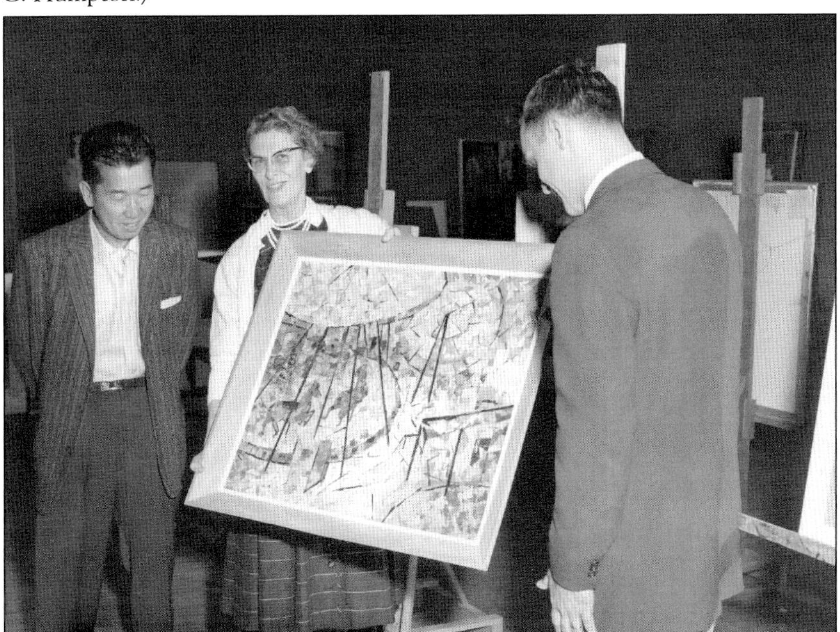

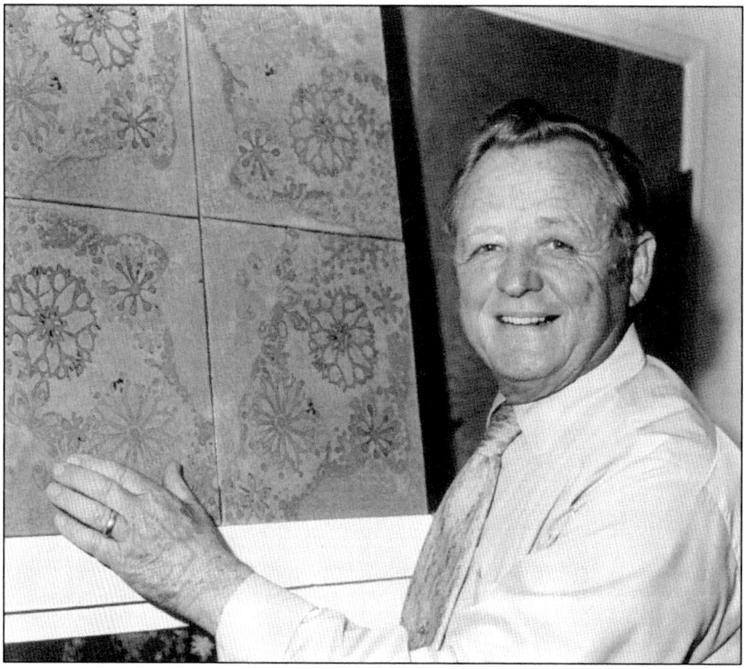

Millard Sheets. Perhaps the most famous artist to emerge from the Claremont art scene, Sheets had an impressive career in several fields, including painting, murals, mosaics, and architectural design. Born in Pomona in 1907, Sheets studied at the Choinard School of Art in Los Angeles before moving back to the Claremont area. From 1936 to 1955, he served as the director of painting at Scripps College.

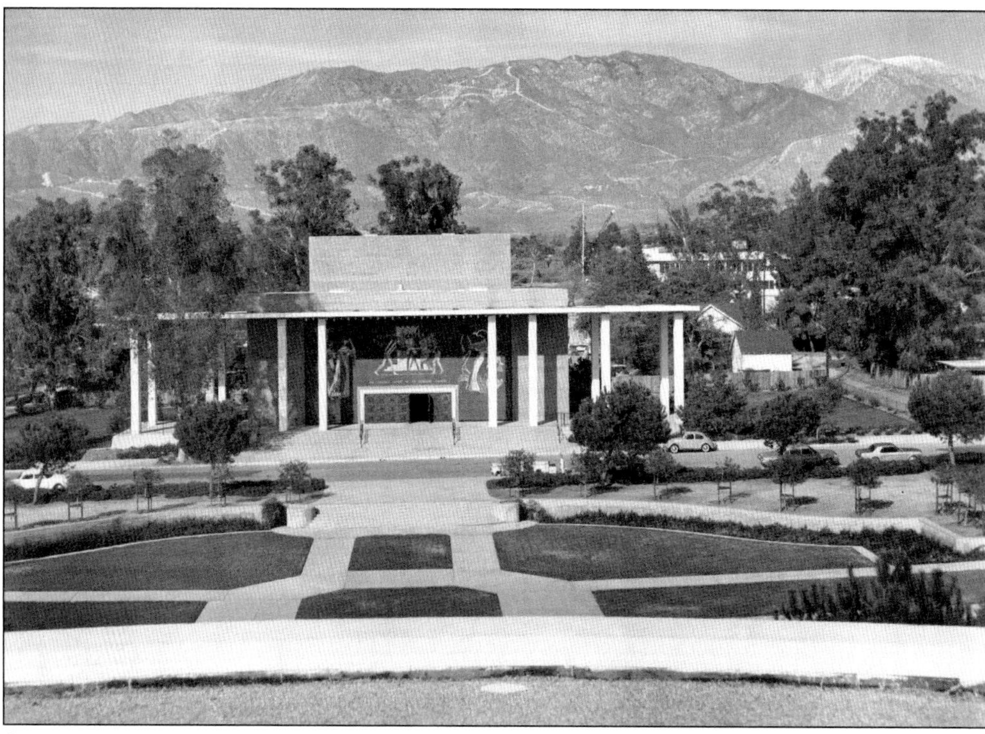

Garrison Theatre, c. 1960s. A multitalented artist, Millard Sheets also worked in architectural design. Despite the growing popularity of modern architecture, Sheets preferred to adorn his buildings with classically inspired architectural elements and mural, sculpture, and mosaic work. Scripps College's Garrison Theatre, designed by Sheets and built in 1963, also contains a Sheets mosaic depicting characters from *Antony and Cleopatra*, *Romeo and Juliet*, and *King Lear*.

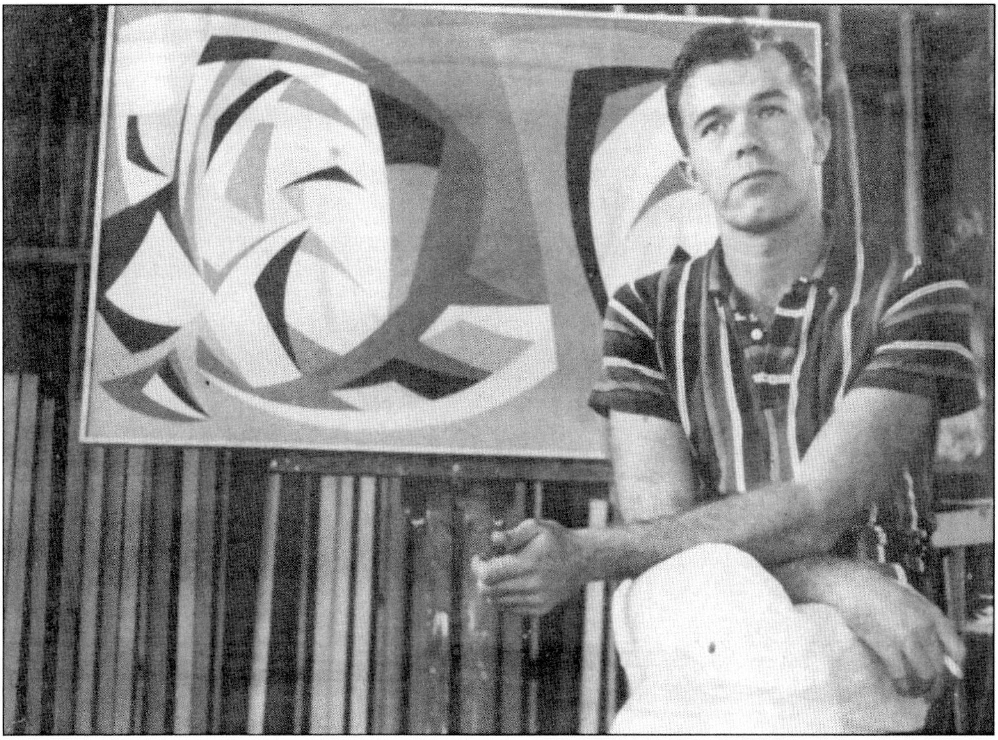

Karl Benjamin in Studio, 1959. Abstract Expressionist painter Karl Benjamin moved to Claremont in 1952 to teach elementary school. While developing an art curriculum for his students, he became enamored with painting, and, as he had no prior formal training, began taking art classes at Claremont Graduate School. He received his master's of arts in 1960 and later became a professor of art at Pomona College.

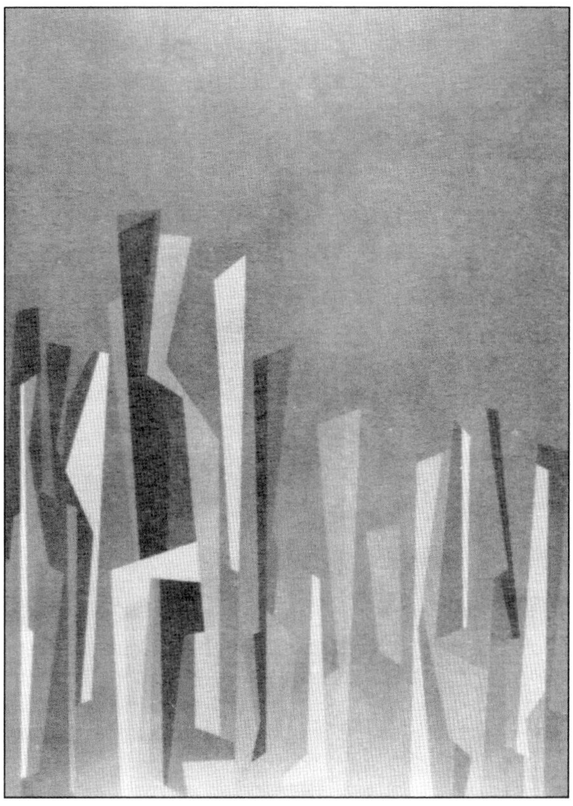

Karl Benjamin Artwork. Benjamin's first show at the Pasadena Art Museum in 1954 marked the beginning of a shift in Abstract Expressionism on the West Coast. Benjamin's paintings mixed abstract lines with bold colors, placing emphasis on how colors change when juxtaposed with other shades. This so-called "West Coast Hard-Edged" style was seen as a direct counter to the style of contemporaneous East Coast Abstract Expressionist artists.

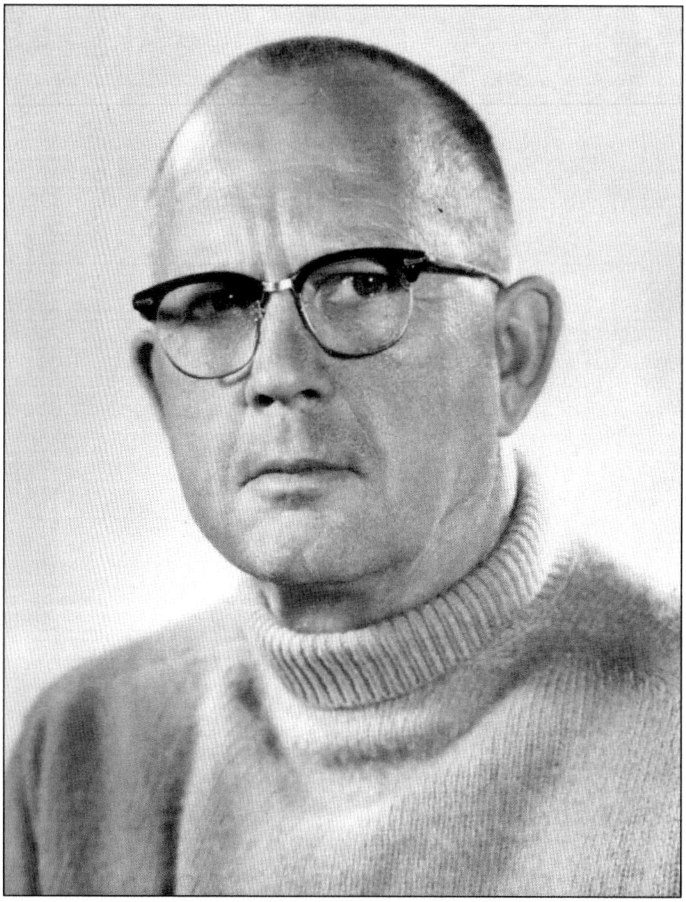

Milford Zornes. A renowned watercolor painter, Zornes was born in Oklahoma and moved to Los Angeles in 1930 to study with Millard Sheets. Zornes became active in the "California Style" movement, later joining the California Water Color Society. Following World War II, Zornes taught at Pomona College, showcasing his unique style of expansive watercolor painting. Zornes's works can be seen at museums throughout the country.

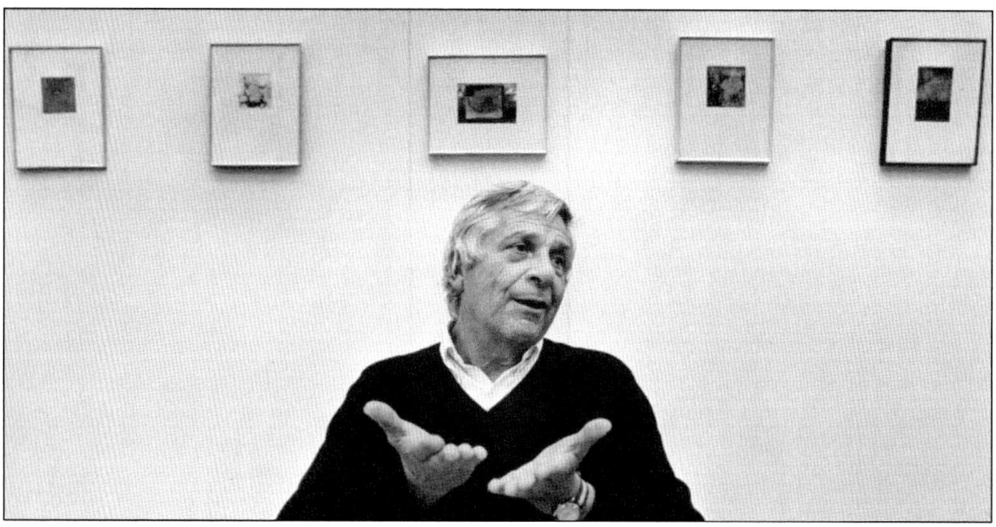

Paul Darrow. Cartoonist, satirist, and painter Paul Darrow taught for many years at the Claremont Colleges, serving as a professor of art at Scripps College and teaching mixed media and advanced drawing at Claremont Graduate School. Today, Darrow still creates art in his Laguna Beach seaside home, painting large abstract pieces that focus on his love of nature and art.

Harrison McIntosh. After attending Claremont Graduate School from 1949 to 1952, McIntosh soon made a name for himself as a renowned ceramic artist. His exquisite bowls, vases, and sculptures show painstaking attention to detail and are valued collectors' items. Despite his work being housed in museums worldwide, McIntosh remains a proud Claremonter, stating, "I have lived in Claremont since 1949 and traveled a lot; this is the best place in the world!"

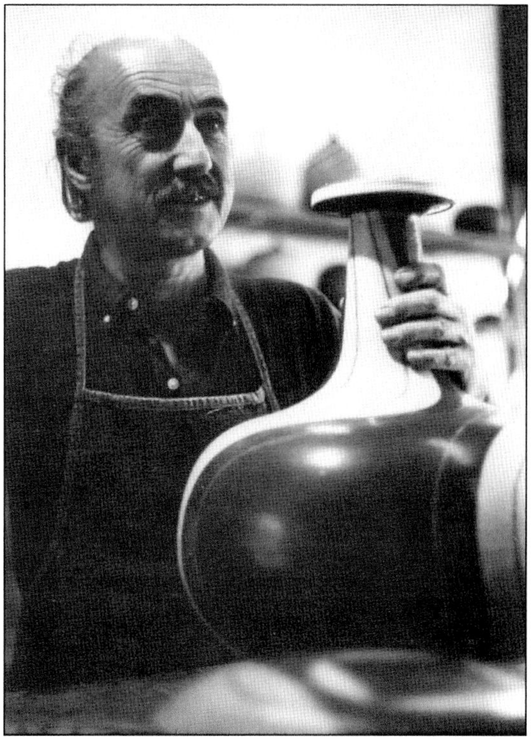

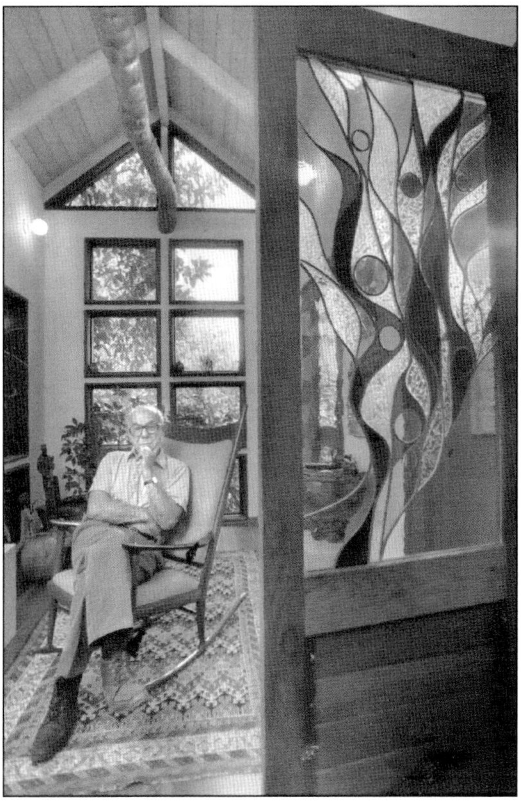

Sam Maloof. Woodworker and furniture designer Sam Maloof, known especially for his rocking chairs, is another great artist with ties to Claremont. After working for Vortox Manufacturing's art department, he set up a woodworking shop in his garage to build furniture for his home. In 1985, Maloof received the MacArthur "Genius Grant" in recognition of his extraordinary craftsmanship.

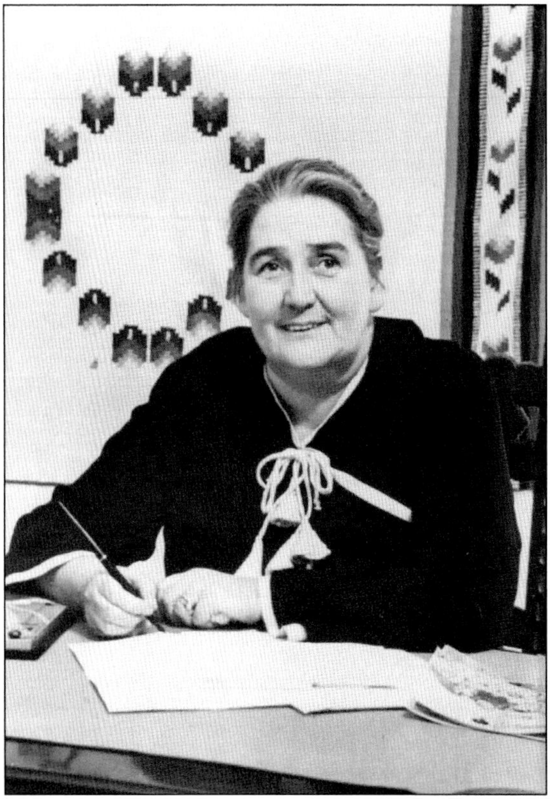

Bess Adams Garner. Garner, appropriately nicknamed "Mrs. Claremont" by many townspeople, was an important and influential figure in the city's history. After growing up in Pomona, Garner and her husband, Herman, moved to Claremont in 1925. Their beautiful adobe home, situated in what is today Memorial Park, is now home to Claremont Heritage. Garner was a true community leader, particularly focusing her efforts on theater and the arts. (Courtesy of the Judy Wright collection.)

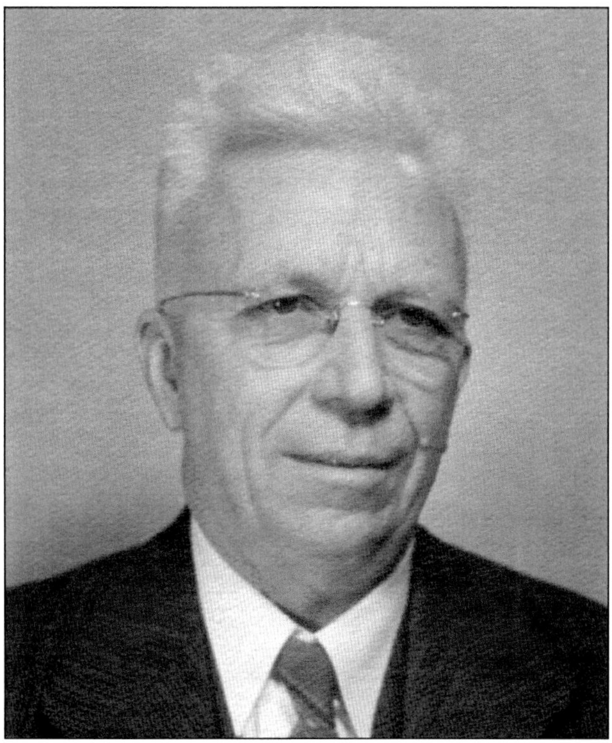

Herman H. Garner. An influential figure in his own right, Bess's husband, Herman Garner, served as president of Padua Hills Inc., which bought land in the foothills of Claremont in order "to save the foothills from other 'Honky Tonk' developments" and create an artistic community there. All houses built there had to be personally approved by Garner. Also an influential businessman and inventor, he owned Vortox Manufacturing and invented the Vortox Air Cleaner.

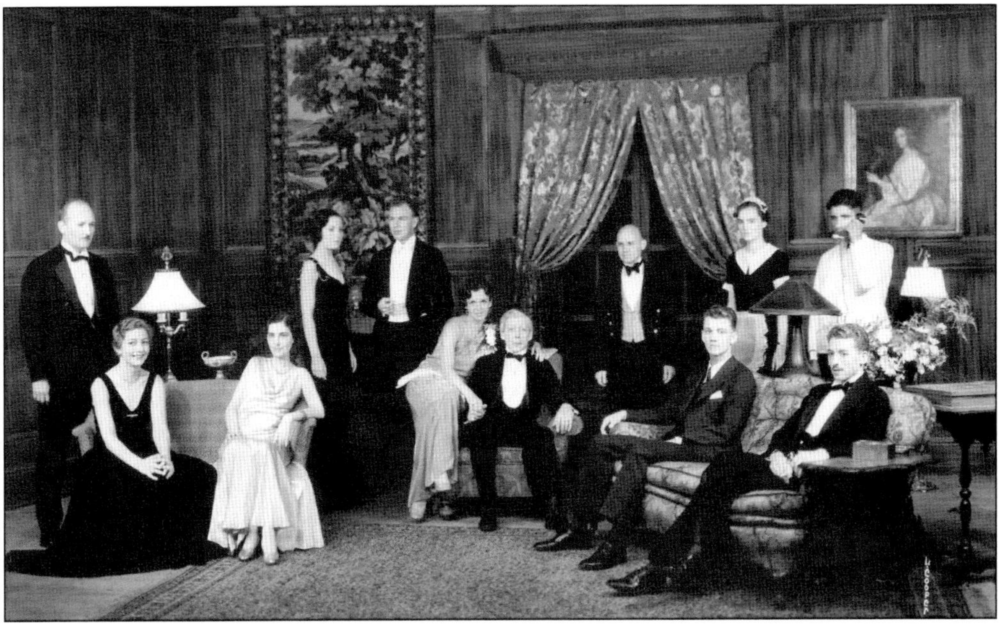

Claremont Community Players. In 1928, residents interested in theater joined together to form the Claremont Community Players, an amateur acting troupe. Their first performance took place at a Halloween party at the Garner home, and it was the Garners who would later construct Padua Hills Theatre to serve as a permanent home for the troupe. It is said that at one point, nearly one-third of residents were members of the Claremont Players.

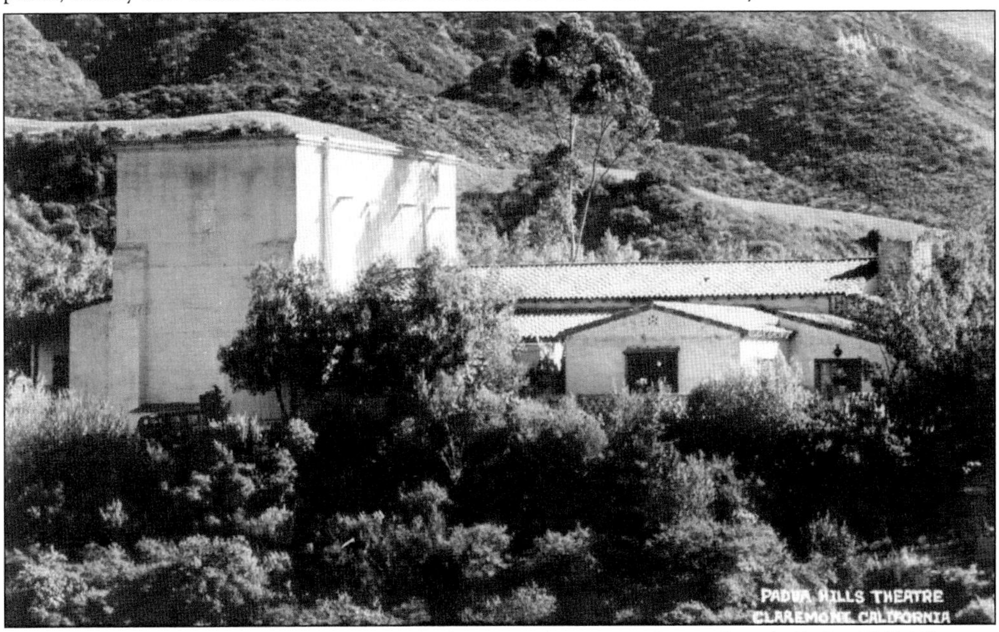

Padua Hills Theatre. The Garners built the Spanish Mission Revival–style Padua Hills Theatre in the foothills above Claremont in 1930 to give a permanent home to the city's thespians. The theater, which also featured a dining hall and a large kitchen, was surrounded by tiled patios and small artist workshops. The Padua Hills area, with its careful planning and pristine natural beauty, would soon become an artistic haven.

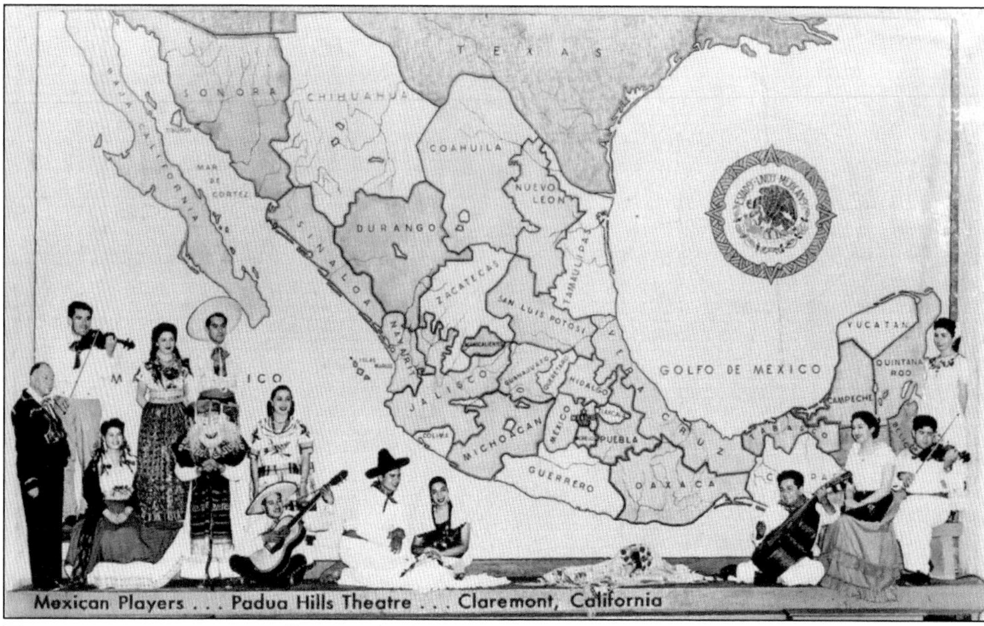

The Mexican Players. Following the loss of Claremont Community Players during the Great Depression, another group of performing individuals, known as the Mexican Players, found success at the Padua Hills Theatre. The new group was initially made up of Mexican American kitchen and dining room attendants who had little or no stage experience. The early days saw the Mexican Players perform simple shows with no memorized dialogue, all based on Mexican folklore and showcasing a variety of traditional songs and dances. As the years went on, actors, singers, dance instructors, and music teachers came from all over California and Mexico to perform and work at Padua Hills. The theater became a premier destination for many years for those seeking to experience Mexican culture or simply enjoy some entertaining song and dance.

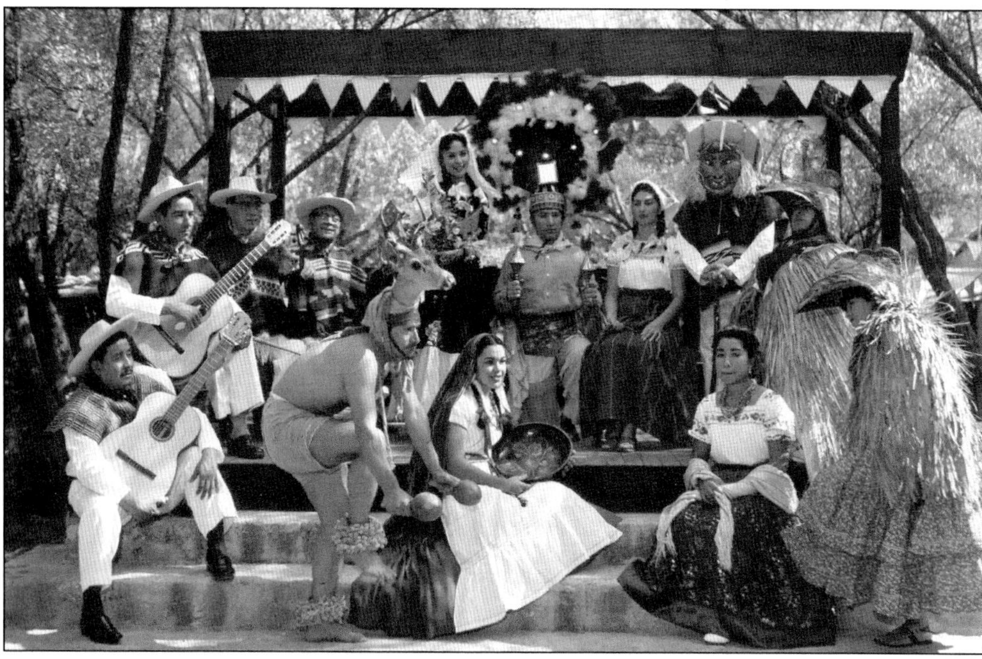

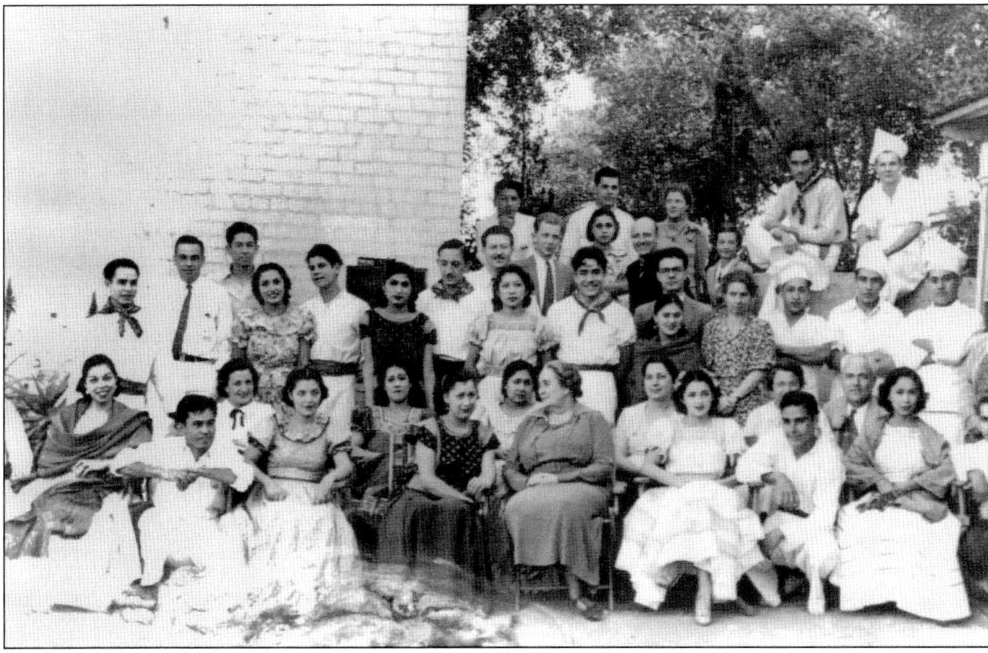

Mexican Players with Bess Garner. As the Mexican Players shows increased in popularity, Bess Garner was inspired to start the Mexican Art Institute to help preserve the vibrant Mexican culture that was on display in Padua Hills. Garner sponsored and chaperoned trips to Mexico with the performers, visiting small villages to bring back regional costumes, customs, folk dramas, songs, and dances to improve their shows and make them as authentic as possible.

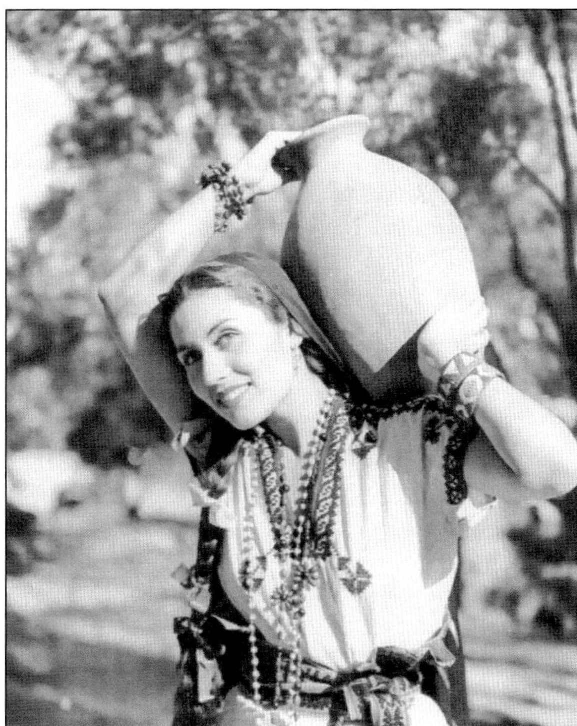

Actress in Traditional Mexican Costume. Performers dressed in traditional Mexican garb captured the hearts and imaginations of visitors from all over Southern California. The Mexican Players were even featured in Walt Disney's 1944 feature film *The Three Caballeros*. They continued performing until 1974 and were not only great contributors to the entertainment field, but were also a source of cultural pride for Mexican Americans living in Claremont and throughout the region.

Bibliography

Acuña, Mark Frank. *The Place Below Snowy Mountain*. Claremont, CA: League of Women Voters of Claremont Area, 2010.

Brackett, F.P. *History of Pomona Valley*. Los Angeles: Historic Record Company, 1920.

Claremont: Profile of a City. Claremont, CA: League of Women Voters, 1976.

Claremont . . . Then and Now. Claremont, CA: Citizens National Bank of Claremont, 1954.

Davis, Harold H. *This is Claremont*. Claremont, CA: Saunders Press, 1941.

Deuel, Pauline B. *Mexican Serenade: The Story of the Mexican Players and the Padua Hills Theatre*. Claremont, CA: The Padua Institute, 1961.

Galloway, Anne. *Tovangar: A Gabrielino Word Book*. Banning, CA: Malki Museum Press, 1978.

Garner, Bess Adams. *Windows in an Old Adobe*. Claremont, CA: Bronson Press, 1970.

Johnston, Francis J. *The Serrano Indians of Southern California*. Banning, CA: Malki Museum Press, 1978.

Lyon, E. Wilson. *The History of Pomona College: 1887–1969*. Claremont, CA: Pomona College, 1977.

McIntosh, Catherine, ed. *The Fiesta Artists of Padua Hills: 1953–1959*. Claremont, CA: Claremont Museum of Art, 2011.

Pomona: A Calendar of Events in the Making of a City. Los Angeles: Title Guarantee & Trust Company, 1936.

Price, Ryan Lee. *Glendora*. Charleston, SC: Arcadia Publishing, 2008.

Starr, Kevin. *Commerce and Civilization: The History of Claremont McKenna College*. Claremont, CA: President and Trustees of Claremont McKenna College, 1998.

Wright, Judy. *Claremont: A Pictorial History*. Claremont, CA: The Claremont Historic Resources, 1999.

About Claremont Heritage

Claremont Heritage is a not-for-profit 501c3 organization formed in 1976 by citizens of Claremont to preserve our unique community for future generations. Our mission is to advance, preserve, and celebrate our historic architectural, natural, and cultural resources of our community through collaboration, education, and advocacy. Working closely with the community, Claremont Heritage collects, catalogs, and preserves historic materials, making them available to the public digitally. Claremont Heritage also works with homeowners, advising on historic preservation issues, as well as city planners and developers to protect our local history while also advancing our economic development for our community.

Claremont Heritage also strives to ensure that our community's historic buildings and neighborhoods are protected. Over the years, our organization has helped to save numerous important buildings, including the College Heights Packing House, the historic Santa Fe Train Depot, the Old School House, and the Padua Hills Theatre, among others.

Located at the Historic Garner House, a 1929 Spanish Colonial Revival home in Memorial Park, Claremont Heritage places great importance on community outreach. Our organization offers many educational programs, such as film series, symposia, and city tours that help inform and educate community members and visitors about our wonderful community and its residents. Through these educational means and collaboration with community groups, we hope to promote and preserve the cultural heritage that has made Claremont the special place it is.

For more information on Claremont Heritage, please visit www.claremontheritage.org.

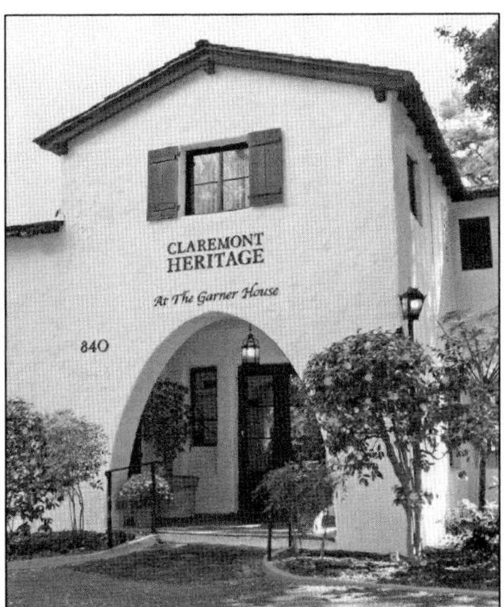